Café con leche
Race, Class, and National Image in Venezuela

Café con leche

Race, Class, and National Image in Venezuela

by
Winthrop R. Wright

 University of Texas Press, Austin

Copyright © 1990 by the University of Texas Press
All rights reserved
Printed in the United States of America

First Edition, 1990

Requests for permission to reproduce material from this
work should be sent to Permissions, University of Texas
Press, Box 7819, Austin, Texas 78713-7819.

♾ The paper used in this publication meets the minimum
requirements of American National Standard for
Information Sciences—Permanence of Paper for Printed
Library Materials, ANSI Z39.48-1984.

Library of Congress Cataloging-in-Publication Data

Wright, Winthrop R., 1936–
    Café con leche : race, class, and national image in
Venezuela / by Winthrop R. Wright. — 1st ed.
        p.   cm.
    Includes bibliographical references.
    ISBN 0-292-71128-X (alk. paper)
    1. Blacks—Venezuela—History.   2. National
characteristics, Venezuelan.   3. Venezuela—Race
relations—History.   I. Title.
F2349.B55W75   1990
987′.00496—dc20   90-32669
                                           CIP

To Polly with love and thanks

CONTENTS

PREFACE

LIKE MOST BOOKS, this one has resulted from a number of personal experiences. For that reason, it is as much the product of my wife, Eleanor, as it is of myself.

In June 1966, we moved from Birmingham, Alabama, to Cumaná, Venezuela. We left behind George Wallace, his wife, Lurleen, and their variety of racial hatred. The universities and colleges of Alabama steadfastly refused to integrate their campuses, at either student or faculty levels. In Cumaná we encountered a radically different Caribbean society. A black governor served the people of the state of Sucre. At the Universidad de Oriente, I worked with colleagues of all racial and ethnic origins and taught a multiracial student body. The Oriente section of Venezuela has one of the most racially mixed populations in the Americas. Small black communities, remnants of runaway-slave settlements, dot the landscape of the states of Sucre and Anzoátegui. Descendants of East Indian and black refugees from nearby Trinidad inhabit the small towns of the eastern reaches of Sucre. Mulattoes, zambos, and mestizos make up most of the population. But a substantial portion of the elite trace their ancestry to Europeans. For whatever reason, no one somatic type dominated the racial spectrum of *orientales*.

On our return to the United States in 1967, we reencountered North American racism in Maryland and Washington, D.C. This culture shock set us to rethinking our recent experiences. In Alabama we had thought that we understood the nature of racism and knew what we had to do to combat it. In Venezuela we lived seemingly free of racism. But on rethinking our Cumaná environment, several incidents led us to believe that we had overlooked some rather obvious facts. On one occasion, a young black acquaintance told my wife that she would never steal from an employer because in Cumaná the blacks were the most likely to be accused of crimes. As for my students, I often noted that they sat in the classroom in a rainbow fashion, with some of the darkest sitting at the back and the two whitest, two young women of Spanish and French descent, sitting apart from all of their classmates, at the front.

In pondering our experience we realized that although Venezuela's racial situation varied from Alabama's, some sort of racial divisions did exist. Thanks to grants from the National Endowment for the Humanities, the Social Science Research Council, and the Graduate School of the University of Maryland, I returned to Venezuela in 1969 to undertake a comparative study of race relations in Venezuela and Alabama. During 1974–1975 and 1978–1979, I spent time in Caracas as a Fulbright lecturer at the Universidad Central de Venezuela and the Universidad Católica Andrés Bello. During that time I completed much of my archival research on the topic of elitist attitudes toward race.

There is no way that I can thank everyone who has helped. For one thing, I spoke to hundreds of black Venezuelans throughout the nation on all sorts of occasions. I vividly remember conversations with street cleaners, police, politicians, poets, and laborers. One took place on the beach at La Restinga, on the island of Margarita, where a young black Venezuelan complained that he did not know why blacks could not have access to the same hotels and beaches open to whites. I also owe a debt of gratitude to all of my Venezuelan friends who have shared their thoughts and experiences with me. If they read the book, they will readily recognize their contributions.

Many friends in the United States and Venezuela have helped me at all stages. Judy Ewell and Ira Berlin read earlier drafts of the book. Allison Blakely, Herbert Eder, Judy Ewell, Robert J. Ferry, Harrison Howard, Arturo Muñoz, Robert P. Matthews, Thomas Orum, Vince Peloso, George Schuyler, and Kathy Waldron have all generously shared information with me and advised me. Dolores Moyano Martin, editor of the *Handbook of Latin American Studies,* also played an important role by encouraging me to finish this book. I owe a special debt of gratitude to my children, Lisa, Jed, and Christopher, for the many sacrifices they made to make this book possible.

In Venezuela I was helped by a number of people. I want to thank the entire staff of the Biblioteca Nacional for their professional zeal and interest in my work. The same goes to the staffs of the Hermética of the Academia Nacional de la Historia and the Archivos of the Academia Nacional de la Historia. The staff of the Archivo General de la Nación also assisted in many stages of my research. The following individuals also provided invaluable assistance and insight: Miguel Acosta Saignes, Federico Brito Figueroa, Pedro Grases, Manuel Pérez Vila, Angelina Pollak-Eltz, and the late Walter Dupouy. I also want to thank my former students Alejandro Mendible and the late Luis Peña.

Above all others, I can never thank Eleanor Witte Wright enough for the help she has given, not only for supplying me constantly with ideas but also for carefully editing the final draft.

Café con leche
Race, Class, and National Image in Venezuela

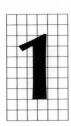

THE MYTH OF
RACIAL DEMOCRACY

IN 1944, the poet-politician Andrés Eloy Blanco wrote a column in the partisan *El País* in which he likened the racial composition of Venezuela to *café con leche*. He did so in response to a letter from a friend in Brazil which informed him the Brazilian government intended to solve its "Negro problem" by offering stipends to whites who married blacks. Blanco considered the idea both offensive and unrealistic, more in keeping with the thinking of Anglo-Saxons than Latin Americans. Venezuelans, after all, had already achieved racial balance through centuries of racial mixing. To illustrate his point, he recounted a recent conversation with a group of North American professors during which he compared race relations in the United States and Venezuela to the preparation of coffee in the two nations. In that conversation he told a guest: "That is how it is, dear professor, with the question of your blacks. In my humble opinion, you have never known how to treat coffee or Negroes. The former you leave too light, the latter too black." He concluded: "Therefore, if it is proven that America ought to be white, I prefer our method of roasting coffee. And our form of preparing *café con leche*. It will prove a bit slower, but it is better."[1]

Blanco, a founding member of the populist Acción Democrática party (AD) that emerged in the decade following the death of the dictator Juan Vicente Gómez in 1935, expressed the openly ambivalent racial attitudes held at the time by middle- and upper-class Venezuelans. On the one hand, he repeated the widely accepted myth of racial equality that had become an official doctrine in Venezuela and elsewhere in Latin America during the twentieth century. Adhering to this belief in racial equality (termed racial democracy by many North American scholars), he argued that prejudice and discrimination were nonexistent in Venezuela. Accordingly, he attacked any expression of racial discrimination in Venezuela as un-Venezuelan. Given the fact that by the mid–twentieth century approximately 70 percent of a population of some eight million belonged to a racial amalgam known as *pardos,* which blended African, European, and Indian elements, Blanco's statement had credence. Moreover, when compared to the United States and its virulent form of antiblack racism, Venezuelans thought they had a right to believe that they lived in a racial utopia, without violence or other overt manifestations of discrimination against blacks.

On the other hand, Blanco's words contained aspects of a second current, an implicit reference to lingering racial prejudices dating from the past century and before. Since the 1890s, the nation's elites had advocated the whitening of their population. They planned to accomplish this in two ways. First, they openly encouraged the immigration of white Europeans, while they excluded the entry of nonwhites. Second, they called for miscegenation, along with cultural assimilation, as means of further reducing the size of the "pure" black racial minority. The latter they hoped would either blend gradually into a whiter mix or retreat to isolated enclaves in the less populated regions of the nation. In other words, despite the pride they took in their mixed racial background, many Venezuelans wanted to dilute the *café* as much as possible with more *leche.*

In theory, then, Venezuelans had achieved a society free of racial tensions. At least they thought they had—and claimed as much. But, in fact, they accomplished this at the expense of blacks, whom they overlooked as a major class. This seeming paradox should come as no surprise to anyone familiar with race relations in modern Latin America, as well as to the many blacks of the region. Recent studies of Brazil's multiracial society show similar problems for that nation's black and colored groups. George Reid Andrews found a more exaggerated version of the same phenomenon in his study of Afro-Argentines in Buenos Aires. There the white elites resisted the integration of blacks into the society of Buenos Aires during the nineteenth century and literally created a separate class of blacks, who still identify themselves as *la clase de color* or *gente de color.*[2]

Similar evidence of the systematic rejection of blacks as a group comes from numerous studies of race relations in Colombia, Mexico, and the Caribbean Spanish islands. In all of these cases what sociologists Mauricio Solaún and Sidney Kronus have termed nonviolent discrimination has characterized relations between white elites and black minorities or majorities. As Harmannus Hoetink has argued in his survey of slavery and race relations in Latin America, racial prejudice occurred in all of the multiracial societies of the region. So, too, did racism—at least in that dominant groups showed preference for individuals who most conformed to their own social definition of race.[3]

Discussions of prejudice and discrimination, like those of race, can bog down in semantics, especially when dealing with a society as multiracial as Venezuela's. To avoid this pitfall, the following definitions of prejudice, discrimination, and racism are used in this study. Prejudice refers to attitudes held by a group or an individual toward another group or individual based on generalizations that may or may not be correct, which nevertheless determine opinions. Discrimination relates to behavior, or the way in which groups or individuals act out their social relationships with other groups or individuals. Usually, discrimination takes an overt form and works against the interests of a specific social or racial group. But in a more subtle guise, discrimination can lead to favoring a particular group, to the detriment of others, without the use of laws, codes, or other strictures aimed at restricting or destroying the victims of prejudice. Racism, as used here, constitutes an ideology held by a dominant group, which leads that group to attribute inherent inferiority to another group because of its race. As for race, Venezuelans do not accept exact definitions. They traditionally used the terms *negro* and *africano* to describe obviously black or African people, the so-called pure blacks of the nation. For that reason light-skinned mulattoes typically did not form part of the black population in the minds of the elites. Rather, they belonged to the colored, or *pardo*, majority.

In this important way, the Venezuelan's visual perception of race differs from that of white North Americans. The latter have argued that origin determines race and that, by definition, any negroid features automatically make an individual black. Thus, a drop of black blood makes an individual black in the eyes of the dominant white group in the United States. But Venezuelans consider only those individuals with black skin as blacks. Color rather than race—appearance rather than origin—play far more important roles in influencing the Venezuelans' perceptions of individuals. In the words of Juan Pablo Sojo, one of a handful of Venezuelans who have studied the culture of black Venezuelans, "Here we only have prejudice against the color of the skin."[4] By that he meant that white Venezuelans looked down on black-skinned people. To use an old adage, their prejudice was only skin deep. Thus, a mulatto became a *pardo*, a nonblack, and therefore more acceptable. By the same token, Venezuelans did not adhere to the Anglo-Saxon belief that a drop of African blood made an individual black. Actually they altered the perspective: they considered individuals with a drop of white blood superior to blacks.[5] Furthermore, they usually rewarded such individuals by bestowing upon them the advantages that accrued from whiteness rather than penalized them for their blackness. In such a situation, race represented more a state of mind, as well as an economic condition, than a physical fact.

As additional factors to consider, prejudice and discrimination existed at both individual and institutional levels. In most Latin American nations, institutional forms of discrimination were banned by laws and constitutional guarantees after the emancipation of slaves. But, nations differed as to how they handled discrimination, and subtle forms of discrimination against blacks persist throughout Latin America despite official efforts to ban such practices. Individuals coped either through racial mixing or by dint of their own abilities to succeed in economic and political careers.

A decade ago, Hoetink noted other reasons why no hard-and-fast rules applied to the study of prejudice and discrimination in Latin America. As he observed, demographic factors within individual countries brought about diverse situations between localities. In one locale, the blacks might comprise the majority and hold leadership positions as well as middle- and lower-class status. But at regional or national levels the blacks might not make their presence felt and might not hold any positions of power.[6]

Moreover, few scholars of any nationality have studied race relations in postemancipation societies in Latin America, as Magnus Mörner observed some two decades ago. A decade later, Leslie B. Rout, Jr., discovered little change.[7] Unfortunately, the observation holds especially true for Venezuela. Any scientific study of the blacks in twentieth-century Venezuela must overcome a surprising paucity of statistical data. Symptomatic of the professed racial harmony found there, no census taken since the abolition of slavery in 1854 mentions people by race. According to the historian José Gil Fortoul, writing in the late nineteenth century, the censuses purposefully lacked racial categories because the elites did not want to remind blacks of their painful experience as slaves.[8]

For all intents and purposes, after emancipation took place the blacks simply disappeared from the official records of modern Venezuela. National historians further contributed to the process by overlooking the presence of blacks as a separate racial group following emancipation. When they did mention blacks in their works, they treated them only in the distant past as colonial slaves, as participants in the wars of independence, or as secondary contributors to the formation of the colonial society. Of course, their disappearance constituted a paper one only, for the blacks' visual presence remains obvious, especially along the Caribbean coast between Coro and Carúpano. But in government documents, court records, and national histories, blacks receive no attention, as such, and remain hidden from sight. Even their cultural contributions to Venezuelan society went unnoticed, for the most part, especially in the history texts used in the nation's schools. Whether this implies racial equality, as some Venezuelans have claimed, seems doubtful. More likely the lack of official concern manifests the subtle but certain rejection of the pure black as a racial type by modern Venezuelan elites.

Because of the lacunae in the data on postemancipation blacks, a review of the attitudes of elites toward blacks serves a useful purpose. These elitist attitudes show that since the late nineteenth century, Venezuela's dominant classes held antiblack prejudices similar to those of their colonial ancestors, who believed that the African's presence in the New World owed to their enslavement. In their eyes, slaves worked. In a slave economy, blacks did the work that the whites refused to do. Important as they were to driving the colonial economy, their slave status placed them in the lower echelons of the social hierarchy. Skin color and other basic physical characteristics further identified blacks as a separate caste. Their race and slave status kept most blacks at the bottom of the social and economic pyramid throughout the colonial period and well into the independence period.

After emancipation in 1854, blacks continued to live in the shadow of their slave background. Throughout the present century, most Venezuelans have denied that they had a racial problem, especially one like that of the United States, with its segregationist practices. But, nevertheless, they placed blacks in an inferior social position. In their minds, they had a chromatic scale that linked dark skin and African characteristics with lower-class status. Even today most Venezuelan elites do not want their children to marry blacks, for fear of losing important social status as a result.

In their own minds the Venezuelans substituted economic discrimination for racial discrimination. Rather than attribute their antiblack feelings to racial attitudes or racism, Venezuelans argued that they did not like blacks because they lived in poverty. The result has much in common with North American racism, for, like Yankees, during the twentieth century Venezuelans blamed economic failure on cultural and physical inferiority. Moreover, they argued—circuitously—that they disliked blacks only because they were poor; the majority of blacks, however, were poor because they were black.

Following such logic, whiter Venezuelans refused to see themselves as racists. Instead, they claimed that they discriminated against individuals for economic reasons alone. For them race remained largely a social concept, for when a black escaped poverty, he or she ceased to be socially black. Successful blacks accepted the same attitude, adopted the norms of the white society to which they had been admitted, and broke with their black past.

As far as race is concerned, pure definitions become obscured. Until black men or women proved their merit, the elites judged them by their appearances, along a chromatic scale that placed negative social values on blackness. During the twentieth century, in popular parlance whiteness described a state of positive social and economic achievement as well as racial characteristics. The racial lexicon of Venezuela abounds with phrases that show change toward social whiteness. The most widely used adage, that "money whitens," also suggests that Venezuelans do not base their prejudices primarily on racial criteria. In the materialistic and multiracial society of twentieth-century Venezuela, individuals' jobs, education, and wealth determined their opportunities for social mobility.

Blacks carried the stigma of their slave heritage and suffered from discrimination as long as they remained poor, but they never lost the opportunity to improve their socioeconomic condition. Occasionally, financial and political success socially whitened black Venezuelans, a fact that José Gil Fortoul recognized in the 1890s, when he first applied the term *social race* to describe such a phenomenon.[9] Others entered white society through marriage and miscegenation. But in the long run, such individuals provided the exceptions that proved the rule. Furthermore, those few successful blacks lost their ties with the less fortunate blacks. They made no attempts to call attention to their race. Nor did they lead efforts to establish black political or cultural movements. Rather, they accepted the doctrine of nondiscrimination as the gospel for social behavior and sought to identify themselves with the culture of their whiter compatriots. For them and their white counterparts, clothes, education, language, social position, and the accumulation of wealth combined to make an individual whiter in the social context. In such a setting the term *blanquear* (to whiten or bleach) had tremendous social significance.

The emphasis placed on whitening as a prerequisite for social and political mobility suggests the antithesis: black characterized backwardness, ignorance, poverty, and failure. Only a generation ago, Venezuelan aristocrats considered blacks as people whose ancestors climbed trees; in the words of one of their members, blacks spent their lives "like Tarzan of the Apes." Venezuelan elites judged people by their appearances. Accordingly, individuals with "anxious hair" or "hair like springs" lived in the shadow of their black slave ancestors. The elites considered respectable the whiter Venezuelans who had "hair flat as rainwater, of an indefinite light brown color which is neither fair nor dark." "With us," wrote Olga Briceño in the early 1940s, "one of the first things you notice is a person's head. In the long run you will base your judgment on what there is inside, but you will inevitably begin by seeing what you can learn by looking at it. That is why the mulatto and the half-breed find it so much harder than the white man to achieve success and why, when they do, it is due solely to merit."[10]

By the mid–twentieth century, Venezuelan elites held attitudes toward blacks like those found elsewhere in Latin America. In particular, they accepted a fluid concept of race which obscured definitions between black and white. A series of contiguous racial categories marked the gradations of a racial continuum. Socioracial mobility occurred as the descendants of blacks moved along that continuum by mixing with individuals from whiter groups. The resulting fluidity allowed Latin Americans to avoid using a simple black-white racial dichotomy like that employed in the United States, since even though they placed blacks and whites at opposite ends of a racial spectrum, they did not create endogamous groupings from which individuals could not escape. Moreover, they demonstrated an amazing propensity to assimilate miscegenated individuals into whiter groups, which also mitigated a dual racial system.

Observers agree that miscegenation is the most salient feature of Latin American race relations. Since the colonial era, large numbers of the region's Afro-American population blended into a third racial tier of colored people, between the black and white levels. In most cases this neither-black-nor-white colored category served as a socioracial buffer or transition between white elites and black masses. Carl Degler called this a "mulatto escape hatch" in his comparative study of slavery and race relations in Brazil and the United States. Miscegenation, or whitening as it came to be known, permitted socioracial movement along a continuum toward the somatic norm established by white or Europeanized elites who defined their status in cultural and economic terms as well as by race. This common acceptance of a neither-black-nor-white category throughout Latin America enabled individuals to escape blackness while moving toward whiteness. It also made segregation impossible.

Despite the omnipresence of miscegenation, the process did not lead to similar results everywhere in Latin America. For instance, miscegenation did not establish a predominantly *pardo* or colored population in eastern Argentina. There, miscegenation became a partial explanation given by Argentines for the apparent disappearance of blacks as a separate group in their nation during the nineteenth century. However erroneous the myth of the vanishing black population may be, Argentines continue to attribute the lack of blacks in the Rio de la Plata area to racial mixing, along with losses sustained by the black population during the nineteenth century as a result of warfare, epidemics, low birthrates, and high mortality rates. As a consequence of their mistaken beliefs, Argentines discounted miscegenation as a major factor in the formation of their modern society, which, instead, they attributed to the massive influx of European immigrants after 1880. They chose to emphasize the European origins of the majority of their citizens, using whiteness as an important part of their national image. In so doing, they ignored the small black group in their midst, reducing them to a separate class.[11]

Brazilian attitudes toward miscegenation differ sharply from those of the Argentines. Since the 1930s, Brazilians have thought of miscegenation as an essential contributor to the formation of the national image forged by cultural nationalists, such as Gilberto Freyre, who referred to multiracial Brazilians as "a new race in the tropics." Like Venezuelans, Brazilians prided themselves on their tricolored heritage. Indeed, as in Venezuela, Brazilians made an official doctrine of nondiscrimination and nonprejudice. In that manner, Brazil more nearly fits what social scientists have termed an infused, or open, system of race relations, which gives individuals of all races more social and racial mobility than found in the closed, or segregated, variant of the United States. But as Florestan Fernandes, Anani Dzidzienyo, Carl Degler, and Pierre-Michel Fontaine, among others, have demonstrated, prejudice and discrimination against blacks still exist in most parts of Brazil, and the Brazilian claim to have achieved racial equality seems exaggerated.[12] Racial inequalities, along with prejudices and discrimination, mar the landscape of Brazil's self-proclaimed racial paradise. Moreover, Brazil has a large black population, many times larger than that of Venezuela, in both relative and actual terms. For the great majority of blacks, the openness of Brazil's racial system remains illusory.[13]

For their part, Venezuelans believed that by midcentury they had reached an advanced stage of racial mixing. Venezuelans constituted a mixed racial group whose members could truly join with the poet Rafael Castro in saying; "I am white, I am Indian, I am black; I am American," except for the small black and white minorities, which combined accounted for no more than 20 to 25 percent of the population.[14] Their long-held self-image as a *café con leche* people reflected this view. Significantly, Venezuela had neither a white majority, as in Argentina, nor a large black minority, as in Brazil.

Culturally as well as physically, Venezuelan society manifested the combining of African, Indian, and European elements. For that reason, most Venezuelans rightfully considered themselves members of a hybridized race. During the past sixty years or more, white elites have openly acknowledged the black part of their ancestry. The Venezuelans' music, dress, language, food, tools, religious cults, folklore, and political and economic institutions all showed contributions of the three racial groups. Venezuelan anthropologists and sociologists may have disagreed about whether the formation of modern Venezuelan society resulted from the indigenization and africanization of the Spaniard in Venezuela, or from the hispanization of the Indian and the African, but all agreed that a long process of cross-cultural exchange and racial mixing took place.[15]

Comparisons between postemancipation racial attitudes in Venezuela and other Latin American countries illustrate subtle differences. Not enough empirical data exists to draw strong conclusions from a comparative perspective. Even the works on Brazilian race relations (which outnumber by far all of the studies on Spanish American racial attitudes) cover mostly local conditions. Although they provide a great deal of enlightenment, they fall short of giving enough information to write a definitive synthesis of race relations in Brazil, let alone to draw conclusions that apply to all of Latin America.

Venezuela and Argentina would sit near opposite poles if a scale existed for measuring the relative amounts of racial prejudice and discrimination found in Latin American nations. Brazil would fall somewhere between them, closer to Venezuela than to Argentina. Historically, blacks and nonwhites have played a more important role in political and social institutions in Venezuela than in any other South American nation, with the notable exception of Guayana and Suriname. Argentines simply purged blacks from their national image and presented themselves to the world as white Euro-Americans. For their part, Brazilians compromised their racist instincts by showing an ostensible tolerance for blacks, even though they kept them from holding powerful positions in government and social institutions. But since Venezuela's inception as an independent nation in 1830, its blacks and *pardos* have held powerful positions in regional and national elites. The process actually began in the colonial era and continued through the wars of independence. Since 1830, each subsequent generation of elites experienced the infusion of new members from nonwhite groups. During the better part of the nineteenth century, and again after the death of Gómez in 1935, blacks and nonwhites gained access to political power at regional and national levels. This social and political mobility of Venezuelan blacks differed markedly from the experiences of blacks in Argentina and Brazil, where the elites remained white and enjoyed far greater continuity from one generation to another.

These comparisons between nations provide a useful background to the historical review of elitist attitudes toward blacks in Venezuela since the mid-nineteenth century. Such comparisons serve to illustrate national differences in prejudice and discrimination. This book concentrates on one country, Venezuela, to study the changes in race relations and attitudes over an extended period. Such an approach permits analysis of the role of various political, social, and economic factors in creating changes in a complex of issues including race, prejudice, and discrimination. In particular, the work examines the evolution of the concept of racial democracy in a multiracial society.

Before the 1890s, Venezuelan elites did not pay much attention to race as such. In the absence of strong central governments, caudillos ruled most parts of the nation. They comprised an assortment of racial types, across the spectrum from white to black. Since many based their power on their military prowess, race did not play an important role in their selection as leaders. Blacks and *pardos* not infrequently held high positions in federal agencies and military organizations as well, and they certainly formed an important segment of the various bandit factions that operated in the more remote regions of the nation, especially in the llanos. Indeed, the tendency for blacks and *pardos* to hold influential posts in federal military services lasted well into the first decade of the twentieth century.

But during the 1890s, intellectuals and politicians reinforced latent ideas concerning race. These individuals, most of whom resided in Caracas, composed an integral part of the elites who associated themselves with the liberal factions that sought to create an increasingly powerful centralized government. Clearly influenced by Spencerian positivism and related European racist theories, these individuals worried publicly about Venezuela's national image. At their urging subsequent governments began a campaign to whiten Venezuela's population. In their writings they lamented the lack of whites in Venezuela and stated that Venezuelans owed their political instability and economic stagnation to the presence of a predominantly mixed racial population.

Flatly put, this group did not believe that *pardos* and blacks could rule themselves through a democratic process. Because of their mistrust of the mixed racial majority, they advocated the creation of a centralized dictatorship like that which Porfirio Díaz established in Mexico. When General Juan Vicente Gómez provided just such leadership, they readily associated themselves with his administration and supported it until its end. Moreover, they supported white immigration as a panacea for Venezuela's many social and economic problems.

Following Gómez's death in 1935, these racist views gave way to more moderate attitudes. Both Eleazar López Contreras (1935–1941) and Isaías Medina Angarita (1941–1945) permitted opposition political parties to form during their respective administrations. As a result, the populist Acción Democrática party came into existence under the leadership of a number of dedicated *café con leche* activists from the nation's middle class. Inspired in part by the Peruvian Víctor Raúl Haya de la Torre's multiclass Alianza Popular Revolucionaria Americana (APRA) party, the leaders of AD soon formed an alliance with the *pardo* and black masses. In so doing, they adopted the myth of racial democracy as their party's official position on race. Rather than attempt the division of Venezuela's electorate along racial lines, between white elites and mixed racial masses, men such as Rómulo Betancourt, Andrés Eloy Blanco, and Luis Beltrán Prieto Figueroa stressed class differences.

Acceptance of the doctrine of nondiscrimination fit the needs of the populists who comprised AD's leadership. Of mixed racial origin themselves, they readily welcomed a cultural nationalism that recognized the triracial nature of Venezuela's masses. During their ascendancy they did not attempt to extol the virtues of hybrid Venezuelans as some new type of race in the tropics, as Brazilian sociologist Gilberto Freyre did of his mixed-race compatriots. But they nonetheless expressed pride in the contributions of Indians and blacks to the formation of Venezuela's society and clearly understood that most Venezuelans had mixed ancestry. When they clashed with members of the white aristocracy, they did so along class lines and excised racial distinctions between the classes from their official party rhetoric.

For their part, white elites felt the pressure of increased political participation by colored and black Venezuelans. As one of their representatives, Dr. Gustavo Herrera, the minister of education, reputedly said in 1942, "If the little Venezuelan blacks are so uppity without knowing how to read and write, where are they going to stop if we educate them?"[16] But Herrera and his contemporaries felt threatened more by the rise of the lower classes than by any particular racial group, and although they maintained certain prejudices against blacks, they did not openly advise any institutional discrimination against them. As in the past, struggles between factions of the elites and their popular opponents could just as well have resulted from any number of causes besides race, among them the fact that AD drew its leadership from individuals who came from outside of Caracas, attended public high schools rather than the exclusive private ones, and came from mostly middle-class families. Their race, though noticeably different from that of the elites, played only an incidental role in their political careers.

Between 1945 and 1948, Acción Democrática enjoyed a short-lived political supremacy, thanks in part to an alliance with military officers who opposed the moderate president Medina Angarita. During the *trienio,* as this interlude came to be known, AD leaders tried to implement a broad-based reform program aimed at improving the lot of the nation's nonwhites. Among other things, they tried to remove the lingering vestiges of racism found in the nation's immigration laws and in the practices of hotels and other public facilities that catered to North American oilmen. They also opened up positions in the nation's bureaucracy for colored and black employees. Though their efforts failed in the short run with their over-throw in 1948, the leaders of AD remained committed to opening up opportunities for social mobility for individuals of all races.

As Andrés Eloy Blanco's 1944 article demonstrated, some *adecos* (members of Acción Democrática) personally favored the gradual whitening of Venezuela's population. But the party's official rhetoric denied any such position and upheld the concept of racial democracy. It seems certain that most Venezuelans believed that individuals of any race could experience some degree of social mobility, based on their own merits. That did not make pure blacks equal to whites or *pardos,* unless they escaped the poverty that characterized most blacks. Nevertheless, AD populists did not consider themselves racists, at least in the North American sense of the word, and thought of racial democracy in terms of the right to whiten socially, either through racial mixing or by economic success.

By the 1940s, Venezuelan society had achieved a remarkable level of racial integration. The expanding wartime economy, spurred on by oil revenues, opened up many jobs in an underpopulated nation. The liberalization of the nation's political system after 1935 sped up the process. Although they had not eliminated either prejudice or subtle forms of discrimination, Venezuelans had made a *café con leche* society a viable one, one in which people of all races belonged to all social strata. Obviously, the myth of racial democracy does not stand up under the scrutiny of historical review. But all the same, Venezuelans lived in a primarily mixed society in which race, while an important factor for poor blacks, did not serve as an impenetrable obstacle for mobility. Historically, changes in political rhetoric, accompanied by scholarly works and legal developments, have been important in the move toward racial democracy.

THE COLONIAL LEGACY: RACIAL TENSIONS IN A HIERARCHICAL SOCIETY

THE RACIAL attitudes of twentieth-century Venezuelans have strong colonial roots. From seeds of myth and reality, the present concept of racial democracy grew, beginning with the racial interaction of the first century of settlement. In the eyes of modern observers, this early miscegenation and *mestizaje* (racial and cultural mixing) combined to produce a uniquely Venezuelan society. As the historian Guillermo Morón expressed, "The most interesting moment of Venezuelan history, from the sociological point of view, is to be found in the process of Spaniard turning into Venezuelan." He thought this process took place through the first three generations of the colonial experience. According to Morón: "The conqueror lost his Iberian home, yet retained his way of life. For how long? Perhaps until the second generation, when the encomendero was a creole, born in America. But perhaps it was not until the third generation that there appeared the notion of 'land of our fathers', the homeland, applied to Venezuela, although this did not imply the idea of separate statehood, but only that of land, land rendered human by possession." [1]

This popular view rested on a few simple premises. First, as Angel Rosenblat argued, liaisons between white men and Indian and black women occurred during the sixteenth century because "Spanish women arrived late to the Indies, and in small numbers." [2] Demographic data for the colonial era gives this opinion some credibility. Since the late eighteenth century, travelers to Venezuela repeatedly identified racial mixing as the most striking feature of Venezuelan society. At the dawn of the independence movement in 1810, as many as 780,000 people lived in Venezuela. Of these, approximately 45 percent belonged to a multiracial group known as *castas* or *pardos*, that included mestizos, mulattoes, and zambos, as well as other mixtures, the majority of which had traces of African descent. Slaves accounted for another 15 percent of the total figure. In other words, about 60 percent of the total population at the end of the colonial era had African origins, with a substantial Indian influence. Indians made up another 15 percent of the inhabitants. So-called whites, comprising *peninsulares*, creoles, and Canary Islanders, formed the remaining 25 percent of the population.[3] Of these, some 90 percent were creoles, of somewhat dubious racial origin, many of whom probably had African ancestors.[4] Small wonder, indeed, that Morón felt that "the colony, then, is not merely one moment in the story of Venezuelan history. It is much more than that, much more than a period: it is a whole complex life in which the Venezuelan came to know and respect his own nationhood."[5]

Second, something like what modern Venezuelans call racial fusion must have occurred during the colonial era. In effect, over the years, blacks became absorbed into an increasingly European culture. Of major concern, most of this absorption took place at the lower strata of the social order. The Venezuelan blacks spoke Spanish dialects, laced with African and Indian terms, and manifested little of their African origins. They abandoned their own religions, as such, and either joined the brotherhoods, or *cofradías,* of the Catholic church or became followers of the various syncretic cults that flourished throughout the colony, such as that of María Lionza. Even their music lost most of its African identity and blended into dance forms such as the popular *joropo,* which retained the polyrhythmic beat of African music but otherwise adhered to European themes and forms. The fact that no one African group formed a clear majority of the slaves transshipped to Venezuela also played an important role in the metamorphosis of African to Venezuelan. With no single strong African faction to hold them together, the blacks of Venezuela failed to preserve a cohesive culture of their own.[6]

The colonial period between 1520 and 1810 deserves some attention, first because of the interaction of the races which took place then. Venezuela developed a heritage of miscegenation accompanied by a racial dualism in which most blacks found themselves exploited socially and economically. Moreover, both the kind of society the Spaniards established in Venezuela and its location at the periphery of the Spanish empire contributed in large part to these unique features of Venezuelan society. After tracing the economic and social factors contributing to *mestizaje* and describing institutions which illustrate its growth, this chapter explores the nature of racial dualism in Venezuelan society. During the first half of the sixteenth century, Indian societies resisted the encroachment of Europeans in their territories. They fought with some success to expel the interlopers, restricting European expansion to a few small enclaves. Nevertheless, a few

Spaniards began to gain small fortunes, especially those who first exploited the pearl beds near the eastern islands of Cubagua and Margarita. Slowly, others established small agricultural, mining, and cattle ranching enterprises and produced enough wheat and other foodstuffs for local and regional markets, as well as enough surplus to export to Colombian and Central American markets. But with no major mining potential, the area attracted few settlers from Spain, who preferred the get-rich atmosphere of Mexico and Peru to that of the peripheral colonies. Like the Rio de la Plata region, Venezuela remained largely outside the main trade routes, at the fringe of the Spanish empire.

Between 1522 and 1542, Germans occupied parts of the colony under grants given to Swiss banking houses as repayments of loans negotiated by Charles I, further complicating the process of development. Dutch also arrived, first as contrabandists from nearby Curaçao and later, between 1542 and 1606, when they controlled the salt flats at Punta Araya, across the Gulf of Cariaco from Cumaná. English, French, and Portuguese traders, smugglers, adventurers, and corsairs rounded out the picture of a disparate group of European males who frequented the coastal waters of Venezuela during the first half century of settlement.

Colonial Venezuela differed from major centers of the Spanish empire in several other ways. Most notably, it lacked highly developed Indian societies, such as the Inca and Aztec; provided no easily exploited, export-oriented economic benefits, such as mining; and remained administratively fragmented through most of its existence as a colony. By the mid–seventeenth century, Venezuelan colonists established a diversified agricultural and pastoral economy. They produced a wide variety of crops, including cacao, wheat, indigo, tobacco, and hides, as well as cotton, gold, and copper for export, mostly to Mexico, New Granada, and Spain. But the majority of the colony's agriculturalists met the demands of local subsistence markets. Only gradually did the loose collection of small towns break down their isolation and draw together to form external and internal trade systems, which enabled the colonists to withstand the rigors of frontier life.

The lack of any central administration hampered their efforts to unite. Until well into the eighteenth century, Venezuela actually constituted six to seven separate provinces, within three distinctly different economic zones. To the west, the provinces of Barinas, Mérida, and Maracaibo formed a basic unit, which drew the pastoral production of the western llanos into the agricultural orbit of the Maracaibo basin and Andean highlands. Both Maracaibo to the north and Bogotá to the south served as termini for the region's diverse products. In eastern Venezuela, the towns of Cumaná and Barcelona served the scattered cattle-raising enterprises of the southern plains of the province of Cumaná, forming another unit. Caracas, the third and by far the most extensive region in economic terms, stretched from Lake Maracaibo on its western frontier along the coast and central plains and valleys to the Unare River on its eastern flank.[7]

During the first half of the seventeenth century, Caracas emerged from this melange as the most prosperous and populous province. By 1650, a small group of Caracas-based encomenderos began to realize substantial profits from the sale of cacao to the Mexican market. A number of factors explain their initial success. First, wild cacao trees flourished along the river valleys of central Venezuela. Second, these *caraqueño* encomenderos took advantage of lax governmental controls in the colony by putting Indians to work gathering cacao from the wild trees. Although the New Laws of 1542 ostensibly ended the use of the encomienda in the Americas, Venezuelan encomenderos enjoyed the privilege of demanding personal service from Indians through encomienda grants until the last decade of the seventeenth century. Third, thanks to the presence of a number of enterprising Portuguese traders, the Caracas cacao growers found a means of shipping their product to Mexico. Fourth, the high prices the cacao fetched in Mexico provided more than enough profit to permit the expansion of production through the introduction of plantation cultivation. Finally, the profits also allowed the emerging cacao elites to supplant unreliable Indian labor with slaves from Africa.[8]

Once the cacao boom started, the Caracas hacendados needed a larger work force. Indians simply did not conform to the disciplined plantation regimen. Many men ran away rather than work under unacceptable conditions. The wealthier encomenderos acquired African slaves to do their work. Africans not only provided the needed labor but also brought their own agricultural technology to the arduous tasks of clearing land, digging irrigation ditches, planting shade crops to protect the cacao seedlings, and caring for the trees as they matured. Farmers in western Africa employed similar methods in their agriculture, so individuals from that region adapted to the work on plantations with little difficulty. They introduced the plantain as a shade crop, as well as a basic foodstuff, and employed metal hoes in tending the newly planted cacao saplings.

The importation of African slaves into the province of Caracas during the seventeenth century far exceeded previous use of slave labor in Venezuela. During the sixteenth century, a small number of slaves worked at the pearl fisheries of eastern Venezuela. Another handful made up a portion of the work force at small mines that dotted the landscape of the fledgling colony. But in Caracas slaves were a majority of the rural laborers by the end of the seventeenth century and constituted a substantial part of a growing domestic servant class in the city of Caracas.

Besides launching a new economic era for the province, the ever-increasing number of blacks had a profound demographic impact. By the end of the 1600s, blacks transformed the population of the central coastal sections of Caracas into a predominantly black, zambo, and *pardo* majority. For the most part, Indians left the area, alienated both by the onslaught of the plantation economy that they abhorred and by the nature of the forced labor they had to perform. Few whites lived outside the urban centers. Thus, by the end of the colonial era, blacks and their descendants accounted for nearly 75 percent of the population of central Venezuela.[9] In surprisingly short time, black enclaves came into existence in Barlovento, as well as along the eastern shore of Lake Maracaibo, and numerous coastal hamlets from Coro to Carúpano.

In many important ways, Venezuela's economy determined the nature of its society. Venezuelans not only produced a variety of cash crops, but they adopted a wide range of land tenure and labor arrangements. By the end of the eighteenth century, the colony had a thriving agricultural and pastoral economy, much like that of the preceding century. Cacao still led as an export cash crop, but indigo, coffee, sugar, and tobacco combined with livestock to form a highly diversified agricultural economy. Unlike large-scale enterprises, that existed in other Latin American countries, such as the Mexican and Peruvian mining industries or the boom-and-bust sugar production of northeastern Brazil, in Venezuela no one system prevailed. Thus, slave gangs worked on some of the large cacao estates, and on the sugar plantations, but many of the former used a mixed labor system of day laborers, or *jornaleros,* and slaves. Tobacco and indigo planters depended almost entirely on free day laborers to grow their crops. Landowners who switched to coffee in the late eighteenth century found it cheaper to use slave labor if they could, but many had to hire free workers to meet their production demands. As for livestock, most of which went to domestic markets, the owners of *hatos* on the llanos took what workers they could get, a smattering of slaves along with freemen who pushed southward into Venezuela's long-lasting frontier.[10]

Land tenure also varied. The wealthiest cacao hacendados owned their land, although the size of their holdings never matched those of large landowners elsewhere in the Americas. Ownership of land protected these individuals from their rivals, especially export-import merchants, and gave them much broader leeway in land usage. They could turn some excess land over to tenants, if they chose, or they could sell land if economic difficulties arose. But many cacao and indigo planters rented their haciendas, particularly those who operated in the Aragua valleys. In these cases, as with the major cacao hacendados of Caracas, the scale of production remained small. Only the *hatos* of the llanos took on the classic characteristics of the latifundia, and even there a surprising number of cattle ranches remained moderate in size. Finally, a significant number of subsistence-level farmers produced a relatively high proportion of Venezuela's cash crops on small holdings.[11]

The proliferation of small landholdings in Venezuela stands as one of the colony's outstanding features. Despite the importance of cash crops, the majority of Venezuela's freemen lived on small plots, as tenants, squatters, or owners, where they raised foodstuffs such as maize, beans, rice, cassava and plantains for local consumption. These *conucos*, as such lots were known, permitted Venezuela's rural workers to shape their relationship with the hacendados. Since they met their basic needs on their *conucos*, the campesinos remained relatively independent of the hacendados and could determine their work patterns for themselves, for the most part. Though they remained poor, they enjoyed a degree of freedom from forced labor not found in most parts of the Spanish and Portuguese colonies in the Western Hemisphere.[12]

In such an environment, where only a very few select individuals possessed great wealth while the majority lived in virtual poverty, a two-tiered society developed. A white elite of high-ranking Spanish officials, rich creole hacendados and ranchers, along with a few wealthy merchants and professionals occupied the top levels, and colored agriculturalists, day laborers, artisans, and slaves the bottom. Remarkably unostentatious in their style of living, the elites nevertheless established their identities separate from the mass of poor Venezuelans. They used their wealth and their ethnicity to differentiate themselves from the average inhabitants of the colony. Over a long period of time, the elites jealously guarded the prerogatives of their self-defined status as whites. In essence, they based the division of society between themselves and the popular masses on economic and cultural criteria, namely wealth and a pure Christian lineage.

Most Venezuelans shared the plight of the poor. Not white in the bureaucratic meaning of the term, and living on small plots, they lacked the means to improve themselves either socially or economically. One foreign visitor to Barinas in the early 1800s noted that the impoverished disposition of the people even obscured the line between slave and free. "One finds some six thousand slaves in the province of Barinas, and they are slaves only in name, since they live with their masters on a familiar basis and are as well fed and as well dressed as they are."[13] A century later, historian Pedro M. Arcaya used much the same language to describe the colonial society of Coro. "Among the *mantuanos* of Coro figured . . . most of the owners of the haciendas and slaves of the sierra. Nevertheless, they were far from being rich, and they endured a modest life, which suited the poverty of the place."[14]

Throughout rural Venezuela people lived in simple one- or two-room dwellings, known as *ranchos*, with few furnishings, if any. Most owned no books, pictures, or other nonessentials. Indian hammocks served as beds, and cooking took place outside of the house. Only a smattering of material possessions distinguished the average hacienda or *hato* owner from the laborers and slaves. Away from urban centers, few people had more than one change of clothes, and even fewer wore manufactured hats, shoes, or fineries of any sort. Campesinos and slaves alike dressed in simple white cotton shirts, cotton drill pants, homemade hats, and sandals (if they had any footwear). Almost everyone, regardless of caste, suffered from a lack of the good things in life and a surplus of the bad. Among the latter, tropical diseases, parasites, dysentery, and wretched living conditions ravaged generations of the region's general population.[15]

According to modern historians, these impoverished conditions promoted racial mixing among the common classes. In most of their interpretations of the colonial period, they depict a society marked by smooth cultural fusion and racial toleration.[16] Poverty clearly served as the common denominator. As Juan Pablo Sojo casually stated, "The process of racial fusion took place more rapidly and thoroughly in Venezuela than in other parts of the Americas, where the Spanish conquistadores emphatically guarded their purity of blood."[17] Though not well documented, his statement gains credence given the nature of the mixed labor system employed throughout Venezuela, whereby *jornaleros*, black slaves, and personal service encomienda Indians frequently worked side by side at similar and complementary tasks. It stands to reason that their proximity to each other gave impetus to racial intermingling.

In his analysis of the composition of a seventeenth-century mining community near Barquisimeto, Miguel Acosta Saignes gave a clear picture of how this process formed the basic culture of the Venezuelan campesinos. At Cocorote people of African and Indian descent worked together as miners, carpenters, cooks, farmers, and cattle hands under the direction of white administrators. They taught each other their respective construction methods as they put up buildings for the mining encampment. On lands surrounding the mines, they exchanged their agricultural knowledge as they supplied food to the miners. Blacks and Indians tended cattle and other livestock and prepared meals blending American and African cuisines. Venezuela's popular diet depended on meat and maize, supplemented by black beans, plantains, yams, cassava, rice, and squash, along with some poultry and fish.[18]

The *conuco* method of agriculture, part of the campesino way of life, gives further proof of the *mestizaje* process in Venezuela. Like many Venezuelan institutions, it had Indian and African antecedents. Both African and Indian farmers used techniques suited to tropical soils and climates. Their respective agricultural systems also employed labor-intensive methods of crop production. The same individuals usually performed all of the tasks on the *conuco,* using human energy to clear the land, break the soil, sow the seeds, and harvest the crops. On most *conucos* in Venezuela, farmers used only rudimentary tools, usually machetes, axes, and hoes. As in other tropical regions, the campesinos practiced slash-and-burn methods to prepare their land for planting. After they cut and piled the brush, they burned it to ashes to put nitrogen into otherwise unproductive tropical soil. For a year or two they raised mixed crops on the cleared plot, while they prepared another for future use. Usually Venezuelan *conuqueros* planted three or more compatible crops. The Indians, for example, planted legumes, tubers, and corn as their basic produce. Africans substituted plantains and bananas for corn and raised yams instead of potatoes. Manioc, or cassava, also served as a basic foodstuff for both groups and their racially mixed progeny.[19]

Mestizaje also influenced religious practices. One of the longest-lived cults, that of María Lionza, illustrates well the combining of Indian, African, and European cultures. The cult originated in the mountains of Sorté in Yaracuy, near a cacao-growing region in which racial and cultural mixing began in the late sixteenth century. It took its name from the Indian legend of María Lionza and her association with other natural divinities. As in most Indian religions, the followers of María Lionza worshiped the forces and spirits of nature they believed inhabited the rivers, forests, and caves. As Africans and Europeans added aspects of their religions, an increasingly diverse cult developed.

Over the years, practitioners of the religion changed some of the worship ceremonies, but they kept intact the essential blend of nature worship, magic, and faith healing as new groups merged with old. Its many African characteristics included the adding of West African deities to the spirits upon whom the priests call during their services. Emphasis on magic and on intervention of supernatural beings in the personal relations between humans and spirits also manifested the African origins of the sect. The belief in magical cures and the knowledge of special medicines derived from both African and Indian sources. The use of tobacco, which played an important role in the services and in the cures effected by the priests, evolved from Indian religious practices. Africans and Europeans often substituted rum for tobacco, especially to achieve a trancelike state in which they claimed to communicate with spirits. European adherents gave the cult several Catholic characteristics, including the association of the name of María Lionza with the Virgin of Coromoto, the patron saint of Venezuela. Other aspects of Catholicism reflected in the cult's syncretistic worship included the symbolic use of the cross, the burning of incense and candles upon altars, and the acceptance of an essentially Christian moral code by members of the sect.[20]

For the common masses, *mestizaje* touched almost every aspect of daily life. Besides farming, food preparation, and religion, popular music and language also derived from the mixing of the three major cultural groups. For instance, the *joropo*, called the national dance by many, placed African polyrhythms with European instrumentation and themes. The orchestration combined Spanish guitars, four-stringed *cuatros*, and harps with instruments of African and Indian origin, such as drums and maracas. Common language followed a similar pattern. Spanish-speaking people from other Latin American nations complain that they cannot understand Venezuelan llaneros from the central and eastern plains regions, whose dialect confuses even other Venezuelans because of repeated use of Indian and African words and exclamations.[21]

Given the nature of Venezuela's colonial society, mixing had to occur. Always underpopulated, situated at the fringe of the empire, largely rural, with a majority of colored citizens in most sections—the structure of the colonial society lent itself to an intimate relationship between various racial groups. As time passed, individuals who wanted to escape the overcrowding around the city of Caracas could push southward onto the expansive llanos. No land shortages confined the population, as on the Caribbean islands. But, by the same token, the concentration of economic activity along the coastal crescent of northern Venezuela tended to keep most people from drifting off to the more isolated regions, except for Indians, renegades, and fugitive slaves, or *cimarrones*, who sought freedom in the remote reaches of the interior.[22]

By all accounts, racial and cultural mixing affected the inhabitants of Venezuela more than almost any other American society. Everywhere they went, travelers in Venezuela encountered signs of miscegenation and *mestizaje*. One such account, written near the end of the eighteenth century by Archbishop Mariano Martí following a trip to the Barlovento district just east of the city of Caracas, pointed out the degree to which racial mixing determined the racial composition of parts of Venezuela's interior. As he reported his impressions, "In this town [Curiepe] there are so many zambos, blacks, and mulattoes that it is rare that one sees anyone other than blacks or those with burnt color, and one sees more blacks than in Nirgua or Pao."[23] A short time later, during the first decade of the nineteenth century, Frenchman Francisco Depons made a similar observation about Caracas. "In proportion to other social classes, there is not in all the West Indies a city with more *pardos* or descendants of freed slaves" than Caracas.[24]

Nevertheless, the mixing of races did not breach the wall that existed between the colony's common folk and the elites. By 1700, a socioracial dualism had also become an important feature of the emerging Venezuelan society. White elites occupied one pole of a paternalistic social system, black slaves the other. Between them ranged Canarians, poor Spaniards and creoles, and the mixed racial groups, including *pardos,* mulattoes, and zambos. Already Indians formed outsiders, pushed more and more to the interior districts. A white creole planter elite and their allies among Spanish bureaucrats and wealthy merchants controlled the economic and governmental institutions. Another white group, comprised of poorer Spaniards and Canarians, made up a class of small planters, farmers, renters, artisans, day laborers, and muleteers. Some of these individuals resided in rural districts, others in urban centers. Below the identifiably European groups in towns such as Caracas, the *castas* held even more menial positions. Some owned land and worked as artisans and farmers. But more often they never rose above making their living as vendors who sold fruits and vegetables, sweets, and other foodstuffs in the towns. In the rural areas they served as laborers, or eked out an existence on their *conucos.* As for blacks, most slaves worked as field hands and agricultural laborers, although a large number worked as domestic servants in Caracas. Free blacks performed similar tasks, although many lived as fishermen, *conuqueros,* and artisans.[25]

Race, as such, became a systemic factor in the division of colonial society into distinct castes. Spaniards originally based their social structure on economic and cultural criteria, which emphasized such characteristics as legitimacy of origin. The use of *limpieza de sangre* (purity of bloodline) allowed them to distinguish themselves from illegitimate individuals in subordinate groups. Their economic and political power gave them further reasons to set themselves apart from the common castes. But even though ethnicity and caste played central roles in determining social status, race entered into the equation by readily identifying the subservient castes, which comprised Africans, Indians, and their mixed racial descendants.

During the seventeenth century, a series of codes and ordinances of a basically racist nature also restricted the privileges of nonwhites in Venezuela. Of both royal and local making, these laws purposefully split the population into separate parts to weaken resistance to the crown's authority. Like a number of similar measures that appeared in Lima and Mexico City during the 1550s, the Venezuelan ordinances also contained explicit racial biases. By the end of the colonial period, laws set tight parameters around the social mobility of all nonwhites. Slaves and free blacks could not travel freely, nor could they bear arms. Free blacks, mulattoes, and zambos could not wear fancy clothes or jewelry. They also faced the possibility of having to return to slavery as a result of some misdemeanor they committed. Blacks had to marry within their own caste and could not have Indian servants. A seldom enforced regulation of 1609 ordered free blacks, mulattoes, and black slaves to pay special tributes. Later laws placed similar constraints upon *pardos,* such as one introduced in 1621 that temporarily banned them from public employment. Laws published on July 22, 1643, and March 23, 1654, declared that *pardos* could not serve in the royal armies, although they could hold ranks up to captain in *pardo* militia units commanded by white officers. Eighteenth-century codes, including supposedly liberal ones of 1785 and 1789, also limited the social movement of nonwhites, and forbade marriages between whites and members of black and mixed racial castes.[26]

Though enacted partly in emulation of more advanced parts of the empire, such as Lima, and partly as a form of social control of the lower castes, these statutes also reflected growing fears and prejudices of white elites who dreaded that nonwhites might achieve some sort of equality. As free blacks, mulattoes, and *pardos* became traders and artisans in urban centers, they quickly adopted European customs to speed their assimilation into higher social levels. They especially copied the elites in dress, which they thought the most notable mark of success. To socially conscious whites this behavior obviously posed a basic threat, particularly to their status. While they did not necessarily oppose social mobility, they were offended seeing descendants of African slaves dressed in apparel similar to their own.

By the later eighteenth century, the elites' antipathy toward blacks and *pardos* took on an emotional quality akin to modern racism, but different in important ways. They made no attempt to attribute inferiority to innate racial characteristics. But they publicly demeaned blacks and zambos as cultural inferiors and accused them of any number of vile crimes and vices. For instance, in 1785 an official document supported laws that prohibited blacks from living with Indians "because they only corrupt them with the bad customs which they generally acquire in their breeding and with the bad example of their parents, besides which they enslave them and endeavor to become owners of their labor, their property, and even their common holdings, and they sow discord among the same Indians, . . . mixing themselves up in interminable lawsuits by which they profit."[27] As for zambos, French traveler Jean Joseph Dauxion-Lavaysse commented that in Caracas and environs "the word Zambo is synonymous with worthless, idler, liar, impious, thief, villain, assassin, etc. Of ten crimes that may be committed in the province (Caracas), eight are said to be done by zamboes." Supposedly the evil nature of the zambos owed to their being "born of clandestine and adulterous unions, of natives who have contracted only the vices of civilization, and of African slaves: what can be expected of children born of such parents, whose minds are totally neglected, and in a climate that invites to sloth and indolence."[28] About the only positive piece of information Dauxion-Lavaysse picked up about zambos reputed that mixed Afro-Indians led healthier lives, resisted diseases better, and seemed better suited physically for life in the tropics than any of their pure-blooded ancestors.

The resistance with which *caraqueño* elites met a royal decree of 1795 that granted nonwhites the right to purchase certificates known as *gracias al sacar* (literally, "thanks for the exclusion") that gave dispensations from color and illegitimacy also testified to their nascent racial prejudices. Sparked in part by class and ethnic considerations, the elites' opposition to permitting *pardos* and blacks to buy the prerogatives of whites demonstrated their strong feelings that *pardos* were illegitimate and inferior persons whom they could not trust.[29] Not only did they not want individuals from lower castes to encroach upon their previously white institutions, such as the university, the church hierarchy, and the militia, but they did not want those institutions contaminated or tainted by the presence of nonwhites.

Following his voyage to Venezuela during the first decade of the nineteenth century, Francisco Depons alluded to similar manifestations of prejudice against blacks and *pardos*. According to him, about the only benefit one *pardo* family acquired through the purchase of a racial dispensation certificate was the right for the women to carry rugs to the church so as not to get their dresses dirty as they knelt to pray during the mass, a privilege previously granted only to elite white families. With the exception of this ostentatious display of status, no other favorable changes occurred for the family. Not one of its members received a public office, and the family's skin color continued to identify its lowly origins in the opinion of the elites. As Depons concluded: "This evinces how far prejudices are paramount to laws. They are formed and destroyed by time, or by the aid of those political commotions, which, by deranging the head, derange likewise the opinions of men."[30] White elites also avoided marriage with *pardos* and blacks. If white men desired lovely *pardo* women as sexual partners, they rarely married them, for in a country as Depons indelicately explained, "where there are so many means of gratifying passion, such a sacrifice is hardly to be expected."[31] Even Canary Islanders whose own ancestors had once shown no reluctance to marry *pardos* now shunned mixed marriages upon achieving some semblance of social well-being.

Assessing the role of fear of slave uprisings and racial wars in determining race relations during the late colonial era proves a problematic venture. So far, Venezuelan historiography of slavery has produced an inconclusive treatment of resistance and rebellion.[32] Nothing in the literature suggests that before 1791 Venezuelans feared slave revolts more than any other people who lived in slave economies. During the 1730s and 1740s, slaves, free blacks, and zambos participated in a series of disturbances, none of which constituted a slave or race insurrection, per se. The presence of blacks in these movements may have resulted in part from their desire to gain freedom or racial parity. But since the uprisings included a significant number of whites and Canarians, whose primary aim amounted to ending the cacao monopoly imposed upon them by the Caracas Company, it seems that issues related to slavery played only ancillary roles. This fact holds especially since slaves as well as free blacks stood to gain economically by the removal of the detested Basque entrepreneurs. Moreover, none of these movements met with success, and government officials moved quickly to crush them, with relative ease.

As another factor, the presence of a seemingly large number of fugitive slave settlements, called *cumbes,* in Venezuela apparently caused some concern, at least in larger urban centers, such as Caracas. Although such scholars as Miguel Acosta Saignes and Federico Brito Figueroa presented exceedingly high figures for the number of *cimarrones* and *cumbes* extant in Venezuela at the end of the colonial period, without doubt many illegal settlements existed, especially surrounding Caracas and in the llano districts.[33] Perhaps incorrectly identified as *cumbes,* the majority of these isolated rural communities actually comprised groups of free blacks, mulattoes, zambos, *pardos,* Indians, and poor whites for the most part. Most likely, criminals rather than runaway slaves made up significant portions of these so-called *cumbes.* Yet, all obviously attracted some runaway slaves who assumed that the relative longevity of so many *cumbes* assured their own safety. Indeed, some, such as Nirgua, actually achieved legal status. Others simply persisted, sustained in large part through the efforts of *conuqueros* who raised enough food to supply the small populations. Although authorities did not look upon these places with favor, they seldom made them targets of attack, with the exception of a brief campaign in 1749 to rid the province of Caracas of *cumbes* in the aftermath of an abortive conspiracy that reputedly involved a large number of *cimarrones.*[34]

After 1791, this generally relaxed atmosphere changed noticeably due to the major slave revolt that broke out in Haiti. As the Haitian revolution ran its bloody course, individuals who previously felt secure became increasingly apprehensive about possible slave revolts. The first real scare came in May 1795 near Coro, when a free zambo tenant farmer named José Leonardo Chirinos led an abortive three-day uprising of slaves, free blacks, *pardos,* zambos, and Indians. Much like the revolt led by Nat Turner several decades later in Virginia, the Chirinos insurrection began with the killing of several slaveholders and members of their families. By May 12, 1795, this phase of the movement had lost much of its impetus. Indeed, Chirinos abandoned his followers the previous day, after they murdered the owner of his wife and children. Without leadership, the insurrection succumbed with little resistance to the militia forces sent to Coro to put down the revolt.

Despite its brevity, the Chirinos rebellion raised the specter of race wars. Its inherent danger lay in the fact that free blacks joined slaves in a struggle to gain equality with whites. In his initial fervor, Chirinos proclaimed the establishment of a French republic in the Coro district. Whatever this meant, it appealed to large numbers of free blacks and zambos who opposed newly imposed taxes. At the time, the Coro district had a large proportion of free black and zambo farmers, including several hundred fugitive slaves from Curaçao, known as *loangos* (so called because the Dutch took slaves from the Loango coast of West Africa), who enjoyed the status of free persons in Venezuela. For the small minority of white *corianos* (residents of Coro), the combined uprising of slaves and disgruntled free blacks took on the appearance of a racial conflict like that which raged on in Haiti. Actually, no serious alliances between slaves and free blacks developed there or elsewhere during the next decade, and royal and local authorities experienced no difficulty in restoring order.[35] Minor revolts that occurred in 1796, 1798, and 1799 in Coro and Maracaibo nevertheless kept alive the elites' lingering fear that racial warfare might break out in areas of Venezuela with heavy concentrations of slaves and free blacks.

In the long run, the real threat to white supremacy in colonial Venezuela came from *pardos,* not free blacks and slaves. Just as in contemporary Haiti and Jamaica, enterprising people of color wanted to achieve legal parity with whites. No longer content to remain second-rate citizens, they looked for opportunities to advance themselves socially and politically. Thwarted by white elites in their attempts to purchase the prerogatives of upper-class status through the *gracias al sacar,* their next chance came with the outbreak of the wars of independence. As their participation in that struggle revealed, they held the balance of power in the colony. Ultimately loyal to neither peninsular nor creole white elites, *pardos* set their own path toward self-aggrandizement. For example, when it suited their own needs, they supported the royalists against Simón Bolívar and his creole associates in

1813. But in 1816, they seemingly switched sides, joining the same creole faction against which they had recently fought a battle to the death.

In 1816, upon his return to Venezuela, Simón Bolívar appealed to Venezuelan *pardos*, blacks, and zambos to join his cause. His defeat in 1813 by José Tomás Boves, whose llanero troops shouted "Death to the whites!" as they rode against the creole forces, convinced Bolívar of the efficacy of employing the same llaneros against the royalists. Similarly, he appealed to slaves to join him by promising them freedom in return for their support of his faction. Obviously an uncomfortable move from a social point of view, the inclusion of masses of nonwhite soldiers in his armies proved politically wise to Bolívar. Llaneros comprised one of the basic elements of the loyalists' fighting force. Now they shouted "Death to the *godos!*" and struck terror into the hearts of the Spaniards.

The inclusion of colored and black troops in the independence movement shattered the old colonial social order. *Pardos* literally came of age as a result of their involvement in the hierarchy of Bolívar's military organization. Slavery also began to disintegrate. The fighting between 1811 and 1821 provided slaves with ample opportunities to escape their masters. Some simply fled the haciendas in the war-torn parts of the colony. Others joined in various factions, although Bolívar frequently complained that not enough slaves fought in a struggle for their own liberation. These actions caused radical changes, for as John Lombardi correctly noted: "It seems certain, however, that these years of devastation, confusion, and disorganization greatly hastened the eventual abolition of slavery. Because the army remained the ultimate refuge for runaway slaves during the war, plantation discipline collapsed. More importantly, black slaves discovered a sense of power during these years as the contending armies wooed their support."[36]

Bolívar certainly understood the racial ramifications of the presence of large numbers of nonwhites in his movement. To his credit, he cautioned his creole followers to recognize the broadened racial and class base of the loyalists. In 1819, he admonished the members of the Congress of Angostura to comprehend their own mixed origins.

We must keep in mind that our people are neither European nor North American; rather, they are a mixture of African and the Americans who originated in Europe. Even Spain herself has ceased to be European because of her African blood, her institutions, and her character. It is impossible to determine with any degree of accuracy where we belong in the human family. The greater portion of the native Indians have been annihilated; Spaniards have mixed with Americans and Africans, and Africans with Indians and Spaniards. While we have all been born of the same mother, our fathers, different in origin and in blood, are foreigners, and all differ visibly as to the color of their skin: a dissimilarity which places upon us an obligation of the greatest importance.[37]

But Bolívar also shared the creole elite's antipathy, fear, and distrust of blacks and nonwhites. Having witnessed in 1813 what he termed the *castas'* hatred of whites, Bolívar expressed his aversion to blacks on numerous occasions during and after the wars of independence. The death of so many whites in Venezuela during the protracted struggle against Spain obviously affected his thinking. As much as he wanted to create an egalitarian society, without classes, Bolívar ever increasingly feared that the dark-hued Venezuelan masses would exterminate the privileged creole class.[38]

During the 1820s, as he realized that the llanero caudillo José Antonio Páez would lead Venezuela and its predominantly *pardo* people out of its union with Gran Colombia, Bolívar expressed his belief that Páez and his ilk meant to establish a "pardocracy." As he bitterly lamented in 1826 to his Colombian associate Francisco de Paula Santander:

We are far from emulating the happy times of Athens and Rome, and we must not compare ourselves in any way to anything European. Our origins have been of the most unwholesome sort: all our antecedents are enveloped in the black cloak of crime. We are the abominable offspring of those raging beasts that came to America to waste her blood and to breed with their victims before sacrificing them. Later, the illegitimate offspring of these unions commingled with the offspring of slaves transplanted from Africa. With such racial mixtures and such a moral history, can we place laws above heroes and principles above men?[39]

Bolívar expected the worst, for as he told Santander: "We shall have more and more of Africa. I do not say this lightly, for anyone with a white skin who escapes will be fortunate."

Without doubt, the Liberator proved far too pessimistic in his prognosis. Following Venezuela's split from Gran Colombia in 1830, *pardos* and whites shared power with little sign of racial acrimony. To outsiders at that time familiar with race relations in the West Indies or the United States, Venezuelans appeared to have achieved a surprising degree of racial harmony. According to the English traveler John Hawkshaw, whites would soon share their control of society with nonwhites because racial mixing had altered race relations in Venezuela. By 1830, in his estimation, over half of Venezuela's population belonged to "a mixed race between the negro, the Indian, and the Spaniard, amongst this class there is every shade of colour, from the bronze of the zambo, to the lighter shades of the mulatto and Mestigo [*sic*]." In his enthusiasm, Hawkshaw thought that "this light yellowish-looking race may be the type of the future nations of South America."[40]

In Venezuela Hawkshaw encountered people of mixed race who had access to power, as in no other part of the Western Hemisphere he knew. To his surprise "the highest offices of the state are open to the man of colour, Páez, the late president, being of the class." Thus, he concluded, "In this country, therefore, the negro is not an object of prejudice, and, if free, immediately takes his stand as high up the scale of society as his capacity and intelligence may entitle him." Moreover, he believed: "It would seem as if these countries were not to be beneath the sway of the white man. He has had his feet upon the soil for centuries, but as an alien he has been cast off. The white man's caste was not there to be supreme."[41]

Hawkshaw, an astute observer, readily saw the significant political gains made by *pardos* in newly independent Venezuela. But his words about "the negro" require some qualification. For one thing, he used the term in its European and North American sense, applying it loosely to any person with negroid features, as he defined them, not just to the so-called pure blacks as identified by Venezuelan usage of the term. Furthermore, on at least one occasion when he did specifically refer to the latter as "negroes" he made it painfully clear that most had not escaped poverty and enslavement. The Englishman somewhat optimistically attributed the plight of most blacks to a lack of education. As much as he felt that being placed on equal footing with others would enable the blacks to make further advances, he did not predict rapid changes. As he said:

Of course the effects that have been created by ages of neglect are not to be remedied by one age of culture. Just as the muscles of the arm become enlarged by the use of the arm, so does the size of the brain become enlarged by the use of the brain; and just as it would be unreasonable to expect muscular limbs in a race of men who had little occasion for the use of either legs or arms, so also it is equally unreasonable to expect a large development of brain in men who, for generations, have had little occasion to exercise their thoughts.[42]

That specific lack of education entrapped most blacks at the bottom of the social order. But they also remained objects of fear among white elites, especially that segment of the white population who lived in urban centers in parts of the country with proportionally high numbers of slaves and free blacks, such as Caracas, Maracaibo, and Coro. No one word better describes the attitude of many elites toward the black masses than *fear*. Born out of the tensions of the late colonial era, and fostered by the bloody nature of the wars of independence, the fear of black insurrection gripped the imagination of remaining descendants of the creole aristocracy.

In part, the fear owed to the political uncertainty of the postindependence period. When Páez took Venezuela out of Gran Colombia, he did not inherit a nation in the modern sense of the word. Rather, Venezuela existed as diverse and separate provinces only loosely tied together by a weak central government. Caudillos and local elites controlled their own districts, each with their own economic bases. To further complicate the unification efforts of such individuals as Páez, between 1830 and 1865, bandit gangs and dissident political factions held vast parts of Venezuela, particularly in the llanos. Although these groups often professed loose political affiliations with national parties, they expressed no clear-cut ideologies.

This confused political ambience resulted in part from deep-seated economic problems. The nation's planters and cattle ranchers paid a heavy price for the more than a decade of fighting that preceded Venezuela's independence from Spain. Cattlemen who were once relatively prosperous never achieved their prerevolutionary levels of production as their holdings languished for want of labor and capital. Planters also experienced a number of difficulties, as many of them shifted from cacao to coffee as their principal cash crop. They, too, lacked an adequate work force and always found themselves dependent upon wealthy bankers and merchants, as well as subject to the vagaries of world markets.

In this context, between 1830 and 1865, free blacks and slaves lived much as they had during the late colonial period. Most free blacks worked at menial tasks and at best aspired to become military chieftains, bureaucratic functionaries, small landowners, or small-town entrepreneurs. The artisan class also continued to include free blacks.[43] Despite promises by Bolívar to end the institution, slavery continued to exist, shedding its lingering shadow on all blacks in Venezuela. Thus, for blacks the colonial caste system seemed intact. Some twelve thousand to thirteen thousand blacks remained slaves, while as many as three thousand risked their futures by running from their masters. Those blacks who lived free experienced different forms of discrimination, but most markedly they faced the perception on the part of white elites that not only did they represent an uneducated body of individuals but they belonged to a racial faction that plotted the violent overthrow of the existing social order. For the most part, the elites wanted to dominate the black underclass as a means of guaranteeing workers for their own enterprises. But, they also suspected that slaves and free blacks would join revolutionary political bands whose intentions included the extermination of whites.

In large part, between 1821 and 1854, slavery festered as a social lesion. A free-birth law passed by the Congress of Cúcuta in 1821, and subsequently incorporated into the Venezuelan Constitution of 1830, guaranteed the gradual abolition of slavery. But for some slave owners the institution remained profitable. Only as the economic basis of slavery eroded with the shift from cacao to coffee, causing the cost of maintaining slavery to outweigh that of eliminating it, did they reluctantly accept the notion of emancipation. Even then, it took a political decision to emancipate the slaves. In March 1854, President José Gregorio Monagas issued a proclamation that freed all slaves, a decision he made in part as a means of alleviating racial tensions he felt threatened the security of his regime.[44]

Though not a volatile issue in itself, the continuing presence of slavery had contributed to the paranoid manner in which urban elites responded to a series of internal rebellions and conflicts that shook Venezuela over the fifty years beginning with the wars of independence in 1810 and ending with the Federal War between 1859 and 1863. Venezuelans experienced an extended period of alternating anarchy, despotism, and civil war in various parts of their nation, but especially on the llanos. One historical factor, the turbulent nature of Venezuela's nineteenth-century political development, gave rise to the image of blacks as militant warriors who fought against the civilized elements of society. Over that period, blacks, zambos, and *pardos* made up the bulk of all armies that fought each other for local and national control. As long as slavery lasted, whites remained apprehensive that free blacks and slaves would link together, not only to end the bondage of the latter but to secure new rights and privileges for the former as well.

Upper-class fear of black revolts ran highest in Caracas, which at the time had some 58 percent of the nation's slaves in its immediate vicinity. For instance, on December 9, 1824, blacks and mulattoes led a riot in Petare, on the eastern outskirts of the city, during which the participants reputedly shouted, "Death to the whites!" News of this demonstration caused near panic among creole whites and Europeans in Caracas, who anticipated that any moment the black and colored population would rise up in arms against them.[45] For much the same reason during the next few years, Bolívar reacted harshly to end the machinations of black and mulatto officers such as Leonardo Infante and José Padilla, whom he accused of trying to establish a "pardocracy."[46]

The diaries of two diplomats who resided in Venezuela, Robert Ker

Porter of Britain and John G. A. Williamson from the United States, recorded other instances of similar racial unrest, between 1826 and 1840. Both men brought the racial biases of their respective countries with them. And, both often referred to racial strife in cases in which government officials attributed violence to political rather than racial tensions. Nevertheless, their close professional association with the nation's elites gave them access to elitist opinions, which frequently belied strong antiblack feelings and fears.[47]

It would be a mistake to consider Robert Ker Porter an objective observer of Venezuelan social behavior. To begin with, he viewed the behavior of multiracial Venezuelans through the lens of his own deeply held prejudices against blacks.

Although he grew to like Venezuela, he considered aspects of its culture uncouth and crude. He attributed this, in part, to the presence of nonwhites; as he wrote in his diary in late 1831, after an evening at the home of General Páez, the affair was "noisy, and not pleasant on account of the smoke and nuisance of cigars—and here certainly equality was most strongly visible, as well as the *freedom* of *that equality*—without distinction to either *rank* or *colours*. To me it was most irritatingly disgusting. I wish some of our *Noble Liberals,* as well as Philanthropic champions of *Negro* equality of social rights, could but pass a few months in this *Free* and *Independent* country. I think they would soon be disgusted with *equality* on the score of political rights."[48]

Porter seldom made any charitable comments about blacks. He once referred to the exploits of a black renegade who killed a white man as "living proofs of negro *intellect* and *virtues*."[49] On an earlier occasion he demonstrated his inclination to expect the worst of blacks when he accepted as true a rumor that a group of blacks had conspired to kill all whites. As he wrote on December 16, 1830: "Nothing to note save a black man taken up—who wished to seduce the soldiery—stating that it was time to do something here since there was no Government now in the country and that Venezuela ought to become a Second Hayti [*sic*]. That all the whites ought to be murdered—and that he had a strong band of blacks, who would aid them in their glorious task." Porter hardly questioned the veracity of this story and concluded, "There can be little doubt but there *is much in this*."[50]

Though many of his statements about racial warfare reflected his own misgivings about Venezuelan society, they also mirrored the views of many of the elites he knew. From what Porter said about the general concern that racial warfare might break out at any moment, it becomes unequivocally certain that several *caraqueños* felt their lives jeopardized by a predominantly colored majority. The perceived threat far exceeded the probability of a rebellion against whites, but elites believed such an uprising could occur.

John G. A. Williamson agreed with Porter on most points. He, too, noted the antipathy that characterized the relationships between whites and blacks.[51] Like his English associate, he thought that the hostility that existed between races would someday lead to racial violence. When José Farfán led a short-lived rebellion in 1837, Williamson treated it as a racial struggle rather than a fight between vying political factions. A defeat of Páez he thought "would have brought a horde of half civilized coloured people from the plains and interior, to murder pillage and rob under exasperated feelings, the white portion of the population of the cities, and with the cry of colour against colour, would have raised the dormant feelings of those who compose the greatest proportion of the population everywhere."[52] Porter concurred with this opinion; independently he reported Páez as having said that "at present it is but trifling, but from the nature of those sambos and their great number—it may, if not promptly put down, become an *affair of colour.*"[53] The seriousness with which the Caracas elites met the news of the Farfán revolt can be seen in Porter's speculation as to what kind of reception they would extend to the victorious Páez. In his estimation, "Doubtless the *cold-hearted* people of Caracas will give him some public demonstration of their gratitude for again saving them from pillage and death, *which was to have been the case* had the coloured chief and his dark horde have beaten Páez and advanced on this city."[54]

Caracas, with its high concentration of slaves, was not the only city to experience waves of panic among its white citizenry. In December 1838, rumors circulated in Puerto Cabello of an impending attack by a small band of fugitive slaves. The details appear sketchy, but apparently a group of four or five armed runaway slaves had been seen in the area around the city. According to a published report sent by Agustín Hernández to the governor of the province, these men, armed with lances and machetes, joined up with a larger group of runaways. According to Hernández, they evidently planned to "fall upon the whites, to assassinate and rob them." In calling for military assistance from the government, Hernández indicated that nobody really knew what might happen but that "some say they [proclaim] the freedom of slaves, others that [they] come to rob and kill since they were counting on the cooperation of people from Morón and Agua Negro, while some add that they say that two boats have come to their aid with people from Santo Domingo."[55]

Other major rebellions on the llanos during the 1840s provoked similar responses from urban elites. During that decade, rebel organizations and bandit factions controlled extensive parts of the countryside. Weak central governments lacked the police force to control local leaders. Like most nineteenth-century armies, the forces that operated on the llanos involved significant numbers of blacks, zambos, and Indians, but few whites. Some of these groups turned to outright banditry, cattle rustling, and contraband trade as a way of life. Others professed some political ideology or another, or at least associated themselves with one of the principal political parties that emerged during the decade. Allegiances occurred either with the Conservatives who rallied around Páez and his coalition of banking and commercial interests or with the Liberals, who in 1848 wrested power from Páez and set up a dictatorship under José Tadeo Monagas and his brother José Gregorio Monagas, representing the indebted planter class.

As described by historians Robert Matthews and Federico Brito Figueroa, most of the fighting that occurred on the llanos at this time amounted to gang warfare. But the presence of numerous armed bands still posed a potential threat in the eyes of white city dwellers. Not only did fugitive slaves participate in these factions but the rhetoric they used included the old slogan "Death to the whites!" which, even if meant in social or abstract terms rather than in a literal sense, had a nonetheless chilling effect on the whites.[56]

Mistaken or not, white elites still thought that the slaves, free blacks, and Indians who joined the llanero factions wanted to complete a racial caste war that began in the late eighteenth century. As voiced in 1840 by the editor of the Caracas newspaper *El Liberal,* they feared that almost anything could cause "great restlessness amongst a certain portion of the slaves and coloured people, whose views are to put down the influence of the white population by an attempt at Negro freedom entirely throughout the country, with no other view than that of revolution and to change the authority of *colour.*"[57]

To some degree actions by politicians contributed to the elites' anxiety. Before they seized control of the national government in 1848, Liberals encouraged free blacks and slaves to join their cause by advertising it as a campaign against a conservative white oligarchy. After their departure from power, Conservatives made similar overtures for support among the blacks. They openly advocated slave rebellion and promised to liberate all slaves once they regained power. In April 1853, for instance, a Conservative pamphlet entitled "The blacks, zambos, and mulattoes of Coro to the blacks, zambos, and mulattoes of all the Republic" branded Monagas as a traitor to the cause of liberty and proclaimed that he had sent an agent to Coro "to buy infant and young *manumisos* in order to ship them to a Spanish Colony [Puerto Rico] and to sell them there as slaves." This same piece of propaganda also charged that the president intended to enslave free blacks, and to subject them to the whips of the hacendados of Puerto Rico.[58]

But by 1853, the slave system showed every sign of having come un-glued. Newspapers regularly ran advertisements for runaway slaves. In the three decades before emancipation in 1854, some three thousand such an-nouncements appeared in the press. Presumably, the fittest and most ener-getic slaves fled their masters. By the same token, the owners probably ad-vertised only for their most valuable slaves. Nevertheless, the ads shed an interesting light on slavery during the years immediately preceding eman-cipation. The majority of slaves who fled did not fit the description of ter-rorists or revolutionaries determined to destroy the ruling class. Most had special skills which would have allowed them to relocate without much difficulty in regions with labor shortages. Their flight suggests the near collapse of slavery itself rather than a state of open rebellion.[59]

Facing both the disintegration of slavery through flight and the possibil-ity of slave rebellions, José Gregorio Monagas decided that he could avert political disaster only by decreeing the total emancipation of Venezuela's slaves. By a proclamation issued on March 24, 1854, he announced the end of slavery. On that day, he appeared before the National Congress, accompanied by a slave family dressed in the simple white cotton attire of their social class. In accordance with promises that he had made to protect the property rights of the slaveholders, Monagas agreed that his govern-ment would pay for the value of every slave for whom the owners could supply proof of ownership. This promise he never fulfilled.

Sporadic violence occurred in provincial cities following the emancipa-tion decree, but for the most part, the transition from slavery to freedom took place peacefully, with demonstrations of joy rather than anger. Only one potentially ugly incident marred the scene in Caracas, when former slaves refused to carry prayer rugs to mass for their masters' wives and daughters on the Sunday following their emancipation. Over the years this practice had come to represent one of the most humiliating aspects of slav-ery, a public demonstration of obedience and submission. On the Sunday before the decree female slaves who carried rugs for their owners met with jeers of derision from free blacks. The next week, the jeers turned to threats, forcing many of the Caracas elite to return to their homes. In other cases, the former slaves absolutely refused to carry rugs. The hostile atmo-sphere so intimidated many of the elite women that one angry aristocrat lamented that the individual security of the women necessitated their de-fense from unruly mobs of people who deserved to be slaves.[60]

Contrary to Monagas' design, emancipation did not end fighting be-tween political factions in Venezuela. In 1858, a coalition of moderate Liberals and Conservatives overthrew the regime of the Monagas brothers in a relatively bloodless coup. By 1859, a short-lived peace gave way to open warfare as demagogues calling themselves Federalists stirred up racial and class feelings by leading a revolt against the government of the politically moderate and inept General Julián Castro. Popular leaders, such as Ezequiel Zamora and Juan Crisostomo Falcón, with the intellectual guidance of Antonio Leocadio Guzmán and his son Antonio Guzmán Blanco, plunged the nation into one of its most sanguinary civil wars, the Federal War, which lasted until 1863. During that war the oppressed masses, including many former slaves, joined the Federalists in their struggle against an elite group known as Centralists. Tens of thousands perished in one of the most chaotic chapters of Venezuela's history.

As perceived by contemporary Venezuelans, and later interpreted by most national historians, two diverse groups faced each other in the Federal War. The Federalists represented groups who wanted autonomy for the states of Venezuela. They passed themselves off as egalitarians, appealing to oppressed persons of every class and race to join them in a struggle for "liberty, order, morality, and justice." They opposed centralized government, which they thought only served an oligarchy of rich landowners, bankers, and commercial interests. The oligarchy flocked to the banner of the Centralists, who thought of themselves as the last defenders of civilization and order.[61]

For their part, the Federalists wanted to overthrow the rich financial class who dominated both urban and rural sectors of Venezuela's predominantly agricultural economy. They identified their enemies as whites, although they used a social definition of the term instead of a strictly racial one and applied it to anyone "who could read or write, or who used shoes or neckties, and possessed the privileges of wealth."[62] They adopted the battle cry "Death to the whites!" as an inducement to the colored masses to join their troops. Moreover, they made direct appeals to blacks and Indians in their recruitment of troops.[63] Their propaganda stated that the Centralists planned to reenslave blacks. One llanero leader even spread the story that the government would brand former slaves they captured in battle before returning them to their former masters. Another claimed that the government planned to sell prisoners of war to foreigners. So effective were these charges that on one occasion when a British ship sailed from Ciudad Bolívar to Nutrías to pick up conscripts for the government's armies, the poverty class in that area believed the Centralists would carry out their threats to enslave them and sell them into bondage.[64]

The Centralists feared the racial consequences of the conflict. Like Bolívar, they inherited the prejudices of the old creoles who abhorred the creation of a pardocracy. To their way of thinking: "It is three quarters of Venezuela that conspires against the few good that there are in this unfortunate land. It is the blacks against the whites: the vicious and idle against the honest and industrious—the ignorant against the learned."[65] Centralists thought that the government had to take extraordinary measures to stop the pillage of the nation by satanic monsters and incendiaries. As one of the more reactionary members of the faction put it, "Let us be Turks rather than Haitians."[66]

In the eyes of the conservative Centralists, the Federalists comprised hordes of colored barbarians who wanted to destroy civilization in Venezuela. To their way of thinking, civilization amounted to a combination of class privilege and the accumulation of wealth and property at the expense of the uneducated workers. In effect, when the latter destroyed property and records of their indebtedness to the propertied class, they attacked civilization. For that reason, Centralists referred to the Federalists' troops as "Huns and Vandals," colored masses, and savage hordes, the latter word being one of the most frequently used in the nineteenth century to describe participants of popular movements. The word suggested an unstructured and undisciplined body of people who held no firm political beliefs. Centralists also depicted Federalists as "inflamed masses" of the criminal elements who had been whipped into action by savage propagandists. Without the latter, they argued, the vagabonds and criminals who fought to end civilization would not have acted, for they were otherwise inherently lazy, drunken, stupid, irreligious, and incapable of taking action on their own. As one Centralist exclaimed: "Poor people! Poor masses! There truly are certain similarities in the sterile sacrifices of these masses and the pugilists and gladiators, who went like automatons to die in cold blood in the Roman circus without knowing why in order to amuse the people."[67]

The absence of whites in the Federalist armies fueled the Centralists' fear of a race war. As one Centralist wrote: "They report, also, that in this number of men you will not see more than one white. If the supreme government does not look at these disturbances with the greatest of interest, these villains will take in greater increments every day, and not only will those of us who might have white skin see ourselves shackled but also they will cut off the only route . . . to the capital."[68] The loss of Caracas would have signaled the end of white rule, in their estimation.

Anticipation of defeat led the conservative Centralists to recall from exile the old caudillo and former president José Antonio Páez. But the once popular Páez failed to rally previously loyal llaneros to his cause. Even his son acknowledged the imminent destruction of whites, despite the efforts of his father to turn the tide of battle. As he observed in 1862, "Shortly after our return from Apure, a revolution broke out among the colored population; a class which until then had been the most peaceful and submissive, but since perverted to such a degree as to require all the energies and resources of the white race to save itself from utter ruin and degradation." Unable to contain the revolt, Páez withdrew. According to his son, the disturbance then spread over the llanos, where "it sowed the seeds of discontent which have since brought forth to the country an abundant crop of revenge, violence, and rapine."[69]

Contrary to such fears, the victory of the Federalists did not lead to a bloodbath. Blacks did not put whites to the sword. Indeed, in both the short and long run, little changed in Venezuela. At first glance, state and regional caudillos appeared to have won the most, for the Constitution of 1864 recognized the autonomy of twenty states and weakened the authority of the national government over local affairs. Other than the economic ruin of many elite families, and their subsequent loss of influence, the Federal War did not change the basic characteristics of Venezuelan society. As the saying aptly goes, The more things change, the more they stay the same. Despite widespread death and destruction, the social order remained intact, changing only in that new members had access to the elites' positions as a result of their association with the winning faction.

In Venezuelan historiography, the Federal War has left the inaccurate but lasting legacy that it marked the end of a series of racial conflicts dating back to the struggle for independence. Since the late nineteenth century, Venezuela's leading historians and social scientists have subscribed to this interpretation. Aristedes Rojas, Lisandro Alvarado, José Santiago Rodríguez, José María Rojas, José Gil Fortoul, Francisco González Guinán, Laureano Vallenilla Lanz, Pedro Manuel Arcaya, and other writers—all treated the period 1810 to 1863 as one rife with racial struggles. Recently Guillermo Morón and J. L. Salcedo-Bastardo have continued this argument. Subsequently, current textbooks continue to give these ideas wide circulation in the nation's secondary schools.

According to this consensus, a struggle for racial equality began during the wars for independence. Between 1810 and 1821, slaves fought for Spaniards and loyalists alike in an effort to obtain their freedom and to gain political rights. Thus, the troops of Boves represented part of a movement by free blacks and slaves to get the upper hand over the white master class.[70] Following independence, *pardos,* free blacks, zambos, and slaves agitated both to liberate slaves and to secure more political rights for themselves from the whites who controlled the new government. The fact that slavery lasted through the middle of the century led the consensus historians to treat the institution as a basic cause of the wars that plagued Venezuela. As a direct result of the seemingly incessant warfare, regional caudillos of all races advanced, largely because of their military careers. The final chapter of this process took place during the Federal War. With its completion, and the rise of the so-called Yellow Liberals under Antonio Guzmán Blanco during the 1870s, racial tensions finally abated. In effect, the turbulent and chaotic struggle for political power between vying factions not only gave way to an era of stability but also introduced a period of racial harmony to Venezuela. In the new order of the post–Federal War period, nonwhites enjoyed the rights and privileges they set out to obtain nearly fifty years before.[71]

Undoubtedly, after 1863, the common folk of Venezuela experienced a sort of racial parity among their own class. For instance, in the late 1860s Ramón Páez marveled at the racial mix he found among the workers on his father's llano estate: "Our retinue presented pretty much the appearance of an oriental caravan; it consisted of more than a hundred individuals of all grades and colors; from the bright, rubicund faces of England's sons, to the jetty phiz of the native African, all of whom, not withstanding, fraternized as though sprung from the same race." A few years later, in 1874, a German visitor reported of the average Venezuelans: "The white, black, and copper-colored races that form the population of Venezuela have mixed themselves principally in the territories of the llanos in such a varied manner that here it would present a difficult task for the expert eye of the ethnologist. But the quality of the hair is the distinctive characteristic. Short and curly hair like wool shows the predominance of African blood, and long flat hair reveals a lineage of predominantly Indian character. Other than this, skin color and general appearance can be exceedingly similar in both cases."[72]

But those who assumed that the Federal War and earlier conflicts either constituted racial wars, as such, or brought an end to racial divisions rested their conclusions on some flawed thinking. First, white elites never accepted nonwhites as absolute equals after the war ended. At best, they relinquished some political power to dark-skinned individuals, but they refused to accept them as equals in any other sense. Second, neither the Federal War nor any of the other wars that took place in Venezuela had anything in common with the type of caste and race war that engulfed Yucatán, Mexico, at approximately the same time. In the latter case, Maya Indians rose up in arms against Europeanized Mexicans of the region. Race definitely differentiated the adversaries in Yucatán.[73] The Federal War of Venezuela did not match race against race, despite the rhetoric of the participants. For one thing, whites led both the Centralist and Federalist movements. Federalist leaders, such as Juan C. Falcón and Ezequiel Zamora, fit both social and racial criteria for whiteness. So did Antonio Leocadio Guzmán and his son Antonio Guzmán Blanco, who had close ties to the white Caracas aristocracy. Finally, blacks, zambos, and *pardos* made up the bulk of every Venezuelan army. This applied particularly to the forces of the western caudillos who came to power after the Federal War. They, like the eastern and central llanero chiefs who preceded them, pressed the downtrodden, dark-hued Venezuelan campesinos into service as cannon fodder—as did the Centralists.

Contemporary accounts substantiate the predominant role of black soldiers in all armies, especially in the ranks. Visitors to Venezuela, such as Charles Daniel Dance, Thomas C. Dawson, Edward B. Eastwick, and Friedrich Gerstacker, often commented on the ubiquitous black forces. In the 1840s, Dance described in detail one such individual he had seen in Maturín. "The Commandant of the troopers—a tall, portly Sambo, of the negro and Indian races—with whom a child might fearlessly have played, but who, in times of Presidential faction fights, kept his enemies in fear, and his soldiers under discipline." During the Federal War, Eastwick reported meeting a "gigantic negro artilleryman, on the side of the aristocrats [Centralists]" at La Guaira. As one Englishman depicted the Coro troops of Falcón, they looked like "lean old scarecrows and starveling boys not five feet high, the greater number half naked, with huge strips of raw beef twisted around their hats or hanging from their belts. Their skins seemed to have been baked black with exposure to the sun and their arms and accessories were of the most wretched description." At about the same time, a German traveler encountered an equally bedraggled force at Calabozo, led by a black general. The army had just taken the city and presented a "uniformly tattered" group which had "all of the shades of skin but scarcely any white, and presently very dirty." Dawson wrote of the armies of Guzmán Blanco in much the same terms: "With a terrific insurrection raging against him, he concentrated power in his hands, suppressed the peculations of his agents, and relentlessly dragged the half-breeds and negroes into his armies." A pencil sketch drawn by Dawson of a typical soldier of the 1870s showed an individual of distinctly negroid features, dark skin, and few possessions.[74]

The wars that devastated Venezuela during the nineteenth century neither stemmed from nor led to racial hatred. The majority of blacks who took part in the many struggles did so for more than one reason. Admittedly, some desired their liberty, others basic equality. Most arrived in the armies as unwilling conscripts, victims of forced recruitment by the regional caudillos. It seems unlikely that many of them ever fully understood the causes for which they fought. Social gain attracted some, but mostly in a limited sense. A few individuals, such as José Félix Mora, met with considerable success because of their military prowess. Mora, who led black troops from the region around Puerto Cabello, eventually joined Guzmán Blanco's Federalist armies and rose to positions of power after the war ended. But most blacks and zambos did not have such good fortune. They died forgotten on the battlefields, or they eked out wretched lives as foot soldiers, unless they deserted. Forced recruitment accounted for most of the nation's troops. In fact, conscription became so widespread that laborers often fled any strangers, including foreigners, rather than run the risk of falling into the clutches of the recruiters. As one planter despaired, "We will continue indefinitely to witness the ruin of our fields and to wait for an end of recruitment, as the pastor of Manzanares waited for the river to stop running in order to go across high and dry."[75]

The case of Cecilio Padrón, a black leader from La Victoria, points up the danger of making any hard-and-fast conclusions about the racial aspects of nineteenth-century warfare. For a brief period, Padrón, the son of prominent free blacks descended directly from slaves, led a "miserable faction" against the Centralists. He already enjoyed social prominence in La Victoria before the war broke out. His parents had considerable wealth and social status. He had married a white woman of French ancestry. Moreover, he numbered among his own friends many of the elite of La Victoria. It seems that he rose up against the government in an effort to usurp more power for himself in local affairs. He certainly did not act for racial reasons, or for social advancement. Apparently he had no clear ideological reasons for supporting the Federalists, nor did he harbor strong racial antagonism toward whites. When his followers deserted him because of his shortcomings as a military leader, he petitioned President Manuel Tovar for peace. In his letter to Tovar he revealed his confused thinking, simply attributing his decision to stop fighting to his newfound religion and his desire to go abroad to do God's work. An accompanying letter from the Frenchman Luis Delpech, who knew Tovar well enough to address him as "my dear Manuel," noted that Padrón resigned because he no longer had any followers. But the white Delpech made no mention of racial strife, and the whole incident suggests that Padrón left the struggle as but one of many frustrated figures for whom the conflict had no clear meaning.[76]

In the final analysis, class not race explained the presence of most nonwhites in the Federalists' armies. As in the case of the llanero uprisings of the 1840s and 1850s, many indebted laborers, subsistence farmers, sharecroppers, and other rural campesinos rose up against the merchants and landowners who controlled their lives. Primarily, they wanted to throw off the burdens of debt. They also wanted to end unjust and strict penal codes and laws that bound them to their debts and lowly stations in life. But they did not necessarily take at its face value the Federalists' promise to create a classless society. Nor did they have a clear idea of their own class identity. It only seems certain that they wanted to overthrow a class which they believed oppressed them and to destroy the government supported by that class.

WHITENING THE POPULATION, 1850–1900

BETWEEN 1850 and 1900, Venezuelan elites experienced several political and philosophical transitions affecting the history of race relations. By 1870, followers of the dictator Antonio Guzmán Blanco, who called themselves Yellow Liberals, replaced the so-called conservative Centralists as leaders of the nation's political structure. Although many of these individuals could trace their families back to traditional regional elites, their move to Caracas marked the efforts of Guzmán to centralize authority in Venezuela and to modernize the nation's infrastructure. In effect, Guzmán brought fresh faces to governmental positions. Philosophical changes occurred along with these political shifts. After 1870, elites moved increasingly toward adopting European intellectual solutions to Venezuela's endlessly nagging problems of development. By the end of the century, positivism became the leading philosophy of influential elites, with close connections to the often shaky political leadership.

With the acceptance of positivism, Venezuelan elites began to formalize their view on race, while making modifications to contemporary European racist theories. As in the past, their folklore conveyed their long-standing dislike of blacks and doubts about the blacks' ability to form an integral part of a stable and modern society. During the last half of the century, elites did more than openly attach positive values to whiteness and negative images to blackness. They actually called for the whitening of the population, by attracting European immigrants to Venezuela, and by effecting the virtual disappearance of blacks over an extended period of time. This movement, while not overt or institutionalized as in the United States, slowly led the Caracas-based elites who ruled most of Venezuela to agree that they could indeed improve their nation's population by whitening.

During the nineteenth century, the whites actively fostered a demeaning image of blacks to keep the impoverished black minority subordinated, depicting them disparagingly in folklore, literature, and other cultural genres. In contrast to North Americans, who created a racial stereotype in the bumbling, fawning, foot-shuffling and obsequious black known as Sambo, Venezuelans made no effort to categorize their black population in any narrow manner. Nor did they turn to hatred in their efforts to maintain social control over blacks. But, like their Yankee contemporaries, they attributed to blacks a number of singularly negative characteristics—namely, stupidity, improvidence, conceit, contentiousness, pretentiousness, ugliness, laziness, dirtiness, sensualness, and slyness.

Historically, negative images dated back to the colonial era. They developed from the attitudes of those colonists who enslaved black Africans and their descendants to do their work. Social control, pettiness, and jealousy had much to do with their origin. As the colonial society evolved, the white creole aristocracy attempted to block the social progress of nonwhites; in so doing they not only used a series of codes that restricted the privileges of blacks and *pardos* but also fostered a negative image of blacks.

Even the adage "Money whitens" took on great significance in this context. For one thing, it suggested a corollary: that poverty blackened. Thus, of itself the adage implies the great social obstacles blacks and *pardos* faced in their efforts to achieve social mobility. Furthermore, during the late colonial era, their attempts to whiten and improve themselves socially by using their wealth to purchase certificates of dispensation from racial restrictions met with considerable resistance from white elites. Thus, though the political turmoil of the nineteenth century offered many more opportunities to black men to achieve powerful positions through military and political careers, their progress did not occur in a vacuum. As in the past, whites resented the upward mobility of nonwhites and resisted change in numerous ways.

Certainly, the type of folklore collected at the end of the century by Aristedes Rojas attacked the personalities, mores, and ethical values of Venezuela's blacks. Although some of the more innocuous refrains merely poked fun at blacks as simple people or depicted them as sexual objects, most insulted them.

Throughout the second half of the nineteenth century, urban elites kept alive the notion of black sloth and indolence. In particular, they used deprecative folk sayings that reinforced existing stereotypes of blacks as ignorant, dirty, and ugly persons, with evil dispositions. With reason, the Brazilian writer Paulo de Carvalho-Neto once referred to such folklore as "fakelore," because he considered it the product of a conscious effort by white elites to demoralize blacks.[1]

One form of resistance to accepting blacks appeared in the coining of a number of popular sayings that referred to blacks in derogatory ways. As the following expression reveals, many whites despised "uppity" blacks who did not conform to the stereotype of blacks as humble people who smelled bad, looked ugly, and lacked the means to support themselves: "The black woman who puts on powder / And showy muslin / Looks like burnt sugarcane / With ashes on top."[2] Dirty blacks had no place in the supposedly clean world of the whites, a theme that repeatedly showed up in a number of refrains, such as: "I began to wash a black man / To see what color he would turn / The more soap I used on him / The dirtier he became." A variant of the same concept stated crudely: "A black went to bathe / And wanted to become white / The water became darker / And the black remained the same."[3]

A great deal of this so-called folklore undermined the self-esteem of blacks. It also stripped them of the privileges of class. By the same token, it reminded everyone of their lowly origin as slaves. One widely used stanza explained the usual relationship of rich whites and blacks in explicit terms: "When a white eats in the company of a black, either the white owes something to the black or they are eating the food of the black." As in the case of the saying "Money whitens," this adage reinforced the accepted notion that blacks lived in poverty, apart from whites. For that reason, no self-respecting white elites would willingly invite blacks into their homes.

Other proverbs picked out what their authors thought were ugly or negative characteristics of blacks. For instance: "Blacks and vultures / Look just alike / Blacks are malicious / Vultures too." Or another, which associated blacks with evil: "All the blacks are sad / And their disconsolateness is caused / By that which San Benito said / That blacks do not enter heaven." Equally to the point: "Black was Santa Ephigenia / The mother of San Benito / Black were the three nails / With which they fastened Christ."[4]

Even sexual allusions put blacks in subservient roles. As the following verse points out, relations between races often led to friction and seldom met with social approval among elites: "The woman who because of madness / Has a black for a lover / Always sees a dark house / Even though the sun shines brightly."[5] Ironically, black and pardo women epitomized sexuality, sensuality, and beauty in Venezuela, and lovers often used the words *negrita* and *morena* as terms of endearment. In fact, even to this day Venezuelan men consider tan-skinned women, or *morenas,* the most appealing type of beauty. As one refrain put it: "The man who might die / Without loving a *morena* / Leaves this world for another / Without having known a good thing."

Folklore, or what passed for folklore, mostly kept blacks in their place from an elitist social perspective. In a real way, this type of imagery mirrored the perceptions of the elites, who had definite ideas about blacks and their place in the work force. Even though Venezuelan elites did not arrive at a rigid concept of "niggers' work," as had their North American contemporaries, they nevertheless believed that most blacks performed the dirtiest and most menial tasks. They expected to see blacks do the work that whites most disdained. Perhaps this attitude originated during the colonial era, when a more rigid social hierarchy existed. Whatever its origins, the image of blacks as lowly laborers lasted throughout the nineteenth century. As seen in the 1890s, in a series of photographs published in the elitist publication *El Cojo Ilustrado* under the title "Typical *Caraqueños*," blacks comprised a disparate and motley group of vendors, porters, street cleaners, gas lamp lighters, itinerant repairmen, and cooks. By implication, they made up a group of quaint and picturesque personalities, vestiges of the past who would disappear as Caracas became increasingly modern.[6] In other words, despite a high degree of racial mixing, and social advance for the nation's mixed racial population, whites still followed long-held convictions when it came to their evaluation of blacks. As trite as it sounds, blacks lived in the shadow of their slave past.

In contrast, by the last decades of the nineteenth century, a white elite came to think of themselves as a distinct nobility. Some could trace their ancestry back to the original conquistadores. Others claimed their privileges by boasting that among their ancestors there numbered only freemen. White skin became, in the words of one traveler, the "real badge of Nobility." As the same visitor noted: "Since the emancipation of the slaves, the white race cultivate a sentiment of equality which seems to have penetrated every bosom. It is their proud boast to never have reckoned among their ancestors any but *freemen*, and they found their Nobility on hereditary liberty. Every Biscayan calls himself noble; and to their credit be it said, they have in no small degree contributed to propagate in the colonies that system of equality among all men whose blood has not been contaminated by the African race."[7]

In general, a socioracial division of society lingered on in practice, as it had during the colonial era. This followed very closely the class distinctions between white elites and colored popular masses. Even visitors to Venezuela noticed the fine racial divisions in all social groupings. As Edward B. Eastwick reported of Valencia in 1864, a clear racial hierarchy existed in Venezuela. "Now, mark me; the white creoles live at this end of the street, near the Plaza; lower down we shall come to the trigueñas, or 'brunettes'; and beyond these we shall find mulattas and mestizas, and we shall finish up with some beauties of a downright black, who are not so much to be despised as you would imagine."[8]

Social customs also recognized class and color lines in Venezuela during the second half of the nineteenth century, though sex allowed for variation. The isolation of upper-class white women persisted as it had during the colonial period. Elite males, on the other hand, enjoyed extraordinary freedom with women of all classes and races and mingled freely at public functions. Travelers to Venezuela reported having seen upper-class men dance the *joropo,* Venezuela's fast-moving national dance, which featured complex polyrhythms of African origin. To most elites the *joropo* represented a common dance. But few could resist its inviting strains. As one European observer noted, while upper-class men joined in the merriment of dancing the *joropo* with people of the lower classes, their women did not. "In Venezuela the *joropo* serves as a dance of the popular colored lower classes, but appropriately it is one of the favorite dances by custom. Upper-class gentlemen do not think it unworthy to take part in a *joropo,* but white gentlewomen are absolutely excluded."[9]

Among other long-lived racial stereotypes, zambos continued to have a reputation as dangerous and shifty individuals, the word taking on an opprobrious meaning, much like that given to the term *half-breed* in the United States. Venezuelans and foreigners alike believed the worst of this mixture of Indian and African. They saw none of the "civilizing" characteristics in the zambo that they assigned solely to European influences. A particularly harsh judgment made in the 1880s by William Barry, a bigoted Englishman, recalled a similar comment made at the beginning of the century by Jean Joseph Dauxion-Lavaysse about Venezuelan attitudes toward zambos, "A peculiar race called Zamboes, a combination of imported African slaves with some of the original Carib Indians, has produced a breed, which, even in Venezuela, is looked upon as singularly ferocious, and out of ten crimes committed, at least eight are attributed, and with reason, to Zamboes." During the Federal War, he concluded, the zambos had proven "the most cruel and blood-thirsty of all troops, neither taking nor giving quarter, and have fairly outrivalled, in that respect, the Llaneros, or men of the plains."[10]

Near the end of the nineteenth century, the degree of miscegenation led many foreigners to notice this factor first before assessing the economic and racial aspects of social class. Ira N. Morris summed up the consensus of most foreigners who wrote about Venezuela when he said: "The color line, while at present still noticed in Venezuela, is not nearly so marked as in the countries to the North. Here are often found inter-marriages, and it is no break of social propriety for a white person to marry one having a taint of colored blood."[11]

In 1896, William Curtis made similar comments about the effect of miscegenation in Venezuela. "While the color line is not entirely obliterated in Venezuelan society, it is not so strictly drawn as in the United States, and the fact that a man has negro blood in his veins does not debar him from either social, professional or political honors." Curtis added, "It is a common thing to see a white woman with an octoroon, or even a mulatto, for a husband, and even more common to see a white husband with a tinted Venus for a wife." At public places, such as resorts, hotels, or the theater, as well as in commercial and political establishments, he found racial mingling without distinction. "It is an ordinary sight to find black and white faces side by side at the dining-tables of the hotels and restaurants, and in the schools and colleges the color of a child makes no difference in his standing or treatment." He met black scholars, jurists, lawyers, doctors, and priests, none of whom he felt suffered from any prejudices. As for the agricultural sector, Curtis stated: "Some of the wealthiest planters in the country are full-blooded negroes, but they are not often found in trade. This is probably because most of the merchants are foreigners. The natives are commonly engaged in agriculture and the professions." [12]

But, as Curtis pointed out, most pure blacks and Indians never escaped a social position much like perpetual peonage. According to him, "While the laws of peonage have never existed in Venezuela, the relation between the planter and his laborers, particularly in the interior of the country, is equivalent to this form of slavery, and it is tolerated by both classes as the natural consequence of the difference in their wealth and social position." [13] For the most part, whites and Europeanized creoles dominated the upper levels of society. They manifested European and North American social behavior, at least in their dress and demeanor, as well as their professed value systems. Below them ranged the Indians, blacks, mestizos, and other admixtures, with the pure blacks and Indians at the bottom. As Curtis concluded: "The full-blooded negro, like the full-blooded Indian, seldom rises above the level of laborer, and the zambo is the lowest of them all. . . . The army, like the laboring classes, is composed of Indians, negroes, and zamboes, while the officers are either white or have white blood in their veins." [14]

In this respect, throughout the nineteenth century the Venezuelan landed elites held laborers of all races in low regard. In their eyes, Venezuelan day laborers did not know the importance of regular work. They lacked a sufficient work ethic of the sort found in Europe and the United States. According to the planters, the *jornaleros* were irresponsible, at best, and only worked intermittently at their own convenience. In an early example of this attitude, one planter complained, "A day wage earner in this land, as abundant as it is, lives for a week with what he earns in one day, and with what he produces in a day of hunting and fishing, so that the laborer does not want to work another day because he does not need to." [15] Sometime later, the Englishman Eastwick, in Venezuela to drum up business for British firms, came to a less charitable conclusion. He depicted the popular mass of Venezuelans as improvident, lazy, and scornful people who shirked all responsibility when it came to work.[16]

Following the disruptions of the Federal War, planters felt the need to force a work ethic on their workers, who otherwise behaved in what they considered an irresponsible manner. In 1864, one representative of the Puerto Cabello planter class actually established a newspaper, appropriately called *El Comercio*, in which he wrote that "to govern is to work and to make work."[17] Building upon the famous Argentine dictum that "to govern is to populate," he argued for himself and his peers that the nation needed laws which would make the masses appreciate the value of hard work. Another contributor to *El Comercio* called work "sacred" since it assured the health, prosperity, and well-being of the nation. "We work then," he wrote, "to be free and happy. We work in order to be great. We work so that we will not be taken ill."[18]

Planters believed that the salvation of the masses would only result when the individual workers learned to love work. Put in its most direct and idealistic form: "The love of work is the most efficacious means of obtaining material well-being. Since the fall of Adam, we remain subject to the law contained in this simple and brief phrase, 'With the sweat of your brow you will eat bread.'"[19] From the planters' perspective, society needed laws to govern workers, since all individuals were not created equal. Without strict laws which forced laborers to learn the value of work, the nation would not develop beyond its present condition.[20] The laws were necessary for the progress of their nation. Such thinking obviously reflected the objectives of an economic elite who equated increased production of their goods with improved living conditions for all Venezuelans.

On their part, the impoverished masses held a contradictory view. Ravaged by malnutrition, parasites, endemic diseases, and tropical heat, they found working day to day a debilitating experience, not religiously uplifting. To them, life amounted more to daily survival than to progressive movement aimed at building a new nation. Nor did the average campesino share the optimism of the elite about the future. Gastrointestinal diseases remained a leading cause of death in Venezuela (as they do to this day). Under such circumstances, the rural masses held a far more conservative view of their lives. They worked, but for their own basic comfort, not to fatten the elite. Even foreign visitors noted with surprising frequency that Venezuelan laborers worked as hard and as well as any workers in the world.[21]

Nevertheless, in the early 1850s, planters pressed for the passing of vagrancy and work codes which gave them the right to coerce unemployed laborers to work on their properties. They had feared that the freeing of slaves would exacerbate a perceived labor shortage. Theoretically, this gave them access to an otherwise unproductive labor force. In fact, the laws failed to achieve the desired results. Before the mid-1870s, no central government could enforce the vagrancy codes for want of a large enough rural police force. Workers either refused to work or moved from one state to another with impunity rather than accept the regulations imposed upon them by the elites. In the same manner, they escaped debts and other obligations. Often they received the support of desperate landowners who wanted laborers. These planters encouraged such behavior by advancing salaries to workers without asking questions about their past, rather than have them arrested and sent back to their home states as the laws required.[22]

In such an environment race alone did not impede most blacks from improving their lives. But the economic conditions of Venezuela did. After 1854, uneducated and underskilled blacks had few options for employment, despite the shortage of rural laborers. Freed slaves moved horizontally on the social scale from bondage to peonage. As noted, like many blacks they ended up as soldiers, or bandits, in the nation's many armed factions. Some moved to the coast, where they found work as stevedores and sailors at the port cities, or lived as fishermen along the beaches and rivers of northern Venezuela. In the larger cities they worked as domestic servants, street cleaners, garbage collectors, doorkeepers, and porters or ended up in any number of street professions, such as lottery sellers and vendors of ice, bread, water, coffee, or pots and pans. As such, they became familiar sights in the major northern cities, such as Caracas, Maracaibo, Valencia, Puerto Cabello, and Cumaná.[23]

Black women had fewer economic opportunities than men. Following emancipation in 1854, many black women remained on the land as day laborers, receiving lower wages than men, or shared the misery of their husbands as seasonal rural workers, tenant farmers, or *conuqueros*. Planters often expressed their preference for women, whom they considered more diligent and conscientious workers, as well as cheaper and more exploitable. Women also replaced men on haciendas when the latter went off to war. Under similar circumstances they took over *conucos* to provide for fatherless families during the turbulent epoch of the Federal War. In the cities they continued to work as domestic servants, as they had throughout the colonial period. Black women cooked, sewed, cleaned, washed, and cared for numerous urban households. They also found employment as *amas,* or nurses, who not only suckled the infants but also cared for the sick and infirm, and in many cases they served as counselors for elitist women. Some *amas* also became midwives, not only for prominent urban families but for entire neighborhoods in the growing Venezuelan cities. Indeed, by the end of the nineteenth century, demands for black domestic servants reached such high levels that black women from Martinique, Curaçao, and Trinidad easily found employment in the major cities.

Black women who did not work as domestics worked at other urban professions. Many set up business as street vendors, most commonly selling sweets and candies they made. These *dulcerías* frequented popular street corners and markets throughout the cities. Others made *arepas*, or food specialties, which they sold either door to door or at small stands that they set up along well-traveled routes. Less fortunate black working-class women turned to prostitution to survive. Until the 1920s, when the so-called Frenchwomen took over the prostitution district of Silencio in Caracas, black women comprised the majority of the city's prostitutes. The same occurred in port cities such as La Guiara and Puerto Cabello. In Maracaibo, Guairo Indian women forced into prostitution outnumbered black prostitutes.

But by far the vast majority of black men and women lived impoverished in rural areas as campesinos. Most former slaves never left the land following their emancipation. They stayed on as *jornaleros*, tenant farmers, sharecroppers, or *conuqueros*. Collectively, the rural poor comprised a nondescript populace of all colors known to the planter class as *gente del vecindario*, whom planters contracted in a variety of ways.

During the second half of the century, most arrangements involved sharecropping. Sharecroppers, known as *medianerios* (riffraff), received rights to till marginal lands adjacent to the planters' estates, usually on the borders or on more mountainous terrain. As a condition, they gave the planters half of their harvests and agreed to work as peons on a seasonal basis to cover additional costs, including seeds and tools. By this method former slaves joined free blacks as peons, assuring planters a relatively steady source of labor. For all intents and purposes, in some parts of Venezuela they lived under semifeudal conditions. In 1865, for instance, an advertisement for the sale of a hacienda near San Felipe not only listed twenty thousand coffee trees, three thousand plantains, three thousand cacao trees, a house with a kitchen, an outdoor oven, and animals but it also assured the buyer of an existing labor force of "seventy *colonos*, the majority peons of the hacienda and the rest those who pay rents."[24]

Before the mid-1870s, poverty anchored most blacks and *pardos* to the lower strata. Race alone did not seem of particular importance to rural elites. Most rural Venezuelans lived simple lives, with no splendor or luxury, and barely adequate housing. Only in slight ways did the living quarters of the more prosperous hacendados and ranchers differ from the *ranchos* of the tenant farmers, *jornaleros*, and *conuqueros*. With the exception of the better-off planters, the average rural Venezuelan still had only one suit of clothes, a simple hat made out of palm leaves, and homemade sandals. The hacendados and ranchers, like their poorer neighbors, often shared their homes with their livestock. Pigs and chickens wandered in and out at will, as much at home in the living quarters as in the dooryards. Women and children barely dressed—boys usually wore nothing but cotton shirts until their tenth birthday. As for luxury items, one visitor to the llanos reported, "It is possible that on all of our haciendas there could not be collected ten cases of wine, nor found one jam, nor do they kill a turkey or a chicken each year except in the case of sickness."[25]

In many basic ways, city dwellers did not fare much better. In 1867, a group of North Americans from Williams College described the general lack of wealth in Caracas in the following terms: "In dress, the upper class follow the European systems; the man of modest pretensions considers himself equipped when supplied with pants, *camisa*, which is worn outside the former, wool or panama hat, and leather sandals. Children of the lower class are not inconvenienced by clothing until they have attained the age of eight or ten years, when a camisa constitutes the outfit."[26] Clothes easily distinguished rich from poor, meaning that race, although an issue, played only a secondary role in determining individuals' status.

During the 1870s, this situation changed perceptibly, largely as the result of the introduction to Venezuela of new intellectual currents, especially that of positivism. For all intents and purposes, the introduction of positivism at the university level came in 1861. German scientist Adolfo Ernst, the first professor of natural history at the national university in Caracas, joined Rafael Villavicencio, Aristedes Rojas, and Vicente Marcano as founders of a Venezuelan positivist school of thought. These men stressed scientific inquiry and paid only scant attention to political questions. As expressed in 1869 by Villavicencio, the basic point of departure for the positivists boiled down to the following:

> We believe that the new dogma that has to be used as a foundation for social reorganization is found in integral science, which harmonizes faith and reason, religion and science; and which separates, in the social, AUTHORITY from POWER, subordinating the latter to the former, understanding authority without material force whose influence rests solely upon WISDOM and VIRTUE.
>
> We conclude, there is no difference between our previous ideas and the present ones; the most that one is able to say is that we have passed from monism, agnostic, to spiritualist, which is not a contradiction but EVOLUTION.[27]

When they did treat historical themes, the early positivists concerned themselves with questions related to the formation of Venezuelan society and its structure. They differed from the preceding generation of lyrical historians who dealt primarily with political chronology.

Most important, during the 1860s and 1870s, their writings and lectures introduced a second and far more influential generation of positivists to the works of Auguste Comte, Charles Darwin, Claude Henri de Saint-Simon, Hippolyte Adolphe Taine, Arthur de Gobineau, Gustave Le Bon, Émile Durkheim, Gabriel Tarde, Vachar de Lapouge, and Herbert Spencer. These teachers firmly believed in evolution; moreover, they taught their students well. By the turn of the century, the younger positivists persuaded the members of newly founded academies of medicine and science to endorse evolutionary theories. Given the absence in Venezuela both of a strong Catholic church and of Bible-Belt Protestantism of the type found in the United States, the ideas about evolution met with little opposition.[28]

The positivists brought a new dimension to the discussion of race in Venezuela through their introduction of recent racial theories put forward by European and North American scholars and writers. Their predecessors had largely overlooked race as an important issue. But in their efforts to understand national development, the positivists soon equated white race with progress. The racist theories purported that racial hierarchies existed and that race, like climate and other natural phenomena, might determine the fate of a given people. The obvious success of Anglo-Saxon societies during the nineteenth century supported the notion that some groups seemed destined to become great, others to remain weak.

Although they rejected some of the most blatantly racist arguments held by European and North American writers, Venezuelan positivists assiduously clung to the basic notion of determinism. They accepted climate, race, hygiene, and technology as important factors in determining the evolution of modern societies. They also applied materialistic standards to measure progress and to compare the relative strengths and weaknesses of nations, which, like Spencer, they studied as living organisms.

Ultimately, the postivists' study of race and its influence on national development led them to advocate a policy of whitening the population. To their credit, the Venezuelans adapted the foreign determinist theories to their own reality. They proved an eclectic lot and refused to become bogged down in self-demeaning or fatalistic arguments about the future of their nation. This optimistic streak eventually took them down some interesting and twisted paths as they explored the potential of a multiracial population in a world seemingly dominated by Anglo-Saxons.

On the one hand, they partially blamed Venezuela's political instability and chaos on the presence of an inherently inferior, mixed racial majority of *pardos,* blacks, and Indians. They judged this majority incapable of governing themselves under a democratic order. Like their Mexican and

Argentine counterparts, who shared many of their liberal precepts, they simply did not trust political power to an ignorant mass of colored people. On the other hand, the Venezuelan positivists believed that in the long run continued racial mixing would save Venezuela by whitening its population. This last observation they based on a number of doubtful premises, including their belief that mestizos made up the bulk of the population. For some unexplained reason they considered mestizos superior to other colored groups, including mulattoes and zambos, even though their treatment of Indians seemed far more harsh than that of blacks.

The idea that Venezuela constituted a predominantly mestizo nation dated back to the writings of Aristedes Rojas. In some of his early works during the 1860s, Rojas stated his conviction that evolution led to the creation of a new civilization in Venezuela in a direct and progressive way from the society of conquistadores and indigenous people. In his words, "The indigenous race has not disappeared entirely, it has entered into a grand era of metamorphosis." Rojas obviously placed mestizos well above negroid groups because they more nearly fit the somatic norms set for acceptance by his class. Mestizos looked more European than other nonwhites. He also let some of the social stigma attached to slavery affect his thinking, for as descendants of the slave caste, blacks failed to conform to his ideal type of person. But whether or not he let his social biases influence him, he definitely felt that racial mixing with whites had a salubrious effect on the mestizos. He also believed that future mixing with whites would allow the Venezuelan mestizos to achieve even higher levels of organic evolution.[29]

Rojas, who dealt mostly with folklore, tried to minimize the African contributions to Venezuelan culture. By 1893, he insisted in an article he published in *El Cojo Ilustrado* that only a few black enclaves remained in Venezuela, mostly in the valleys of Aragua and Tuy. With the exception of these remote communities, he wrote, the African elements had mixed with other Venezuelans, all but disappearing from sight as a distinct racial group. They left behind vestiges of their music and folklore, but otherwise they no longer played an active role in the national society. Like others who treated blacks as anachronistic segments of a modernizing society, Rojas dismissed them as a part of the future Venezuelan society. Moreover, he did not believe that their limited presence would adversely affect the national character of succeeding generations.[30]

During the 1890s, José Gil Fortoul became the leading exponent of this line of reasoning. He openly declared that in Venezuela miscegenation mostly involved whites and Indians. Like Rojas, he considered this an acceptable mixture. In fact, he acknowledged that most of the ruling class were mestizos, with little or no black ancestry. As he described them:

"This mixture [mestizo] constitutes the directing social class. From it appear the functionaries of all kinds, the writers, the artists, the learned, the most fearless and capable impresarios."[31]

Actually, Gil Fortoul deserves recognition as the first major Venezuelan intellectual to write extensively about questions related to race. During the 1890s, he wrote several positive statements about racial mixing that helped Venezuelan elites accept the *café con leche* status of their society. In this important way he differed from many of his prominent Latin American contemporaries who shared his positivistic philosophy, such as Justo Sierra of Mexico, Alejandro O. Deustua of Peru, Silvio Romero and Raimundo Nina Rodríguez of Brazil, and José Ingenieros of Argentina. All of these individuals considered racial mixing an obstacle to national progress. Unlike these thinkers, Gil Fortoul wrote that racial mixing led to a stronger racial type and that racial mixing with white immigrants would strengthen the Venezuelan mestizos. This idea anticipated by over thirty years similar concepts expressed by the Mexican José Vasconcelos in his famous *Raza cósmica*, and over forty years the world-renowned theories on racial mixing in Brazil written by cultural nationalist Gilberto Freyre.

In 1891, Gil Fortoul published one of his first statements on the racial theme when he responded to a book written by Jesús Muñoz Tébar. The latter argued that race had no influence on human development, that all races were but different species of the human genus, and that anyone could achieve culture through education, regardless of race or climate. In taking Muñoz to task, Gil Fortoul chastised him for having ignored the evolutionists' theories. Humans could not move from one climate to another, he said, "without modifying themselves in some way by this act." Muñoz had, in Gil Fortoul's judgment, erroneously negated the constant influence of race and climate on civilization. "Strange inconsistency!" he exclaimed. "The author began by denying the influence of race and ended by pointing out the lack of changes in Spanish customs as an essential cause of the unhappy politics. . . . Would the author have maintained that the state of South America would have been the same if it might have been colonized by Englishmen or Germans?"[32]

Like most positivists, Gil Fortoul accepted race and climate as determining factors in a nation's evolution. For that reason, he criticized Muñoz for suggesting that just anyone could achieve a high level of culture. To Gil Fortoul, the history of Venezuela would have been quite different under German or Anglo-Saxon tutelage. Obviously, he ignored the fact that during the sixteenth century Germans did colonize parts of Venezuela—with disastrous results. Nevertheless, he sincerely believed that Germans and Anglo-Saxons stood well above Spaniards, Indians, and Africans on the social scale. He also maintained that immigration from Europe would guarantee change for the better for Venezuela. Without white immigrants, he argued, the nation would never move beyond a transitional stage, marked by disorder and political instability, to an era of progress and order.

In his subsequent works, Gil Fortoul manifested a concept of white supremacy found throughout Latin America at the end of the nineteenth century. Most positivists in the region placed Anglo-Saxons at the top of a racial hierarchy of some sort, which they based on a Darwinian concept of societies. Gil Fortoul also insisted that the crossing of races frequently led to the birth of offspring better suited to the environment than either parent.

In 1895, Gil Fortoul explained in greater detail his idea of social race in the first chapter of *El hombre y la historia*. There he clearly showed the inspiration of Jean Louis Armand de Quatrefages, Tarde, and Walter Bagehot. As a starting point, he stated that no racially pure types existed anywhere in the Spanish American world. Rather, centuries of miscegenation and *mestizaje* had created Hispanic peoples of multiracial origin who had strong mutual cultural ties but no recognizably pure racial identity. Neither in Spain nor in the Americas could one encounter whites of pure race, he said, for the conquistadores carried in their veins the blood of many groups. Furthermore, he rejected the existence of anthropologically defined races. In his estimation, "Present day man is a combination of ethnic and cultural alluviums differentiated by heredity and physical mediums." Finally, he announced, "We wanted to make these observations in order to point out that from a racial and intellectual point of view the preponderant influence today does not belong to the pure races in Venezuela."[33]

Because the question of racial purity did not bother him, and because he insisted that most Venezuelans had some white ancestry, Gil Fortoul maintained that the nation's majority would benefit immediately from the infusion of European blood. In his opinion, Venezuelans had an excellent chance of establishing a progressive and vigorous society if they attracted enough whites from Europe. Thus, in 1895, he wrote from Paris: "But the state of things that we observe today in Venezuela is only transitory. . . . To begin with, the future of this country depends entirely upon a strong immigration, and it is evident that some millions of immigrants would soon absorb the indigenous population. It is probable that with the immigration we will have . . . an industrial and capitalist system that surely will produce considerable changes in distinct manifestations of the national life."[34]

Gil Fortoul and Muñoz Tébar agreed that Venezuela needed European immigrants, though for different reasons. Whereas the latter felt that by their example immigrants would educate Venezuelans to understand modern technology, capitalism, and a work ethic, Gil Fortoul thought that the immigrants would play a far more important role by improving what he called the "social race" of the nation. By social race he meant that culture rather than genetic racial origin played the leading role in determining the evolution of a society. Race, for him, only stood as a description of the degree to which an individual had become incorporated into the prevailing culture, which in the case of Venezuela involved the Hispanicized segment of the population. Thus, the process of evolution allowed for a new and stronger race to emerge in Venezuela through racial mixing with European immigrants.[35]

Gil Fortoul's positive attitudes toward racial mixing owed to his belief that Venezuela had a mestizo majority that could evolve into a progressive racial type. But he demonstrated much more antipathy toward blacks. He clearly disliked blacks from the Antilles who came to Venezuela in search of jobs. These individuals he placed in a special category because of their distinct non-Venezuelan cultures and origins. As for Venezuelan blacks, he took a very circumspect and more ambivalent approach. On one hand, he readily acknowledged their contributions to the formation of Venezuela's colonial society, as well as their participation in the wars of independence. On the other hand, he limited his references to blacks to these distant past episodes, overlooking their presence as a separate group in his era. He made no effort to encourage Venezuelans of any race to take pride in or keep alive their African roots. Nor did he even allude to the richness of that African heritage. Rather, he treated black Venezuelans in abstract terms, not as a collection of diverse individuals who belonged to a racial minority.[36]

Part of Gil Fortoul's reluctance to study contemporary blacks stemmed from his desire to avoid racial tensions of the sort that divided the society of the United States into separate black and white castes. He wanted to forget the past, much like those Brazilians of the same era who ordered the destruction of slave records following emancipation in 1888 on the ground that they did not want to keep a reminder of the blacks' lowly and painful history. Indeed, under the misguided impression that reminders of slavery would only embarrass or embitter most Venezuelan blacks, Gil Fortoul once explained that since emancipation the official census of Venezuela made no reference to race "to spare the sensitivity of the blacks and the descendants of slaves."[37]

By avoiding an open discussion of "the black problem," as he saw it, Gil Fortoul hoped to speed up the absorption of blacks into the *pardo* majority. Although he did not call this process racial democracy, his discussions of race certainly contained seeds of just such a concept. He sincerely believed that race in Venezuela constituted a social and cultural phenomenon: miscegenation and cultural fusion would give blacks an opportunity to progress toward higher levels of social development. The fact that exceptional blacks and "men of color" had achieved positions of power in Venezuela as generals, governors, ministers, and even presidents encouraged him to take this position. As Gil Fortoul once claimed, with considerable pride, "Now that the political system is truly liberal, in the sense that it does not place shackles upon any personal ambitions and aspirations, very often one may see men of color occupy the highest government positions, and in general they do not demonstrate governmental capacity inferior to those of whites of pure race." [38]

But Gil Fortoul was troubled that the bulk of the nation's blacks lived under conditions very much like those of their slave ancestors. These poor, uneducated, and alienated blacks served as a too obvious historical reminder of their inherent social inferiority. He thought of blacks as ignorant people prone to violence and believed that they had to be held in check, or in some other way contained, to assure the orderly development of Venezuela. He predicted that in the long run those blacks not absorbed into the new Hispanicized Venezuelan racial type would move farther toward the periphery, removing themselves to remote enclaves, such as those found along the southeastern coast of Lake Maracaibo or in the Barlovento region to the east of Caracas. Although blacks had not disappeared in the literal sense of the word, Gil Fortoul hoped that their virtual disappearance would occur within a few generations. According to him: "With regard to the blacks of pure race, carried to the Americas by the Spaniards after the near destruction of the Indians, one does not find them in great number except in the cities of the littoral, and these come for the most part from the Antilles. Probably they will soon disappear as a race through mixing with the rest of the population." [39]

Gil Fortoul's views on race summed up the core of a concept of racial democracy, as understood by his generation. For several decades a self-proclaimed white minority, which controlled the means of production and the government in Venezuela, shared their power with multiracial *pardos* and a few blacks. Thus, men and women of all races enjoyed some of the privileges of patronage. In effect, Gil Fortoul merely reflected the reality of Venezuelan history, for individual nonwhites had penetrated the nation's elites over a long period of time. By emphasizing the economic and political mobility of these individuals, Gil Fortoul shifted the discussion of blacks and mixed racial groups from race to class. In so doing, he made implicit the Venezuelan desire to overlook obvious signs of prejudice and racial discrimination based on genetic factors alone. Because of the success of a few blacks, discrimination against the majority of their racial group as members of a poverty-bound lower class did not disturb him. Blacks, as such, had always comprised an important subgroup of the poverty class, an inferior social position that elites regarded as natural.

A review of Venezuela's nineteenth-century immigration policies reveals that many Venezuelan elites shared Gil Fortoul's attitude on race. Throughout the independence period, elites showed a preference for white immigrants; and on many occasions they demonstrated latent anti-black feelings in formulating schemes to open up the nation to foreigners. From 1830 onward, Venezuelans actively sought white Europeans as the ideal types to settle the interior with agricultural communities, for they desperately needed to expand their population if they hoped to survive as an independent nation. As summed up in 1831 in a speech to the National Congress by Antonio Leocadio Guzmán, founder of the Liberal faction: "We do not have roads for lack of people; we do not have transportation to the interior for the same shortcoming; and because of this our agriculture is poor, commerce short, industry reduced, art scarce, morale weak, and Venezuela small."[40]

To satisfy this desire to populate the interior with European immigrants, immigration laws of 1831, 1837, and 1840 authorized the national government to subsidize the movement of European agricultural workers to Venezuela. Elites considered this a means by which they could civilize their nation. But they had pragmatic reasons for endorsing this policy, as well. First, Europeans had much-needed agricultural skills. Second, they had reputations as hard workers. Their example, many elites felt, would teach Venezuelan campesinos the value of hard work. Third, several European nations faced serious economic difficulties, which made it likely that large numbers of working-class and peasant groups would jump at an opportunity to move to underpopulated Venezuela. They had already gone to the United States, and in increasing numbers to Argentina and Brazil, where they offered conclusive proof of the beneficial effects of large-scale immigration. Finally, the expense of bringing Europeans to Venezuela seemed worthwhile because, as one Venezuelan official put it, "each immigrant . . . is capital sown in the country, is a living machine in constant activity, is the center of a family whose offspring born on our soil will have our customs and will defend our independence and liberty."[41]

Despite their best intentions, from the beginning Venezuelans failed to attract white Europeans to their shores. Their nation suffered from a bad image in Europe, where people saw it as an unruly and backward place. Between 1832 and 1845, only 11,851 persons immigrated to Venezuela. The majority came from the Canary Islands, a traditional source of Venezuelan immigrants. Few Germans, Irish, or Scots entered Venezuela, and of those who did, the majority left. Robert Ker Porter described in his diary the abortive efforts of Irish and Scottish settlers to establish agricultural communities, which ended in confusion, failure, and misery. Only a handful of white Europeans stayed on, and many of these enjoyed moderate success as merchants, hotel owners, or shopkeepers, but they refused to do agricultural work.[42]

Ironically, if European whites did not come to Venezuela in significant numbers, Antillian and Guayanese blacks did. They worked on the docks of Venezuela's ports and in the larger urban centers as domestic servants. Moreover, much to the alarm of many Venezuelan elites, they rushed to the remote mining region in the Guayana district of eastern Venezuela after the discovery of gold near Callao by four Jamaican miners in 1850. In part, the movement of black Antillians to eastern Venezuela reflected an endemic situation in the Caribbean, where workers constantly migrated from place to place. Hard times at home led them to seek work elsewhere, such as the boomtowns in Venezuela's mining district. But their presence also owed to the departure of Venezuelan workers from Guayana. Owners of the mines at Callao, Upata, and Yuruari could not find an adequate supply of Venezuelan labor. Traditionally, Venezuelans of all classes refused to live in the hot and supposedly unhealthy Guayana region. Of those few who lived there, a good portion left during the previous decades to avoid forced recruitment into the several armies that operated in eastern Venezuela.[43]

Despite the obvious need for Antillian and Guayanese laborers at the Guayana district mines, officials stated that they considered the black foreigners an undesirable element for both nationalistic and racial reasons. They had a low regard of the West Indian workers, whom they believed deserved their reputation as rowdy and disorderly subjects.

For example, in speaking out against a wave of black immigration to his district in 1850, the governor of Guayana, José Tomás Machado, outlined what he saw as the most vexing aspects of the problem. While he readily admitted the need for additional workers, he cautioned that "for the little bit that one can reflect upon the character of these men, one will discover that their entry into the country will be far from suitable as it threatens it with absolute evils." He called the black immigrants "unstable men, without morality and accustomed to vagrancy for the most part, who offer no guarantee that they will live subjected to the laws of the Venezuelan authorities." Accordingly, he felt that the government should use any means at its disposal to stop blacks from entering Venezuela. To Machado, at least, the foreign blacks could only bring disaster and catastrophe to Venezuela. In his view, "That the free blacks from the Antilles are harmful to the interests of the republic is . . . as clear as the midday sun."[44] Some four years later, in 1854, an official publication responded to the movement of

Trinidadian workers to the mining district in much the same manner, by asking, "Aren't there any hardworking laborers to be found in the diverse provinces who want to come to work in Bolívar?" [45]

For basically the same reasons, Machado's contemporaries also opposed Chinese immigration. In 1855, a proposal made by Antonio Leocadio Guzmán to have the government pay contractors twenty-five pesos per head to bring Chinese coolies to Venezuela met a stinging defeat in the congress. Too many prominent Venezuelans did not want Asians to enter the country. Indeed, the National Congress voted sanctions against all Asian immigration. They did so on the ground that Venezuela should avert the situation found in Peru, where Chinese workers seemingly formed a particularly loathsome class of indentured servants. Three years later, Oegario Meneses, a delegate at the constitutional convention at Valencia, restated this attitude: "Asiatic immigration does not suit Venezuela because Asia has a distinct civilization, entirely different from our customs, good breeding, and habits; and if it is important to bring people, it is not people with such different civilization." Moreover, he added that in nations which had encouraged Asian immigration, such as Peru, Chile, and British Guayana, "they want to get rid of them." [46]

In most ways, the aspiration of Venezuelan elites to Europeanize their homeland far exceeded the reality of their times. As of the mid–nineteenth century, Venezuela remained a divided and impoverished nation. The period of the 1850s and 1860s witnessed a series of natural and man-made catastrophes. Cholera and yellow fever epidemics wiped out large portions of the rural population. Frequent wars exacerbated their plight. Agricultural and pastoral enterprises languished as an economic depression swept the nation. Chronic banditry, cattle rustling, and factional strife characterized the extensive region of the llanos. In general, the situation promised little but further decline, continued unemployment among the rural masses, and more sickness. Political instability and local anarchy completed the dismal picture. [47]

Yet at the dawn of the era of positivistic thought, Venezuelan intellectuals and politicians maintained an optimistic view of the future. They convinced themselves that European immigrants would come soon and that they would help to transform Venezuela from a poor and underpopulated nation into a prosperous one, with a large and industrious working class. The 1865 annual report of the minister of development best expressed this attitude. According to that document, "Capital and laborers are, then, the two great coefficients of our prosperity, founded upon the well-being of agriculture." [48] A year later, Minister of Development Jacinto Reyeno Pachano went further when he stated, "In almost all of the countries of the world, the foreigner is inferior in condition to the national: in

Venezuela, as in many sections of South America, under certain respects, the national is inferior to the foreigner." The minister concluded his remarks by declaring that Europeans made the most satisfactory immigrants. Furthermore, he noted that "you should not forget, either, that if the appropriate immigration, that of the European of good physical and moral condition, the industrious, honest, and capable European, is a moral and progressive element, bad immigration, that which lacks such virtues, far from producing positive good for us will become a germ of immorality and decadence."[49]

During the last quarter of the nineteenth century, Venezuelan leaders wanted European immigrants to perform the same miracles they had in Argentina and Brazil.[50] They wanted a white, hardworking, and enterprising work force who would introduce progressive moral and economic values to Venezuela. But they also thought of this as a "transfusion of blood" of a pure grade, which would bring new and vigorous people to the nation's hinterland.[51]

On July 20, 1891, a new immigration code underscored the type of immigrant desired. It specifically prohibited the immigration of blacks and Asians. As promulgated on August 11, 1891, the law read, "Individuals of Asiatic nationality or those from the English and Dutch Antilles will not be contracted or accepted as immigrants."[52] The lack of any public debate preceding or following the passage of the new code hampers any exact determination of its origins. But given the elites' growing opposition to black and Chinese immigration since 1874, the banning of their entry into Venezuela came as no surprise. Furthermore, the new provisions definitely placated prominent landowners, especially those in eastern Venezuela, such as José Antonio Velutini, who worried about the growing number of black, Chinese, and East Indian workers who fled to the South American mainland from Trinidad and Tobago. Finally, the decision to close the nation to nonwhites fit the thinking of a generation of intellectuals and politicians under the influence of positivism and other racist theories that gained acceptance throughout Latin America.

Despite the new restrictions placed on the immigration of non-Europeans, those groups supplied a significant portion of Venezuela's foreign-born work force during the late nineteenth century. Antillian blacks still constituted a major portion of the workers at port cities, on plantations along the Orinoco River, and at mine fields in eastern Venezuela.[53] They appeared in such numbers in the mining districts that in 1887 Rómulo Carnevali, the local agent of Hahn y Cía at Callao, wrote to Tulio Febres Cordero at Mérida the following: "This is a detestable settlement because of its inhabitants (who are all blacks), its society which the latter constitute, in a word because of its heterogeneity! Here they use English,

Spanish, Canarian, French, Corsican, Italian, Cocuili, and Arabic—in fine this is a true Babel and one lives (unhappily) only commercially."[54] During 1888 and 1889, some two hundred black Trinidadian and Barbadian men constructed a British-owned railway at Barcelona. An account left by one of their employers reported that these men paraded around the streets of Barcelona as if the city belonged to them, and "let it be known that they were 'English.' It greatly tickled the fancy of the Barcelonese, who remarked jokingly, 'that the city was taken by the English.'"[55] There, as elsewhere in Venezuela during the last decade of the nineteenth century, Venezuelans often used the word *ingles* (English) to identify black Antillians.[56]

In summary, several interrelated factors explain the presence of such a large foreign-born black work force in eastern Venezuela. First, local and national political struggles had driven away many of the native Venezuelans. They fled the recruiters, or if they failed, they ended up as cannon fodder in the various armies that vied with each other for control of the region. Second, the islanders provided an ancillary source of wage labor. They worked in regions where most native Venezuelans refused to go. Third, West Indians worked for less money than the Venezuelans. Although some Venezuelans complained that Antillians stole jobs from Venezuelan laborers, most of the employers in eastern Venezuela actually appreciated the availability of a reliable source of labor at lower wages in an area that always lacked enough workers. Finally, since immigrants from the islands did not speak much Spanish, Venezuelan employers usually exploited them unmercifully. To add to the problem, they worked in areas far removed from the protection of home-country officials. British officials at Ciudad Bolívar received numerous complaints from Trinidadians claiming that Venezuelan landowners had tricked them into virtual servitude. Working under harsh conditions without adequate food or housing, often unpaid—these wretched individuals frequently turned to British officials in a desperate attempt to get back to Trinidad to escape peonage.[57]

By 1898, the number of Trinidadians alone in the Guayana and Orinoco regions had become so high that the British minister to Venezuela, W. H. D. Haggard, suggested that the Home Office raise the post at Ciudad Bolívar to a consulate.[58] Haggard, who disliked Venezuelans, reported that the consular officer at that city, one C. H. de Lemos, needed to enlarge his office to handle the growing needs of British citizens who flocked to the region in search of jobs. According to Lemos: "In the Guruari district alone between the ports of Las Tablas and El Callao it is estimated that there are at least 5000 resident British subjects. While lower down on the Orinoco a large number of squatters of British nationality have settled. Most of these subjects are natives of the British West Indies and there are also a number of Englishmen. They are employed in different industries like mining, agriculture and trades. Most of them are peaceful and industrious and this country would probably be able to absorb a further large number of tradesmen and agriculturalists."[59]

During the same period, East Indians also arrived in eastern Venezuela from Trinidad, as indentured Hindus fled to escape unjust and impossible working conditions. They justified their flight by arguing that their British employers had deceived them into coming to Trinidad in the first place. Unable to earn a decent wage there, and placed under a slaverylike labor system, these individuals found it easy to flee to the accessible Venezuelan coast. They had only to cross a few miles of water to establish new homes on the South American mainland. Once in Venezuela, the former indentured servants either obtained land of their own or took on contracts to work for one of the large cacao estates.

In 1890, the Trinidadian protector of immigrants reported one such case as follows: "During the last year several Immigrants have returned from the Spanish Main, some of whom have taken contracts on Cacao Estates and are doing remarkably well. One of these men, the father of a family of five or six grown-up children, all of whom returned with him, informed me that there were at Guiria, where he resided, about one hundred coolies from Trinidad, who nearly all had small patches of cacao on contract."[60] Five years later, the same colonial office noted: "The number of absentees is slightly on the increase; this is not to be wondered at owing to the depression in the labour market here, and the advantages that the adjacent coast of the Spanish Main offers where the immigrant can obtain land with great facility, and can not only plant what he requires for ordinary use, but may grow Ganja [marihuana] for the purpose of being smuggled into this colony."[61]

Chinese also came to Venezuela during the last decade of the nineteenth century, although never in the same numbers as to Cuba, the West Indies, or the United States. Their contributions to agriculture elsewhere in the Americas led some Venezuelan landowners to think that Chinese contract laborers might solve their own chronic shortage of workers. Thus, in 1892 they pressured President Joaquín Crespo to modify the 1891 immigration code to permit the entry of Chinese coolies for work on plantations. On January 7, 1893, Crespo revised the code to meet the planters' demands. The new statute read as follows: "Individuals from the Antilles will not be contracted or accepted as immigrants, nor will anyone from other countries who are more than sixty years old, unless the latter might be the mother or father of a family which comes with them or which already settled in the country."[62] On August 26, 1894, this stipulation, which continued to ban blacks, reappeared in a revised law.

The wording of both laws indicated that Venezuelan elites considered the Chinese a lesser evil than West Indian blacks. Necessity led them to permit the flow of some nonwhite groups, but in keeping with their past antipathy toward Antillians, they excluded blacks and in their place allowed another alien group, the Chinese, to enter in limited numbers. In either case, the elites expressed considerable concern about race and its effect upon national character.

Such thinking typified the attitudes of most Latin American elites during the period. As expressed by the newspaper *El Derecho* in 1892: "If to the vigor of nature one joins the perfection of organization, superiority of intelligence, and the active assiduity of the Caucasian race, which one finds for the most part in Europe, the judgment favors European immigration, a decision that becomes irrevocable since experience has confirmed that that race crossed with the hybrid that composes the general population of Venezuela, perfects ours, producing a sane, intelligent, beautiful, and strong generation."[63]

Intellectuals gave impetus to this policy—for instance, José Gil Fortoul, through his "scientific" study of Venezuela's history and social evolution. Lawmakers adapted the new positivistic thought to legislation that excluded nonwhites from entering the country as permanent residents, and devised settlement schemes aimed at attracting large numbers of white immigrants from Italy and other European nations.

Thus, at century's end, Venezuela offered a seeming paradox in its race relations, at first glance. Racial and cultural fusion, as well as political change, had created an environment in which whites and colored mingled freely and shared positions of power and prestige with a handful of so-called pure blacks. But, given their own choice, the elites who associated themselves with national leaders favored the whitening of the nation, preferably with Italian, northern European, and Spanish immigrants. This they desired not only because they hoped to bring an adequate work force to Venezuela but also because they attributed the nation's political instability and economic stagnation to the presence of a colored majority who could not perform on a level equal to that of whites. They literally planned to regenerate their race through whitening.

In spite of their hopes, most such schemes failed, thwarting the elites' efforts. Venezuela did not attract numbers of Europeans, who preferred the economic opportunities of New York, São Paulo, and Buenos Aires to the stagnant climate of Caracas. In 1898, one of the largest immigration programs fell through when Venezuelan officials could not reach an agreement with a Florence firm to contract several thousand Italian families to establish an agricultural community. The project's failure typified government efforts to attract workers from Europe. In assessing the collapse of the proposed immigration plan, British diplomat W. H. D. Haggard summed up the Venezuelans' frustrations with unflattering frankness: "The introduction into Venezuela of a sober and industrious population—to do the work which might be effected by the idle and worthless natives—cannot fail to benefit the country if the terms of the contract are carried out on the part of the Venezuelan Government; but it is hardly to be expected that they will adhere to the money payment as promised, and the best that the immigrants can expect is the grant of land and the advantages of the other clauses."[64]

Several talented and ambitious black individuals held important positions, both in governmental and private institutions. Though not a long list, by any means, enough blacks reached prominence to dispel any lingering doubts about the ability of Venezuelan blacks and their descendants to perform as equals with whites and *pardos,* if given a proper chance. José Victorio Guerra served as minister of development under Antonio Guzmán Blanco, as well as a customs inspector in eastern Venezuela and as a diplomat in Europe. Alberto González, who earned a doctor of philosophy and letters degree, helped to initiate the first pedagogic congress ever held in Venezuela. Marcelino Rojas, a political orator, along with the physician-publicist Gabriel Muñoz Tébar, who wrote for *El Monitor Industrial,* showed further that blacks played active roles in many other walks of life.[65]

Many blacks succeeded as politicians. In 1892, one of these individuals, General José Félix Mora, served as governor of Carabobo under Joaquín Crespo. Since the 1850s, when he joined the forces of the caudillo Ezequiel Zamora, Mora led predominantly black troops from the coastal region near Puerto Cabello. When appointed governor in 1892, he moved to Valencia, state capital of Carabobo, and met with enthusiastic support during his term in office. He surrounded himself with capable advisors, ran an honest and sympathetic administration, and remained loyal to Crespo.[66] Another black ally of Crespo, Natividad Soloranzo, known as "Zambo y Medio," enjoyed popularity in the state of Guárico before he died fighting against followers of Guzmán Blanco.[67]

Nor did Crespo suffer because of his mixed racial background. Like Mora and other military chieftains, he won the respect of his followers because of his intelligence, military prowess, and political sagacity. Moreover, he was but one of many men of color who fought for control of the government following the downfall of Guzmán Blanco. In 1892, American ambassador William Scruggs described those who sought power in a confidential letter he sent to the secretary of state. As he said of the multiracial composition of that group: "Paul and Saria are both of pure

Castillian origin. . . . Monagas is a mestizo of low origin and bad character. Crespo is a half educated mulatto, but a man of military genious and
large political following. Andrueza [Palacio] is a half Indian, a man of
good natural abilities and fair education, but of sluggish disposition and
usually stupified by strong drink."[68]

The inclusion of such blacks as Mora and Muñoz Tébar among the nation's elites suggests that some sort of racial democracy existed in Venezuela during the nineteenth century. But, by the same token, these individuals also turned out to be the exceptions that proved the rule: blacks
could not succeed unless they had extraordinary talents. Most members of
Venezuela's black minority remained entrapped in the same socioeconomic level they had experienced during the colonial era. They comprised
a collection of menial laborers, *conuqueros,* fishermen, domestic servants,
and soldiers, along with a few artisans, small shopkeepers, boatmen, and
lesser bureaucrats.

Few blacks could escape this fate, less because of their race, per se, than
their economic conditions. The nation's economy left few avenues for advancement for uneducated and unskilled people. As a group, blacks did
not improve their lot and seldom competed with whites and *pardos* as
equals, except as the bottom levels of society. Despite arguments which
state that Venezuelan blacks lost their African identities, they lived much as
they had as slaves—impoverished, and overlooked.

During his brief tenure as United States consul at Puerto Cabello between 1906 and 1908, James Weldon Johnson reached a similar conclusion. Noting the success of "colored" individuals, and the absence of overt
discrimination, Johnson described the average blacks and Indians as part
of a definite lower class. Although he did not attribute their condition to
reasons of race alone, Johnson noted, "The fact is, the great majority of
Indians and blacks are poor and ignorant." As for blacks, he added:

> The pure black plays but a small part in life in this country, and there
> are 'very few of him.' It seems that his chief work has been to lend a
> little color to the scene. I judge that soon there will be 'none of him.'
> In the course of years the Venezuelans will become a homogeneous
> race of a Spanish type, in color somewhere between a light brown and
> a yellow. So, the Negro, in spite of the fact that he has not the great
> obstacle of prejudice to overcome, will make no name in Venezuela as
> a Negro.[69]

Johnson's epitaph hit the mark. Although neither violent nor virulent in
nature, Venezuelan elites discriminated against blacks in a number of spe-

cific ways. In particular, they wanted to improve the race by increasing the white population while reducing the black presence. To reach this objective, they used immigration laws that prohibited the entry of nonwhites. Without doubt, Venezuela's elites wanted more cream in their coffee. For the blacks, this meant a bleak future, at best.

POSITIVISM AND
NATIONAL IMAGE,
1890–1935

AT THE OUTSET of the twentieth century, Venezuelan elites made racial regeneration one of their primary objectives. As one of the nation's leading newspapers put it, "It is especially advantageous to cross our race, in which imagination prevails, with those virile ones of the North, whose thought appears more concentrated upon the practical than the theoretical."[1] A year later, journalist Jorge Lima concurred with this opinion when he explained: "In all countries that have started down the road to perfection, immigration has been the primary factor. With it they have obtained moral and material advantages. The regeneration of our masses through crossing the races is the point of departure for perfecting society and its respective growth."[2]

In brief, Lima espoused a widely held belief that Venezuela needed the "diligent and untiring hands of these workers of progress," who would stimulate agriculture and bring foreign capital. Races had crossed and cultures had merged in the United States, France, and Great Britain, where new groups joined old in a process of evolution. Venezuela could experience a similar change. But Lima also understood the ambiguous nature of the word *cruzamiento* (crossing) in the Venezuelan context, for he could not forget his own "primitive background." As he put it: "I have not denied that we are products of mixing; above all, to the contrary, I have affirmed it; but we have not yet arrived at perfection, because of the youth of our nation and because of the constant internal revolts that have paralyzed any notion of progress. At this point, we still need new blood."[3]

The elites' desire for racial regeneration through whitening coincided with a period in which two powerful political leaders brought political stability to the beleaguered nation. With Cipriano Castro's ascension to power in 1899,

Venezuelans began a painful but certain transition toward the establishment of an effective central government. Castro and his stronger successor, Juan Vicente Gómez, ended the internal divisions that had plagued Venezuela. The process took several decades to complete, but between 1908 and 1935, Gómez relentlessly worked to replace a system characterized by local and regional caudillos with a centralized authoritarian rule. He unified the nation by force; in one way or another, he subdued any opposition to his regime. Some opponents went into exile, others ended up in prisons—or at work on the nation's expanding road system. Yet others joined the government as converts. But by 1935, Gómez had assured Venezuela an unparalleled era of peace and economic development.

Castro and Gómez came from the western state of Táchira, a part of Venezuela many people considered a separate province, if not a part of Colombia. Táchirans had long thought of themselves as different from other Venezuelans. According to their own accounts, Táchira had few blacks, boasted a large proportion of mestizos, and had a white aristocracy. Táchirans considered themselves serious, industrious, hardworking people of European origin. They owned their small plots, ate three square meals a day (mostly of meat and wheat), and knew few personal pleasures. Moreover, they contrasted their austere way of life with that of the darker-hued lowland Venezuelans, whom they depicted as being descendants of fun-loving and frolicking slave ancestors.[4]

Yet as a national leader, Castro showed no inclination to demonstrate regional favoritism. Nor did he favor whites over blacks. In fact, during his military campaign Castro received decisive assistance from two black generals, Benjamín Ruiz and Antonio Fernández. Following his victory he rewarded both of these officers. Ruiz, a Colombian from Panama by birth, took part in Castro's western operations. After the struggle ended, he served briefly as a high-ranking official at Maracaibo, despite outspoken opposition to his appointment by influential Zulians. As for Fernández, a leader of a predominantly black army, he betrayed President Ignacio Andrade at a crucial point of the war in 1899 and shifted his loyalty to Castro. His defection assured Castro's victory. Like Ruiz, Fernández received a commission as a high-ranking officer in Castro's army.[5]

Another black, Manuel Corao, also held several powerful positions in the new regime, despite resistance among the *caraqueño* elites to accept him as a social equal. Indeed, blacks played such a visible role in the Castro administration that when James Weldon Johnson arrived in Venezuela to serve as consul at Puerto Cabello, he found it difficult to contain his enthusiasm; he described their presence in a letter to Booker T. Washington. In 1906, shortly after his arrival at Caracas, Johnson met the president's retinue at the opera. He could hardly believe his eyes, he wrote, for "when I

saw in the President's suite, and mingling among the crowd, colored colo-
nels, and generals, and major generals, clad in crimson and gold with gold
handled swords clinking at their sides, I felt like exclaiming with the
prophet, 'Lord, mine eyes have seen thy salvation, let now thy servant de-
part in peace.'"[6]

Caracas whites, in particular, resented the success of men such as Ruiz
and Corao. In 1902, the gifted and prolific writer Rufino Blanco Fombona,
who fled Venezuela two years before, published a pamphlet entitled *De
cuerpo entero: El negro Benjamín Ruiz*, in which he vilified Ruiz by depicting him as an evil and venal political opportunist. Blanco Fombona accused Ruiz of many crimes, including prostitution, impersonation of a
medical doctor, fraud, and robbery. But he also reminded his readers that
Ruiz was "an African of pure race," and a "Nero from Africa." In conclud-
ing his attack he said, "If the portrait of the whole body turns out dark,
nobody should forget that I promised to paint Ruiz with the colors of his
body and his heart."[7]

Corao also became the victim of equally racist assaults. A politician of
dubious distinction, he laid himself open to criticism by his ostentatious
behavior. When he paid for a tombstone for an obscure and impoverished
Venezuelan poet who died in Paris, he received not the thanks of Venezuelans but rather words of derision. Race obviously played a factor in this
case, for in political caricatures he appeared as an apelike black, with stereotypical round face, large white eyes, kinky hair, thick lips, and huge
ears. In 1907, some of his enemies went so far as to call him a "heartless
black," an "opulent orangutan," and "the monkey Corao . . . the leading
orangutan of the American jungles."[8]

Even Cipriano Castro suffered some racial slurs while in office. At their
crudest, his bitterest critics frequently referred to him as the "Monkey
from Capacho." Although this description owed in large part to his bandy
legs and long arms, it nonetheless fit into an overall pattern of racial asper-
sions used by his opponents.[9] Of the Castro years, José María Vargas Vilas
once wrote: "These were very sad times for Venezuelan intellectualism,
in that Gumersindo Rivas was controlling the press, and certain lake-
dwelling little blacks, escaped from the palm trees of Chinquinquira,
slicked down and perfumed with fragrant coco oil, were moving toward
ruin, pontificating hypercritically in the columns of *El Cojo Ilustrado,* exer-
cising from these the pedagogy of Ansalidad; with African candor, of sim-
ian apes who have read from cheap translations of Taine, criticizing great
names, insulting them, and consecrated by heavenly bliss, desiring thusly,
through the excess of their audacity, to save themselves from ruin among
the forgotten."[10]

The outbursts against Ruiz and Corao constituted an exceptional public outburst against successful blacks. Most Venezuelan elites turned their creative energies to extolling the virtues of whitening rather than making racist comments. Racist statements often reflected the fears of elites who did not want to include blacks among their close associates. But the majority of those statements resulted as much from hatred of the Castro regime as from any clear racial motivation. But, individuals such as Rufino Blanco Fombona clearly resented the presence of blacks among the powerful political leadership of Venezuela.

Blanco Fombona was candid about his dislike of blacks. In short order, he became a leading advocate of whitening Venezuela as a means of removing blacks from public view. Without doubt, he held some rather curious ideas about race. For the most part, he agreed with Simón Bolívar that Venezuelans did not know to which branch of the human family they belonged. As he pointed out in 1911, he thought that Venezuelans formed a hybridized race which passed through all of the spectrum from chocolate to *café con leche*. But he departed radically from Bolívar's explanation of the origin of Venezuela's dark-skinned populace in that he borrowed an outrageous theory from Oscar A. Noguera, a Colombian who claimed that the second generation of Europeans in the tropics often proved to be darker hued than their parents, because of exposure to the sun rather than because of their mixed racial ancestry.

Accordingly, Blanco Fombona blamed dark complexions among the Venezuelan elite upon a burning process. He maintained that these colored elites actually preserved their *limpieza de sangre*, or racial purity, in this case, despite their *café con leche* appearance.[11] He adamantly believed that Venezuela had to become a white nation. As he explained in 1912 in the introduction to *Judas capitolino:* "Sí, Señor, Venezuela has no salvation unless it resolves how it will become a Caucasian country. This is the key to the future. In its ethnic tangles resides . . . the cause of its disorders and the secret of its misfortunes." By his estimate, Venezuela could become a white nation within a century. Yet, to date, no Venezuelan leader other than Bolívar had comprehended the need to bring "torrents" of European blood to the veins of the nation's mestizo population. To save the nation, he argued, every sacrifice had to be made. "We are," he warned, "two steps from the jungle because of our blacks and Indians; . . . a great part of our country is mulatto, mestizo, and zambo, with all the defects which Spencer recognized in hybridism; we must transfer regenerating blood into their veins. Do not attempt to finish off the Indians and blacks of the country through destruction, since they are our brothers, but rather, whiten them through constant crossing. In summary, try to assure that a large white population absorbs the population of color." Without whitening, he exclaimed, "*finis patrias.*" [12]

Another relevant factor deserves consideration at this juncture. During the early twentieth century, the expansion of the United States into the Caribbean forced many Venezuelans to think seriously about the racial composition of their population. At the turn of the century, Venezuelans looked upon the United States as a leading representative of modern industrial civilization. But as much as they respected the North Americans for their accomplishments, they also feared them as expansionists. Venezuelans felt vulnerable to growth of U.S. hegemony throughout the Caribbean region. In their eyes, this expansion included the possibility that the racial attitudes that prevailed in the United States might spread southward to Venezuela. They especially believed that the type of segregation found in the southern states, and to a lesser degree in occupied Cuba after 1898, might some day develop in Venezuela and other multiracial societies that could not protect themselves from the influence of the Yankees.

Most Venezuelan intellectuals did not want to create a segregated society like that of the United States, with its separate racial castes. They understood the danger to their nation posed by the spread of the type of racism that gripped their northern neighbor. In 1898, the intervention of the United States in the affairs of Cuba and Puerto Rico brought the North Americans a step closer to Venezuela's shores. Suspicion grew among Venezuelan observers that the United States planned to penetrate the entire Caribbean zone. As expressed in an editorial that appeared in *El Mensajero* of Maracaibo on March 6, 1899, "That which has occurred in Cuba is but the prologue of a drama: the conquest of the Americas." To Venezuelans that conquest did not involve warfare between countries, but rather "it was a duel between two races." A few years later, when protesting the emigration of some fifteen thousand Venezuelans to Cuba, *El Pregonero* claimed that North Americans wanted to control Venezuela, as well as Cuba and other republics, where they exploit colored people whom they believe can work in tropical climates.[13]

Above all, Venezuelans abhorred the racial violence and separatism practiced in the United States. In the United States blacks and colored could not enter the whites' world in any way as equals. Through the use of violence and systematic Jim Crow laws, the white North Americans kept blacks oppressed. The competitive nature of the United States' industrial society contributed to separatism and in part explained the outbreak of racial clashes during the late nineteenth century. By 1900, increased opportunities for education, better employment, and improved living standards closed the socioeconomic gap between members of the white and black races. But as that gap diminished, moderate whites employed physical segregation as a means of assuring the modernization of their country. Segregation maintained the whites' predominant position in society and removed a perceived threat of the rise of the black underclass.

Segregation and violence were the most distinctive features of the virulent North American brand of racism. No other nation in the Western Hemisphere witnessed as many lynchings and racial murders as the United States. Nor did white elites in any other nation attempt to separate racial groups on such a large scale. No other American nation had as many racist organizations, such as the Ku Klux Klan or the White Citizens' Committees, which functioned solely to control the black population by intimidation. Citizens of the United States demonstrated an extraordinary degree of tolerance toward the use of violence against blacks. Even the courts, which applied a dual standard of justice for blacks and whites, supported white supremacy by condoning rather than condemning the activities of white terrorists. Carried to an extreme, as in Mississippi, violence led to a closed society in which the unity of the dominant white group remained intact. As James W. Silver pointed out, once challenged, the closed society "tightly closes its ranks, becomes inflexible and stubborn, and lets no scruples, legal or ethical, stand in the way of the enforcement of orthodoxy."[14]

No such racial orthodoxy existed in Venezuela. By 1900, most Venezuelan elites accepted a concept of racial democracy by which *pardos,* along with exceptional blacks, became equal to their white compatriots if they met certain social and economic preconditions. The entire notion of whitening depended upon the assimilation of nonwhites into a *café con leche* blend. For that reason, most literate Venezuelans could not understand the North Americans' use of violence to maintain white supremacy.

At the beginning of the twentieth century, detailed accounts of lynchings and other antiblack activities in the United States became regular fare in the Venezuelan daily press. Newspapers listed the names of obscure towns in the United States in which crimes against blacks took place. In an early example of such an article, the January 9, 1899, issue of *El Pregonero* stated, "We do not have enough words to describe the indignation caused us by the horrible inequities committed by the white population of the United States against Negroes of the South during the last elections, or the indifference with which the courts and the executive power viewed these events."

Undoubtedly, educated Venezuelans felt humanitarian concern for the plight of the blacks victimized by racism in the United States. But they also discussed the racial implications for Venezuelans of the spread of United States influence through the Caribbean. As the same article in *El Pregonero* asked, "If this is what happens to the American Negroes . . . what will happen later on to the inferior races of those recently conquered people [in Cuba and Puerto Rico]?" A few years later, another editorial noted that the Yankees had enslaved Puerto Ricans, just like Hawaiians, and that the same fate awaited other Latin Americans, including Venezuelans. The prolonged occupation of Cuba by the United States raised serious questions in the minds of Venezuelans about the long-range intentions of the North Americans.

In fact, in 1908, James Weldon Johnson, United States consul at Puerto Cabello, noted the significance of these fears as they related to the strained relations between Venezuela and the United States. According to him: "As to our relations with Venezuela, I don't know whether our government understands that much of the antagonism here to the U.S. really finds origins in our race question at home. . . . I feel sure that here in Venezuela they are constantly fighting against any possible chance of a Saxon standard being set which would place them in any grade below that of equals." He went on to say that the government of Venezuela actually tried to warn its citizens against increased influence from the United States on the matter of racial discrimination.[15]

Anxiety about the United States' domination of Venezuela fueled the rise of cultural nationalism in the latter, as in other Latin American countries. Cipriano Castro's provocation of hostility with the United States during the first decade of the century did nothing to allay such fears. Like Manuel Ugarte of Argentina and Rubén Darío of Nicaragua, who spearheaded a nascent Pan-Americanist movement against the United States, Castro protested the hegemonic tendencies of the North Americans. In 1902 and 1903, he turned many Venezuelans against the British, Germans, and other European powers. By 1906, he made anti–United States propaganda a central part of a nationalistic appeal to his constituents for their support of his faltering regime. His posture lacked the sophistication of many Venezuelan intellectuals, but he effectively portrayed Yankees as materialistic Anglo-Saxons, whose culture contrasted markedly with that of the Latin race. As for the latter, the so-called *raza latina* he often mentioned, he saw Venezuela as part of a hybrid group, with a distinct culture that rejected materialism while valuing the more spiritual virtues of the Latin American heritage.

Obviously, Venezuelan cultural nationalists faced a dilemma in formulating their theories about immigration and whitening. The dilemma stemmed in large part from their need to resolve a basic conflict between two attitudes toward nonwhites, and blacks in particular. On the one hand, they mistrusted blacks and colored people. Their mistrust did not rise from deep-seated racial hatred of the sort that developed in the United States. Instead, their concern resulted from their interpretation of the

Venezuelan past, filtered through the lens of European racist theories. They arrived at an understanding that the violence and political instability that marred the bulk of the nation's history since independence owed to the inability of the multiracial and black masses to comprehend a democratic system of government. On the other hand, the nationalists wanted to assure peace and preserve the ideals of Bolivarian liberalism, without splitting the population into separate racial castes.

To achieve their objective, scholars wanted all nonwhite members of society to be incorporated into an increasingly white racial and cultural body, which they often referred to as a new race. As had José Gil Fortoul during the 1890s, they predicted the eventual disappearance of the black and indigenous peoples, either by their withdrawal into isolated enclaves, far from the growing urban centers, or through their assimilation into a whiter society. In either case, they combined the issues of immigration and racial mixing as part of their long-term solution to Venezuela's political, social, and economic difficulties.

The commitment to whitening the nation led to an equally firm resolve not to let supposedly inferior people enter Venezuela as immigrants. This meant continuing the exclusion of Chinese, Middle Easterners, or *turcos,* and almost every Antillian group. They particularly wanted to exclude blacks, whom the liberal newspaper *Linterna Mágica* depicted in 1900 as a group given to "an exuberant and ferocious disposition." [16]

Accordingly, in 1906, Carlos Gómez warned, "We ought to reject Asians, European and Asian Turks, continental and colonial French, and all immigration from the Antilles for the indisputable reasons of race and future." Antillians, he thought, constituted a "motley mixture of races, distinct and contrary in intelligence and color of face." Moreover, he considered the black Antillians detestable candidates as immigrants because "with their crossing we will never improve our race." Like others of his era, he found many shortcomings in the character of the Antillians, among which he listed ugly instincts and a lack of moral feeling. [17]

A year later, Cristóbal L. Mendoza touched on the shortcomings of the black presence in Venezuela from a somewhat different perspective. In a speech he delivered at the Universidad Central de Venezuela, he cited Haitians as examples of people who could never achieve a superior civilization because of their race. Venezuela, too, had a black minority, he reminded his audience, pointing out, "According to some, we are the descendants of that accursed son of Noah, wretched populator of Africa, whose piety and cupidity was transplanted in America." But, he insisted that Venezuelans did not constitute an inferior race as a result of their African heritage. Rather, like Gil Fortoul, he believed that Venezuela owed its major impulse to the Spanish. Blacks, while present, did not endanger the nation's march toward civilization. In his words:

> Brought in order to take the place of the indigenous American in the rough work of the mines, he always remained separate from the social activities; without liberties, and that which is worse, without aspirations to acquire them, the sad chain of slavery always weighed upon his neck and upon his spirit. . . . A part of the black blood has effectively infiltrated our nationality; but I repeat that this element, inferior in character, inferior in civilization, inferior in number, while it has been able to cause pernicious influences upon the race of the conquistadores, has not had much force in determining the composition of our nationality.[18]

Both Gómez and Mendoza sought to whiten their nation, to preserve it from further pernicious influences from lower racial groups. Typical of their generation, they recognized the hybrid nature of the Venezuelan population. They also wanted further mixing with superior races, which they thought ultimately would save the nation. As Gómez explained, "The crossing of our sickly and old-looking race with vigorous and young races is indispensable." Gómez considered colored Venezuelans equal to any task, for "the PEOPLE of COLOR, as the Spanish despisingly called us and as the Yankees call us today, have proven to be able to govern as well as any other race." Mendoza also thought that the granite base of Venezuela's Latin nationality would support a new civilization if enough Europeans came to Venezuela. According to him, "This is the only sure and easy road we have toward civilization: to educate, to instruct, but not in the stagnant atmosphere in which we have vegetated during centuries, but rather in the powerful ambience of European civilization."[19]

Ironically, despite seemingly strict measures to ban nonwhite immigration since the late nineteenth century, the nation's economy depended on black Antillian laborers throughout the Gómez era. The majority of the stevedores, miners, and coastal agricultural workers came from the Antilles. Owing to demand for workers, some six thousand to eleven thousand Antillian blacks arrived annually to work at the docks, and still more worked seasonally on the private estates of Gómez and his associates. Their numbers remained high in the Orinoco region, and at the gold fields of Guayana. Most of Venezuela's domestic servants came from Martinique, Curaçao, Trinidad, and other Caribbean islands, including Cuba. Once the boom began, petroleum companies took advantage of loopholes in the immigration and colonization code of 1918 to bring in large numbers of

Antillians to work at the oil fields, ostensibly due to the nature of the work and a scarcity of qualified Venezuelan laborers.[20]

Travelers to the interior of Venezuela found Antillian blacks carrying out all sorts of tasks. During a visit in 1912, Lindon Bates, Jr., met with Trinidadians in eastern Venezuela who worked as guards, servants, and rubber traders, as well as miners and boatmen. Some individuals had made fortunes, but others suffered the vagaries of the hard eastern life and its mercurial economy. A travel account published in 1924 reported finding Trinidadian handymen and boatmen for hire in Ciudad Bolívar and other Orinoco towns. They continued to comprise a major portion of the work force at the oil fields in western and eastern Venezuela. In 1936, Leonidas R. Dennison wrote: "Most of the negroes found in the interior of Venezuela are from British, Dutch or French Guiana, or from the West Indies islands of Trinidad, Barbados, Grenada, St. Vincent, St. Lucia, Dominica, Martinique and Guadaloupe." In the gold fields they worked as cooks and watchmen, but the majority earned their living as miners who dug the gravel deposits in the hills and streams of the hinterland.[21]

The influx of black immigrants did not please many supporters of the Gómez regime. Indeed, many *gomecistas* held strong racist views about the innate inferiority of Africans. As much as Gómez may have needed laborers on his estates, many elites moved to tighten up legislation that excluded Antillian blacks, Chinese, and other nonwhite groups. A revised immigration and colonization law enacted on June 20, 1918, continued the ban on nonwhite immigration and stated specifically that Venezuela would not accept "those persons not of European stock, or the islanders of yellow race in the Northern Hemisphere."[22]

During the 1920s, a faction of the pro-Gómez elites also opposed the immigration of blacks from the United States, whom they openly acknowledged as superior to those from the Antilles. When a rumor circulated in Caracas in 1924 that several companies wanted a large group of blacks from the West Indies and the United States to help establish cotton cultivation, the elites made their position on such immigration clear. They announced in an official organ: "Just the idea of such a thing, even if it might be a rumor, justifiably alarms us. The introduction of individuals of this race, under the conditions by which they would come, constitutes a true immigration, and this is not the class of immigration that Venezuela needs."[23]

According to an article entitled "The Danger of Colored Immigration," only European immigration suited Venezuela's needs. Even then, only individuals from certain regions whose populations possessed racial features that made them bearers of civilization wherever they went were desirable. The article went on to say, "We should avoid by any means the introduction and establishment of groups such as blacks and mestizos from North America, the Antilles, or any other country." It cited the United States as an example of a nation which used immigration regulations to conserve its race. This article, which appeared in the bulletin of the chamber of commerce of Caracas, concluded thus: "For us the problem is extremely serious, and a well-intended liberal policy ought to have as its goal to whiten the population as much as possible."[24]

About a year and a half later, the same publication ran a translation of an article from the French journal *L'Ilustration* which cautioned against Asiatic immigration to Venezuela. According to its author, all Asians, with the exception of the Japanese, had inferior capacities for progress, as proven by their inability to maintain any improvements in self-government, hygiene, education, agricultural production, industry, or transportation since the Europeans first introduced these modern institutions to their mainland China colonies. The author went on to urge Venezuelan legislators to end any discussions about changing the immigration laws to permit Asians to enter Venezuela because of the damage such immigration would cause. In conclusion he fell back on the well-worn argument that only white immigrants from certain European countries would achieve the desired results, as they already had in Argentina and Brazil.[25]

Since the turn of the century, the seeming inability of Venezuela's multiracial majority to sustain a democratic system of government also led many observers to conclude that a strong political dictatorship might have to serve as a prelude to the introduction of truly democratic rule. One such thinker, César Zumeta, built upon Gil Fortoul's assessment of political events in Venezuela. According to the latter, neither liberal nor conservative held any special meaning in the context of the recent past. In 1902, Zumeta extended this idea when he argued that Venezuelans fell into two groups: the recruiters and the recruited, or the directors and the exploited. The leaders, a small body of white or mestizo elites, constituted the directing class. They exploited over 80 percent of the population, which comprised an illiterate multiracial group to whom democracy meant nothing more than conscripted military service under the demagogic rule of self-professed liberal regimes. Zumeta felt that Mexico, along with Argentina and Brazil, had overcome similar troubles, largely through the introduction of foreign capital and the application of a new work ethic brought by foreigners, but also because of a "vigorous" leadership.[26]

Mexico offered the most useful model for Venezuelan thinkers to follow. Porfirio Díaz, who ruled that nation between 1876 and 1910, accomplished through the imposition of strong dictatorial rule what many Venezuelans aspired to build in their nation. Thus, many Venezuelans advocated dictatorship as the only means by which the Venezuelan masses could have democratic principles and values forced upon them. Without dictatorship, their argument ran, internal revolts would continue unabated. They pointed out that before Díaz Mexico had experienced political and social problems like those found in Venezuela. In their view, no clear ideology dominated Mexico until the *porfiriato* established the government of Díaz and his positivist associates. Then, and only then, the ironfisted dictator served as a guiding light for Mexico's development.

The apparent parallels between Venezuela and Mexico encouraged Venezuelan intellectuals to think that stable government could be established in their nation through dictatorship. For instance, in 1902, Ramón Tello Mendoza, a close associate of Cipriano Castro, praised Díaz for having transformed Mexico from a poor to a rich nation. Calling Díaz a man "of superior intelligence, of astonishing energy, of progressive vision, and of a humanitarian perspective," Tello detailed the great advances that occurred in Mexico, a nation in which "mendacity is a miracle, vagrancy a surprise, treachery an impossibility, war a myth, and crime an account that seldom appears in the newspapers." In contrast, he stated, Venezuela remained chaotic. Castro had finally brought peace to the republic, but Tello believed that Venezuela needed laws and dedicated officials who would do for it what Díaz and his supporters had done for Mexico.[27]

In 1907, Alfredo Machado Hernández presented an equally strong statement in support of dictatorship in a dissertation that he presented for a doctorate in political science at the Central University of Caracas. Machado Hernández gave a straightforward account of the failure of government in Venezuela. Citing extensively the works of Spencer, Le Bon, and Taine, he blamed Venezuela's political difficulties on the state of crisis Venezuelans had lived in since the founding of their republic. Due to the heterogeneity of the population, Venezuelans had not developed a true national spirit of the sort described by Le Bon. Therefore, leaders had ruled the nation through personality rather than ideology. But, Machado maintained that dictatorship offered certain advantages to Venezuela, where it had prevailed because "dictatorship in Venezuela is a physiological product, that is to say, a normal product of the collective body, as unavoidable and natural as saliva or gastric juice in a superior biological organism."[28]

Machado did not mean that Venezuelans had to perpetuate dictatorship forever, but under the right circumstances such a system provided a workable transition toward transcending the basic internal problems that plagued Venezuelans. As he noted, "Dictatorship, in effect, is a jealous instrument, of double action, which demands prudence and exquisite tact in its handling; well utilized, . . . it gives the most beneficial results; but directed incompetently or maliciously, not only is it inefficacious, but also perturbing and fatal for the nation that endures it." Despite the fact that in Venezuela dictatorship had yet to produce happy results, Machado argued that its success in Mexico warranted its consideration by Venezuelans as a means of bringing order to the nation. In closing, he wrote that if anyone doubted his conclusions he "would respond, murmuring two names: Mexico, Porfirio Díaz."[29]

This support of dictatorship culminated in Laureano Vallenilla Lanz's classic study *Cesarismo democrático*. Published in 1919 by one of General Gómez's staunchest supporters, this short book offered by far the most sophisticated argument to date in favor of dictatorship in Venezuela. Vallenilla Lanz, who edited the official Gómez organ *El Nuevo Diario*, combined sociology, anthropology, and history in his studies of Venezuela. He wrote *Cesarismo democrático* in part to justify the rule of Gómez, who ran Venezuela like a personal estate. But the book offered its readers more than an apology for the Gómez dictatorship. It also fit into Vallenilla Lanz's efforts to describe Venezuela's unique racial ambience in terms that all Venezuelans could comprehend.

Vallenilla Lanz's *Cesarismo democrático* won acclaim from critics throughout the Spanish-speaking world. Like all of his writings, it showed his ability to blend the best-known European thought into his indigenous interpretations of the Venezuelan past. According to Vallenilla Lanz, societies, as organisms, experienced birth, growth, and death. Historical analysis showed Vallenilla Lanz that Venezuela's multiracial majority could not govern themselves democratically. Without dictatorship, he stated, Venezuela had no hope of progressing. Mestizos, blacks, and Indians needed an authoritarian government. Order and progress necessitated the implementation of a white dictatorship, even if the dictator, like Gómez, was probably a mestizo.

Vallenilla and his close friend and associate Pedro Manuel Arcaya best expressed the new racial and political doctrines of the *caraqueño* elites who attached themselves to the Gómez regime. Their view won additional support because of their prominence in the dictator's administration. For that reason, their observations gained a reputation for being quasiofficial statements. By 1917, they had joined Gil Fortoul as leading positivist interpreters of Venezuela's social history.

In their major works, both Arcaya and Vallenilla Lanz attempted to interpret Venezuela's social history along lines first spelled out by Gil Fortoul. Their many speeches, papers, articles, and books applied modern social science methodology to questions related to the formation of a Venezuelan race. Like Gil Fortoul, they eventually used the term *social race* in their discussions of Venezuela's heterogeneous population. None of them believed that the Spanish had represented a pure race at the time of the conquest of the Americas. Rather, they treated the conquistadores as an amalgam of the diverse groups who had intermingled over many centuries of coexistence on the Iberian Peninsula: Moors, Jews, Phoenicians, Romans, Visigoths, Celts, Berbers, and almost every Mediterranean and European people who migrated to Spain at one time or another.

Arcaya wrote the more tradition-bound analyses of Venezuelan society. In his best-known work, *Estudios de sociología venezolana* (1917), he expressed his conservative attitudes about racial purity, European superiority, and national character. In so doing, he reflected the cosmopolitan outlook of most of the ruling elite. His idea of a civilized and progressive society combined the best features of French culture with the best elements of United States and British industrialization. In his treatment of miscegenation, he emphasized that most Venezuelans were mestizos, a combination of Indian and European that he and his contemporaries found much more acceptable than any mixture of African origin.

He also believed that only a few Venezuelans had black ancestors. For that reason, he paid scant attention to the African contributions to the formation of modern Venezuela and wrote mostly about slavery. He did attribute vitality and resistance to disease to blacks, but not intelligence or superior culture; in fact, he claimed that the blacks had come from decidedly uncultured backgrounds. Because of Venezuela's mestizo majority, Arcaya felt optimistic about the nation's future, for he thought that the Indians had already been assimilated into the prevailing European society and that the blacks had become isolated in remote areas as a distinct minority. Consequently, the bleaching of the population through further immigration could occur with relative ease.

During his lifetime Vallenilla Lanz became a leading exponent of white immigration, as well as one of the most brilliant advocates of Spencerian organicism and Comtean positivism. He read widely, especially the works of Gobineau, Le Bon, Tarde, Taine, Darwin, Spencer, and Bagehot. He also made extensive use of Venezuelan archives. He criticized Gobineau, Le Bon, and those who blamed anarchy in Latin America solely upon racial mixing. Like Gil Fortoul, Vallenilla Lanz placed far more emphasis on cultural characteristics than on biological race. He particularly took Gobineau to task for writing what he considered vicious and scurrilous books about racial mixing and lashed out at Gobineau's rigid theory of racial determinism. However, he did not ignore all of the current European thought on the subject of racial mixing and accepted Gabriel Tarde as an authority with whom he could agree. Like Tarde, Vallenilla argued that the mixing of races often had beneficial effects, producing "more complex, richer, and more refined individuals." This especially applied to cases involving the mixing of Europeans with other racial groups.[30]

In a series of speeches, articles, and essays written between 1914 and 1921, he evolved a basic argument that pure race had no meaning in the Americas. He began by restating the belief that Spain had experienced centuries of racial and ethnic mixing before the conquest of the New World and that the same process reoccurred in the Western Hemisphere. For that reason, he felt that concepts based upon pure race did not correspond to the Venezuelan sociological reality, nor did race adequately explain the evolution of the nation's population. According to him, "A Venezuelan type exists, just as do a society, a state, and a nation." In that context, race represented a cultural or psychological condition because "a multitude of Spanish and American people, whose somatic character differ profoundly, think, speak, and write Castillian or Spanish."[31]

By 1929, Vallenilla applied the term *social races* to the various nationalities that comprised the Hispanic republics.[32] By this he meant that culture, not race, determined a nation's ability to experience a progressive future. In other words, Venezuelans formed a subgroup of Hispanic people, whose society maintained European values. Miscegenation produced a new type of mixed racial individual in Venezuela, with capabilities determined mostly by culture. Like so many before him, he thought that the introduction of Europeans in large numbers would offer at least a partial solution to some of Venezuela's most pressing social problems. In keeping with the prevailing view of his day, he favored an immigration program that opened Venezuela to white Europeans but closed the nation to non-whites to encourage further whitening, both racially and culturally.

Like most of his Venezuelan contemporaries, Vallenilla generally overlooked blacks as a separate group. When he did write about blacks, he chose fairly abstract subjects or dealt with them as slaves during the colonial era. This attitude placed him at odds with Gilberto Freyre of Brazil, whose pioneer studies placed utmost importance upon the role of Africans in the formation of Brazilian society. Not only did he overlook blacks in the postemancipation period but he routinely treated them as a monolithic mass rather than a collection of diverse individuals and types. Contemporary blacks literally disappeared in his books. In his last major study, *Disgregación e integración,* published in 1930, Vallenilla Lanz dealt with colonial blacks and mulattoes in flat, collective terms. He showed an awareness of the existence of white supremacy during the colonial era, especially in areas of Venezuela in which blacks formed the majorities. But like most white intellectuals of the early twentieth century, he accepted the notion that the colonial hierarchy ended during the wars of the previous century.

Vallenilla Lanz, Arcaya, and others called for the whitening, or bleaching, of the population to improve the Venezuelan race. In part they thought that a whiter population would be less likely to create political turmoil of the sort that had characterized the nation's history since the 1830s. They also believed that whitening would lead to the formation of a stronger and more useful citizenry. They shaped a cultural nationalism around this objective. Whitening became the cornerstone of their optimistic view of the future, despite their pessimism about the present. In their eyes, Venezuela's already predominantly mestizo people would quickly absorb waves of white immigrants, who in turn would produce a new and vigorous type of Venezuelan. Rather than lament over the presence of a multiracial majority, about which they could do nothing, they rejoiced that miscegenation had already led their fellow Venezuelans on the way to creating a white nation.

Other intellectuals shared these basic ideas. For instance, in 1919 the sociologist Julio C. Salas argued in *Civilización y barbarie* that pure race did not explain the differences between the United States and Latin America. As had other Venezuelan positivists, he chose to emphasize culture rather than race as the leading determinant. Therefore, he felt that European immigration would alter the Venezuelan society radically.

In rejecting race, as well as climate, as the cause of the gap between the two Americas, Salas pointed out that no pure races existed in North, Central, or South America, except for a few "well-tinted blacks" and some "copper Indians." He attributed the so-called retardation of Latin America to Spain's backward economic system and to the Spanish settlers, whom he compared unfavorably to those Europeans who went to North America. Racial inferiority itself had not been an issue. Rather, Latin Americans inherited their well-known laziness from Spanish hidalgos who disdained hard work: everyone in Latin America—white, black, Indian, mulatto and zambo—wanted to be a don. Such attitudes toward work had held back the growth of Venezuela. As Salas remarked: "It has been said 'to populate is to civilize'; we add 'to civilize is to cauterize the national ulcers and to abolish bad political, economic, and social customs, the only manner of forming useful citizens or preparing the natives so that they might triumph in the struggle for existence': this, more than to civilize, is to redeem." [33]

Some individuals, such as Jesús Semprúm and Mariano Picón Salas, went another step in relegating blacks to clearly negative positions. In 1920, Semprúm wrote a review of Rómulo Gallego's novel *El último solar* in which he said, "It is common to attribute all of our bad habits to Indian blood, which least abounds in the population of the coast, truly heirs of the customs of the roguish Spanish and the *cruel* and *slothful African*." [34] The liberal-minded Mariano Picón Salas saw no place for blacks in a new society, other than to add local color as they currently did. He joined his more conservative colleagues in advocating whitening as a means of stimulating the development of the country. In 1922, he contributed an article to the important journal *Cultura Venezolana* in which he argued that miscegenation would establish a new race in Venezuela. This new race, he said, had a better chance of surviving in the tropics because, among other things, the Venezuelans' African ancestry would enable them to endure the tropical climate, while the white blood would let them progress. As for the nation's past political problems, those struggles he wrote off as manifestations of the difficulties associated with all youthful societies. Though hardly scientific in his thinking, Picón Salas concluded that Venezuela had a bright future as the result of miscegenation.[35]

Not all Venezuelans treated the question of whitening in an academic manner. Some turned to humor and satire to make their points. One such humorist, Leoncio Martínez (Leo), started the humor magazine *Fantoches*. This publication both shaped and reflected the culture of Venezuelans of all classes with its cartoons and caricatures. Quick-witted artists captured the spirit of sometimes conflicting and contradictory currents of thought about race. The cartoonists also served as mirrors of the society they entertained. Much of what they drew only repeated in a humorous or satirical form what the public already accepted as true. To succeed, a cartoon obviously depended on the existence of beliefs held in common by readers and cartoonists.

Over the years, cartoonists satirized the racial behavior of black and white Venezuelans in a number of ways. A careful reading of *Fantoches* suggests that Venezuelans continued to treat blacks as a type, not as individuals. As they had at the end of the nineteenth century, artists always drew stereotyped blacks—flat round heads, kinky hair or shiny bald pates, large or bulging white eyes, large thick lips, and huge ears. Though all of the cartoons depicting blacks did not have antiblack content, the majority usually did.

But the cartoons also poked fun at upwardly mobile Venezuelan blacks and the process of whitening. Quite a few drawings simply parodied blacks for their looks or aspirations. Others placed the onus of pretentiousness upon blacks who seemed "uppity," or overambitious. Seldom did cartoonists depict whites or *pardos* in equally demeaning ways.

Such evaluation of Venezuelan humor runs the risk of reading North American biases into the Venezuelan mind. Many cartoons show that the multiracial Venezuelans could laugh at themselves and their racial mixing. Venezuelans took delight in racial situations that would have angered or offended whites and blacks in the United States. Nonetheless, the bulk of the cartoons between 1920 and 1935 that contained references to blacks or race had clear social implications. For instance, one particularly bitter cartoon by "Rivero" showed two white men seated at a restaurant table arguing vehemently. Behind them stood a black waiter with a shocked expression on his face. Entitled "National Problem," the conversation between the two men pointed out the antipathy between some white elites and blacks. One man said to the other, "You ought to understand that what we lack here is emigration!" His friend objected, "Quiet! Don't be ignorant! What you mean to say is immigration!" "No!" shouted the first, "Emigration it is! That all of the bad elements emigrate!"[36]

In 1927, one of Leo's drawings, which he called "Paternal Sacrifices," portrayed a rich black man, his two sons, and an old woman. Both boys had distinct negroid features like their father, but very white complexions. The woman, who registered surprise upon seeing two light-skinned boys, learned from the proud father that indeed they were his sons, but he had bathed them in oxygenated water since their birth. In another version of whitening humor that appeared in 1925, Leo showed a coal black dandy, dressed in a double-breasted suit, standing in front of a mirror with his hand on his hair. Looking at his image, he said: "I have everything but the hair and the color."[37]

Not all humor seemed so lighthearted. In 1928, one cartoonist referred to a well-dressed black as a Rudolph Valentino "after the explosion."[38] Some two years earlier, in another publication, Adolfo Blanco García published a cartoon entitled "Straightened Hair," which presented a well-dressed black gentleman seated in a barber's chair having his hair straightened. Above him, in the rising smoke of his cigarette, appeared his dream of a new self; a handsome profile, without thick lips and flat nose. A poem written by Job PIM (Francisco Pimental) accompanied the drawing. According to the poet, hair straightening did not offer much hope for blacks, whose skin, "like the wing of a vulture," kept them from passing as whites. But the process did provide a remedy for "the intermediate type who had light but very twisted hair." Even so, Job PIM, who considered himself a democratic man, applauded such a simple solution to racial mixing and hoped that some day there would be a preparation that would allow blacks to whiten their pigmentation, thus enabling them to improve in rank. On that happy day, he concluded his poem, "perfect equality will have arrived."[39] One other cartoon, from a 1929 edition of *Fantoches*, also left no doubt as to its social message. Designated "The Newly Rich," it showed a white house painter arriving at the door of a lovely home of a prosperous black couple with four coal black children. In the caption the painter asked, "What do you want done in your house?" In response, the father simply said, "For now, to whiten it."[40]

By 1920, Venezuela's leading publications had devised a fairly uniform array of racial stereotypes. They systematically projected a negative image of blacks as inferior beings and a positive image of whites as ideal types. These stereotypes regularly showed up in newspapers and magazines aimed at middle- and upper-class readers. When depicted in cartoons and advertisements, blacks appeared as featureless nonentities, gross carica-tures of blacks, with the usual exaggerated negroid features. Most often, they represented individuals of humble origin—bellhops, mammies, non-descript male laborers and the like—in ads for common items, such as beer, foodstuffs, or local markets.

During the first four decades of the twentieth century, photos in the leading journals, newspapers, and magazines also showed only blacks from the poverty class, if they showed any. In a way, the absence of any photo-graphic record of blacks in the nation's newspapers reflected or reinforced the decision of elites to ignore the black presence in Venezuela and to an-ticipate their disappearance. Unlike in Argentina, where a black press came into existence during the nineteenth century, no newspapers served the in-terests of blacks. Relegated to the back pages, at best in servile positions, they never seemed important to the readers of the leading newspapers and magazines. Thus, they virtually disappeared from public view.

As characters in mainstream fiction blacks served either as minor figures or as tragic protagonists whose lives proved that individuals of their race could not escape the forces of racial determinism. Mixed racial heroes and heroines inevitably returned to the savagery of their nonwhite ancestors, or became victims of superior whites. For instance, the mestizo author Rómulo Gallegos used protagonists of mixed racial origin in many of his early works. His most common theme traced the regression of these mixed breeds toward the primitive and often savage nature of their Indian or black ancestors. Gallegos thus immortalized the struggle for civilization on the llanos in his *Doña Barbara*. He also wrote the best pre–World War II novel about Barlovento, *Pobre negro,* approaching racial topics from a Spencerian determinist point of view.

During the 1920s, one of the strongest antiblack statements came from Alberto Adriani, a son of Italian immigrants who grew up in the Andean city of Mérida, a region with few blacks. Though a liberal and a self-professed opponent of positivism, he agreed with the basic philosophy be-hind restrictive immigration policies. In a 1926 essay which he published in the influential *Cultura Venezolana,* Adriani warned his fellow Venezu-elans of the dangers inherent in expanding Venezuela's already substantial black population through immigration from nearby Antillian islands or the United States. Because he feared the influx of nonwhites, especially blacks from the islands, he recommended that the government not take a

Top. Paternal Sacrifices
"Oh, my friend, you don't know what these sons cost me." "Ah, but are these your little boys? So blond?" "Yes, Señora, but washed in oxygenated water since infants."
Fantoches (Caracas), September 21, 1927, p. 8.

Right. "I have everything but the hair and the color."
Fantoches (Caracas), April 25, 1925, p. 7.

Top. Straightened Hair
Elite (Caracas), November 6, 1926.

Right. The Newly Rich
Painter: "What do you want done in your house?"
Newly Rich: "For now, to whiten it."
Fantoches (Caracas), May 29, 1929, p. 8.

passive role. He thought that "neutrality of the government and business interests will work so that immigrants will be recruited from among black Antillians, Chinese coolies, Japanese, and East Indians."

In looking ahead, Adriani took for granted that black immigration posed a serious threat to Venezuela. He thought that Venezuela already had a considerable black minority, but he saw no easy way to block the immigration of blacks from the United States. In his mind, no simple solution existed. But he definitely advocated taking a strong stand against immigration from the Antilles. Antillian blacks, he wrote, were at "a level inferior to that of our nationals." He said they would form "a harmful element to our intellectual, social, and political life." Furthermore, Adriani wanted to end all immigration of blacks because he believed "the black has been a factor of deterioration in American countries where the races have mixed, or of disorder where they have remained separated." As proof of this observation, he noted that in Venezuela blacks had been the primary source of recruits in almost every revolution that had occurred since independence. For that reason, he stated, "An appreciable increase of the black population would upset the normal development of our democratic institutions and, above all, jeopardize our moral unity."[41]

Above all else, Adriani was afraid that blacks would account for the greatest number of immigrants if not banned from entry by rigidly enforced legislation. He believed that because of their prolific nature, their proximity to Venezuela, and their penchant for moving to any kind of work to escape overcrowded conditions, millions of blacks would descend upon Venezuela. After all, he argued, recent movement from the islands to Venezuela had been increasing. An alarmist, he used ridiculously exaggerated figures of his own making to purport that during 1919 and 1920, Jamaica alone had sent over two hundred thousand people to Panama, Cuba, and the United States. Adriani further claimed that in 1926 more than twenty thousand Antillian blacks entered the state of Zulia to work at the oil fields. Worse yet, he also believed that Hindus and coolies might invade Venezuela. These latter groups he called "unassimilable immigrants, whose way of life is inferior to ours and whose institutions and customs are strange to our people."[42]

Besides the internal complications, Adriani foresaw international implications of a policy that permitted the free entry of blacks into Venezuela. As he warned, the United States dealt especially harshly with black countries, such as Haiti and the Dominican Republic. "The Americans have certain prejudices against the black race and do not collaborate pleasantly even with their own countrymen of this race," he advised. Venezuela could not risk such a confrontation.[43]

In view of his belief that black immigration would have a debilitating influence upon the nation, Adriani urged the formulation of a careful immigration policy that would whiten the population. He stated that despite higher costs involved in bringing Europeans, such immigration should receive preferential treatment because "the people of Europe possess a superior standard of living and contribute not only to the economic progress of a country but also to its social and intellectual advance." For Adriani, two objectives stood above all others. First, he agreed with Simón Bolívar that Venezuelans should use immigration to educate their population by example. Second, immigration should "increase and improve our white population." Of the two goals, the second seemed most important to Adriani, who observed that in Latin America a direct relationship existed between the relative size of white populations and the degree of general progress. As he put it: "The ideal would be to have a homogeneous white population, which is impossible since our region contains a great proportion of Indians and blacks. Nevertheless, we can increase considerably the white element with great success."[44]

But just as efforts to exclude blacks failed, white immigration schemes did not work either. Europeans refused to move to Venezuela in any significant numbers while Gómez ruled. A few Italians, Middle Easterners, Germans, and Canary Islanders arrived before 1914 and lived as small shopkeepers and merchants, but a wave of European agricultural workers never appeared. The poor economic situation in Venezuela before the petroleum boom meant that the opportunities for social mobility found in other countries, such as the United States, Brazil, or Argentina, did not exist. Furthermore, most government-sponsored colonization projects failed. Gómez treated the nation as though it was his private estate, and he and his immediate family and close associates coveted what wealth they could gain from the land. Their avarice left little room for the average European immigrant "to make it" in the Americas.

Hence, despite ample rhetoric in favor of government-financed colonization programs, such schemes enjoyed only token support from Venezuelan authorities. Only trifling numbers of Europeans came—and then only sporadically. The majority of the government contracts succeeded in placing large tracts of land in the hands of Gómez supporters, rather than in attracting immigrants. Gómez further complicated matters by his intractable distrust of foreigners, especially non-Catholic, non-Spanish-speaking individuals, whose cultures and intentions he did not understand. His xenophobia, and that of his followers, offset any immigration schemes his administration ostensibly sponsored.[45]

With the demise of Gómez in December 1935, the positivists' influence declined rapidly. Actually it peaked during the 1920s, but its chief disciples—Gil Fortoul, Vallenilla Lanz, and Arcaya—remained powerful intellectual figures well beyond that decade. However much positivism may have subsided, its basic impact on the elites' attitudes toward race and racial mixing remained intact as subsequent generations of elites advocated whitening as a panacea.

One of the ironies of the period between 1899 and 1935 resulted from the contrasting views that Venezuelans and foreigners had of Venezuelan society. Even after the waning of the positivists' influence, the predominantly mixed nature of Venezuela's population troubled Venezuelan intellectuals. They felt uneasy about the fate of a seemingly inferior people. Like their predecessors, they wanted to whiten the mass of Venezuelans because they believed that *pardos* and blacks comprised an unruly mass incapable of achieving progress, as they desired it. In sharp contrast, foreigners who left accounts of their visits to Venezuela marveled at the degree of racial harmony they encountered. Most registered surprise at the amount of racial mixing that had taken place and commented favorably on the lack of racial conflict throughout Venezuela. Where the Venezuelan elites saw weakness in a mixed, nonwhite population, visitors perceived strength.

Between 1900 and 1935, foreigners' descriptions of race relations in Venezuela remained consistent with those of previous generations of travelers to the country. Most reacted well to the racial ambience. Perhaps Venezuela impressed them positively because it differed so noticeably from the racist societies from which they came. For instance, in 1900, a letter to the *New York Tribune* described Venezuela as a country in which "the majority of the people are half breeds or a mixture." [46] In 1906, James Weldon Johnson offered a similar account of Puerto Cabello, where he reported: "I see men of Negro blood in all the trades. I find them in clerical positions in the large wholesale houses, they are priests, there is one here who is a successful physician, and one of the richest importing and exporting merchants of the city is a colored man—as we use the term." [47] Some six years later, Lindon Bates, Jr., wrote of a river trip to Ciudad Bolívar, "There is no racial discrimination at this festive board as to race, or colour, or previous condition of servitude." He went on to explain to his readers that only one percent of Venezuela's population were recorded as pure white, "and in the most aristocratic circles the black of Africa is mixed with the blue of Castile." Like Johnson, he saw mestizos everywhere and noted: "Mulattoes are fairly common, and Zamboes, Negro and Indian half-breeds, less so. There is every possible permutation of these race mixtures." [48]

Later accounts left the same impressions. For instance, his arrival at La Guaira inspired Leonard Caro to comment upon the "jostling crowds of all hues from Negro graduating through dark mahoganies, mahoganies, pale mahoganies, on to lighter complexions still, through creams dark and pale, to well sunburnt brick-red of the Northern European."[49] During the 1930s, Hendrick De Leeuw remarked of Venezuela, "As to its inhabitants, who range from brilliant culture to untold simplicity, their pigment is borrowed from the Caucasian, African, Asiatic, and Indian races." Although Venezuelans always faced complex race problems, from a European perspective, De Leeuw felt that they had resolved most of them. He found that "Venezuelan law makes no distinction between races. Here a man is recognized as a man more frankly than in any other land. Negroes, whites, half-castes and Indians sit side by side in the jury box and there cast equal votes."[50]

Lady Dorothy Mills, an intrepid traveler who drove all over Venezuela in a Ford motor car, also found little prejudice wherever she went. Of Caracas in 1931, she wrote: "In the little streets moves a population equally motley. One sees the narrow-featured face of Spanish tradition, one sees a . . . mingling of white and Indian, of high cheek-bones, slant eyes and lank black hair. . . . One sees, too, the thickened features of a negro trend, in fact, one sees such a mixture that sometimes it is hard to tell where one type begins and another ends, for besides these, there are Syrians and French and Germans, Italians and Sicilians, Orientals and Jews." In the interior she discovered racial mixing in varying degrees. Valera, in the Andes, had few blacks. There she saw "fine-looking people with their Spanish-Indian blood. There were no longer traces of negro strain, for the negroes of the coastal regions do not care to work in the mountain regions, preferring the hot relaxing climate of the coast." But in Ciudad Bolívar she once again encountered the black presence, and the accompanying lack of prejudice. She reported: "As one sits or walks on the Paseo, all the facial types of the world seem to pass before one, with their admixture, especially the latter. It is hard to say who are the Venezuelans proper, so much have the lower and middle orders mingled with other races. For there is little colour prejudice, and among the natives of Venezuela one may notice the high cheek-bones and rough-hewn features of the Indian, and the thick lips and kinky hair of the negro. To try and guess the ancestors of a passer-by in the streets of Ciudad Bolívar often presents a problem that would tax the powers of Mendel himself."[51]

On the surface, the Venezuelans' opinion of their own society did not differ radically from those of foreign travelers; they readily acknowledged the lack of prejudice. But their interpretations of the Venezuelan reality clashed with those of visitors. Racial mixing disturbed them and presented what they considered a weak image. Thus, an official publication put out by the Gómez administration to encourage immigration to Venezuela recognized the complexity of the racial situation by pointing out, "The population of Venezuela is formed of European whites, halfbreeds and mulattoes, African negroes, Asiatics and aboriginal Indians, some of these civilized and speaking the Spanish language." But beyond this point the propaganda took a different turn. In discussing the elites the authors stated that the Venezuelan upper class had maintained their racial purity. "When the Spaniards invaded the country they chose for founding the cities, places and climates similar to those of Spain. This is the reason for the development of the white race in Venezuela, the old families of clear lineage being careful to avoid mixing with other stocks introduced by circumstances in Venezuela." [52]

In their analysis of Venezuela's progress as a modern nation, positivists and their opponents agreed that European immigration would transform Venezuela from a chaotic wasteland to a modern civilization. Whitening served as a common theme for all who touched on the subject of development between 1900 and the death of Gómez. For varied reasons, foreign observers described a relatively idyllic racial scene in Venezuela, which contrasted with the race relations in most other American nations. If Venezuelan thinkers sometimes fell into fits of pessimism and despair about the future, foreigners praised Venezuelans for their remarkable ability to transcend racial lines. Venezuelans revealed grave self-doubts about the abilities of their racially mixed population to cope with modern civilization, work, and democratic institutions. They also harbored lingering fears that the much admired but often feared Yankees might think of them as blacks, and thus vulnerable. [53] Whereas the travelers praised the racial mixing that took place in Venezuela, often citing the phenomenon as an example of what could happen when prejudices did not limit open relations between racial groups, Venezuelan elites often saw the actual state of racial mixing as a manifestation of retrogression and a cause of national stagnation and disorder that could be cured only by the infusion of more white blood. For them whitening the population offered the only sensible solution, both to the nation's long-standing labor and economic problems and to its political stability. For the elites of the Gómez generation, an orderly, hardworking European stock held the key to Venezuela's future.

RACE AND NATIONAL IMAGE IN THE ERA OF POPULAR POLITICS, 1935–1958

ON MAY 24, 1945, three prominent hotels in Caracas refused accommodations to the eminent North American singer, Robert Todd Duncan, his wife, Gladys, and his accompanist William Allen because of their race. Despite reservations made previously by his agent, Columbia Concerts, the manager of the Hotel Majestic informed Duncan that he did not have rooms available for the artist's party. Managers of the Carlton and the Ávila Hotels also turned down Duncan's request for rooms. Yet, according to a witness, all three managers gave the impression that they had space until they actually saw the Duncans and Allen. Upon seeing the party, the managers obviously changed their minds and insisted that the three seek quarters elsewhere in the city.[1]

At the time, the incident did not trouble Duncan. He had not understood the rapid *caraqueño* Spanish spoken by his host Héctor Govourneur, chairman of the Caracas Pro Arts Committee, and the hotel managers. Moreover, during his distinguished career as a performing artist, he had learned not to expend energy worrying about matters he could not control. He found it more fruitful to concentrate on preparing for his concerts. Thus, he thoroughly enjoyed his stay at the Hollywood, an older and very comfortable hotel. Not until Duncan reached Bogotá, on the next leg of his tour of South America, did he learn of "the hell" he had stirred up in Venezuela. In Colombia the newsmen who met his plane informed him of new laws against discrimination in Venezuela that had resulted from his exclusion from the three Caracas hotels.[2]

In contrast, though the incident did not bother Duncan, it did rankle people in Venezuela. Its announcement in the United States in June challenged the official ideology of nondiscrimination now espoused by Venezuelans. By 1945, most thinking Venezuelans regularly referred to their multiracial compatriots as a *café con leche* people. Only two years before the Duncan affair, the conservative newspaper *Ahora* stated: "Today our tricolored criollo race, sufficiently diversified by its derivation from intermarrying, finds itself satisfied by the absence of conflict of color. . . . We feel proud that racial problems do not exist in Venezuela."[3]

Therefore, the refusal to let blacks stay at prestigious hotels shocked many concerned individuals and groups. Not only did the hotel managers' actions contradict the policy of nondiscrimination, they also went against changed currents of the post-Gómez era. First, moderates followed in the wake of the Gómez regime. During the 1930s, Venezuela's leaders let several popular political movements expand their membership. By far the most successful of these, a nascent populist movement led by the founders of what ultimately became the Acción Democrática party, organized *pardos*, blacks, and Indians at grass-roots levels throughout the republic. Led by nonwhites, the emerging party with its larger mixed racial population had a profound influence on race relations as it came to power during the middle of the next decade. Second, the rise of Adolf Hitler and the outbreak of World War II heightened the racial awareness of most Venezuelans because of the threat to all colored persons inherent in the aryanism of the German Nazis. Third, since the late 1930s, a small group of Venezuelan writers attempted to awaken an interest in topics related to Venezuela's African heritage. Inspired by such Brazilian scholars as Gilberto Freyre and Arthur Ramos, writers Juan Pablo Sojo, Juan Liscano, Carlos Siso, Eduardo Calcaño, Alfredo Machado Hernández, and others treated a number of positive Afro-Venezuelan themes. As cultural nationalists, they tried to inspire pride in the contribution Africans made to the culture of modern Venezuela.

By the mid-1940s, these convergent currents definitely raised Venezuelans' sensitivity to race. Although the Todd Duncan incident subsequently became a dim memory, its occurrence stirred up considerable debate at the time. Like Brazilians who faced a similar dilemma when the North American dancer Katherine Dunham asserted that a hotel in São Paulo refused to give her a room, Venezuelans found it difficult to face the fact that an overt racist act had taken place. The Venezuelan press disclosed the details of Duncan's experience following his departure. Reaction to the news ranged from stunned disbelief to bitter anger.

Given their advanced state of racial consciousness, Venezuelans moved quickly to resolve the problem. Within a week of the incident, they passed legislation that prohibited all public services from practicing racial discrimination in any form. In general, those responding to the affair agreed that measures had to be taken to avoid future discrimination. They also agreed that the behavior of the hotel managers did not conform to Venezuelans' self-image as a society in which racial prejudice and discrimination did not exist.

From the outset, the debates took on nationalistic overtones. Though hardly partisan in nature, on political terms, the discussion reflected a wide spectrum of Venezuelan society. The most strident voices, nevertheless, belonged to members of the Acción Democrática party. These leaders took the initiative in introducing municipal and federal legislation aimed at prohibiting discrimination. Several factors contributed to the leading role played by the *adecos:* the racial composition of the party and the change in political climate.

At one point or another in their lives, most AD leaders felt the sting of racial discrimination in some form. These individuals comprised a diverse lot of men and women of mixed racial origin: Rómulo Betancourt from the state of Miranda, a self-described *café con leche* politician of middle-class origin; the mulatto educator, Luis Beltrán Prieto Figueroa from the island of Margarita; Andrés Eloy Blanco, a *pardo* poet from Cumaná; and Manuel Rodríguez Cárdenas, a light-skinned mulatto writer from the state of Yaracuy. These individuals came to power in the mid-1940s as outsiders. Born and raised outside of Caracas, from middle-class families, they attended public rather than private schools and universities and shared a nonwhite racial origin.

They organized their new party during the era of political moderation ushered in by Gómez's successors, General Eleazar López Contreras and General Isaías Medina Angarita. Between 1936 and 1945, they worked to create a multiclass and multiracial political movement, based in large part upon the ideas of the Peruvian political thinker Víctor Raúl Haya de la Torre. Like the latter, Betancourt and his associates broke with orthodox Marxists and took over the leadership of the working class by incorporating rural and urban laborers into a party. As in the case of the Peruvian model, middle-class politicians held most of the leadership positions at the national level. Nevertheless, the populist objectives advocated by the party attracted a wide following among workers and campesinos. With this wider base of supporters, the party easily supplanted the Communists as the leading representatives of the masses.[4]

By design, Betancourt and his AD party became advocates for Venezuela's tricolored masses. As Betancourt later wrote, in his mind the Venezuelan population, "formed from various races with all their virtues and faults, are just as capable of creative thought and activity and just as able to live a civilized life as any other."[5] He and his colleagues consistently fought lingering vestiges of racial discrimination. For instance, between 1943 and 1948, they tried without success to change the nation's immigration laws so as to permit the entry of nonwhites. They also incorporated the doctrine of racial democracy into their party rhetoric and applied it in a literal sense. Thus, they frequently referred to their fellow Venezuelans as a *café con leche* people. Finally, they openly expressed their opposition to a predominantly white oligarchy whom they linked with foreign imperialists trying to dominate the Venezuelan economy. During the 1940s, several relatively violent clashes between *pardo* youths from AD and white conservative youngsters occurred in Caracas. Though mostly of a political nature, these disturbances further reflected the efforts of AD to appeal to the large nonwhite portion of the populace rather than pander to the white minority who controlled the nation's wealth. But in this case, as in most others, their strategy counted on class distinctions more than on race, which, in their eyes, remained a sensitive issue.

A brief back track highlights the factors which influenced this change in advocacy. Following the death of Gómez at the end of 1935, the nation's elites had moved slowly toward more liberal positions on many political and economic issues. But their attitudes toward race did not shift perceptibly, at first. In particular, most white elites continued to view white immigration as a solution for Venezuela's basic social and economic problems. Despite oil revenues that allowed Venezuelans to balance their national budget, most elites still thought of the nation as an agricultural producer. Few believed that Venezuela had great industrial potential, beyond that of producing a few basic import-substitution consumer items. Therefore, they perpetuated the theme of populating the uninhabited sections of the country with hardy white agricultural colonists from Europe. Only now, changes in agricultural technology gave them the reason: the Venezuelan campesino lacked both the education and technical skills needed to undertake modern farming on a large scale. They convinced themselves that Europeans could perform miracles by rebuilding the agricultural sector, still languishing since the nineteenth century. Like their predecessors of a century before, they called for the implementation of immigration schemes aimed at attracting thousands of white Europeans, especially from Spain, Portugal, and Italy, as well as the Canary Islands. As in the past, European immigrants remained symbols of rejuvenation.

In many ways, the post-Gómez elites sounded very much like mid-nineteenth-century Argentines in their expectations. In fact, Vicente Dávila, director of *La Esfera* (Caracas), likened the Venezuelan situation to that of Argentina when he urged Venezuelans to heed Juan B. Alberdi's advice to Argentines in 1852 "To govern is to populate." In 1936, Dávila blamed Venezuela's failure to achieve its true destiny on the lack of an energetic population. Venezuela needed to populate its vast frontier, he wrote. Tropical diseases, tuberculosis, syphilis, alcoholism, and malnutrition had debilitated the population. Furthermore, he claimed, most Venezuelans lacked the spiritual, ethnic, and racial strength required to resolve the most urgent problems. European immigration offered a solution. Not only would the immigrants enrich the nation through their productivity, they would also introduce much-needed characteristics presently missing in the native population. As Dávila put it: "In order to help our national evolution, we need the introduction of other races, the joining of other ideas, the transfusion of blood, the example of creative activity, and the fertile stimulation of the spirit of sacrifice."[6]

However much Venezuelan elites wanted agricultural workers to settle in the interior, they virulently opposed the free entry of nonwhites. They did not want more of what they called "culturally inferior" persons to enter Venezuela. Accordingly, in January 1936, Alfredo Pardo argued in the pages of El Luchador of Ciudad Bolívar that the national government should regulate immigration carefully to impede the entry of "undesirable or harmful elements, in that these would only contribute to the degeneration of our race." He, like Dávila, believed that tropical diseases, poor sanitary habits, and primitive living conditions resulting from a generally low level of economic development combined to retard the growth of an industrious population in the interior of Venezuela. The introduction of more people with similar life-styles struck Pardo as an unlikely way to improve the rural population.[7]

The August 27, 1936, issue of the Maracaibo daily Panorama also warned against black immigration, although for somewhat different reasons. That newspaper hoped to weaken a strike at the western oil fields by turning Venezuelan workers against West Indians who worked there. Thus, an editorial entitled "The Negro Danger" suggested that Antillian blacks took jobs from Venezuelans by signing Venezuelan citizenship papers to get around provisions of a law requiring the oil companies to hire a work force composed of at least 75 percent Venezuelan citizens. The article also expressed alarm at the rate at which blacks entered Venezuela from the British West Indies. Panorama claimed that the presence of black Antillians not only posed a threat to Venezuelan workers but also endangered the well-being of the entire Venezuelan society. According to the newspaper's editors, blacks who moved to Venezuela just to take jobs were criminals, for "to renounce the country of one's origin and to adopt another in order to acquire a job with better conditions . . . is a felony, a betrayal of the hospitality that has been received."[8]

In 1937, the influential liberal oligarch Arturo Uslar Pietri made an even more forceful statement against black immigration in a series of articles published in the newspaper El Universal of Caracas. To begin with, he did not think that Venezuelans had the capacity to realize the economic potential of their country because of the indolent nature of their mixed race. He singled out blacks in particular as a negative element and wrote that "the black, for his part, does not constitute a beneficial part of the race." Furthermore, he stated, "That which we may be able to call the Venezuelan race actually is . . . as incapable of a modern and dynamic concept of work and wealth as were its antecedents."

Like other white elites of his generation, Uslar Pietri argued that an open-port policy for immigrants would bring disastrous consequences, since work opportunities in agriculture and oil would attract an invasion of black workers from the Antilles and coolies from the Orient. These types, he felt, would only hurt Venezuela's ethnic composition and lower its standard of living. In short, the introduction of blacks would delay the general progress of Venezuela toward what he thought of as civilization. However, he urged Venezuela to change its ethnic composition in order to alter its course of history. He believed that to become a modern state, "it is necessary to inject a formidable quantity of new blood into the country, with which a new concept of life, with an aggressive economic mentality, will begin the transformation of our ruinous economic and social structure." To accomplish this goal, he concluded, Venezuela needed European immigrants.[9]

When Alberto Adriani framed new immigration and colonization legislation during 1936 and 1937 as a member of the administration, he, too, renewed calls for an exclusive policy of admitting whites only. In 1936, he republished his candid, antiblack 1926 essay on the subject of white immigration. As architect of the immigration policy, he reaffirmed his conviction that permitting blacks to enter Venezuela endangered the orderly development of the nation.

He set as Venezuela's primary objective the entry of thousands of whites, to the complete exclusion of all other racial groups. In that regard his colonization schemes differed from previous administrations only in that he set up a new mechanism by which the Venezuelan government could take an active role in the selection of immigrants from Europe. He created an immigration commission which functioned as an intermediary between Venezuelan mining, industrial, and agricultural interests and the emigration authorities of several European nations. As implemented under the rule of Eleazar López Contreras, Adriani's immigration program steered Venezuela toward whitening its population. Although Adriani died shortly after the program's inception, his policy determined the immigration patterns for the next three decades.[10]

Very clearly, the populist leaders of Acción Democrática eschewed this attitude. During the 1940s, as AD began its ascendancy toward power, adeco leaders repeatedly criticized Venezuela's restrictive immigration policy as contrary to basic Venezuelan concepts of race and democracy. Undoubtedly, they demonstrated mixed motives in undertaking what proved to be an abortive campaign to change the immigration codes. But AD politicians manifested a deep-seated commitment to represent the interests of the nation's multiracial masses. From the beginning of its existence, the party questioned the legitimacy of the immigration laws and called for a more open system that would permit nonwhite immigration.

As Rómulo Betancourt elucidated: "Our immigration policy followed a definite sociological concept. We wanted the immigrant to increase our production and to fill the country. We did not consider the white man as such or the European as superior to the Venezuelan of mixed blood. We were not interested in a transfer of civilization as one might bring some Swiss pine saplings to give style to a tropical garden, filled with our mango and tamarind trees." As for the role of white immigrants, he pointed out that "an immigration policy which gave privileged status to people coming from outside, just because they came from countries with some centuries more of history than Latin America, would not contribute to this goal." [11]

The immigration policy advocated by the members of Acción Democrática included concern over the prohibition of other nonwhites. This became quite clear during the war years when *adecos* worked to remove restrictions on Chinese immigration. They saw the Chinese as beleaguered allies in a worldwide struggle against totalitarianism. In their eyes, Venezuelans and Chinese shared a common cause: the preservation of democracy. In keeping with this spirit, in June 1943 José Antonio Marturet introduced a motion to the House of Deputies that called for modification of the immigration code to permit Asians to enter Venezuela as resident immigrants. A number of factors motivated Marturet. First, he wanted to gain support for his party from Venezuela's small Chinese community by obtaining citizenship for those Chinese who had married Venezuelans. Second, he felt obligated to offer a haven to Chinese who had fought the Japanese but lost. Third, he thought that China and Venezuela stood together in their fight for democracy. Finally, in pragmatic terms, he argued that Chinese immigrants would supply much needed labor in the agricultural sections of the underpopulated hinterland. [12]

Marturet's bill failed to pass. The failure was not because other members of the congress lacked sympathy for the plight of "the heroic sons of China" in their death struggle against Japan, but according to the report of a special commission set up to study the proposed changes in the immigration codes, those Chinese who lived in Venezuela already enjoyed all of the juridical guarantees given to Venezuelan citizens, even if they could not vote. For that reason and several others, the commission recommended no changes in the existing laws. Moreover, the report said, the Chinese who lived in Venezuela had proven themselves responsible social elements. The report concluded that the lack of racial fanaticism in Venezuela assured future Chinese immigrants a protected and cordial atmosphere.[13]

Neither Marturet nor fellow *adeco* Andrés Eloy Blanco accepted the commission's findings. For them, the exclusion of Chinese from a multiracial society such as Venezuela's seemed hypocritical. As Marturet asked: "How is it possible that in Venezuela we speak of white race? Our America, and consequently Venezuela, is essentially a country of hybrids. . . . I, Señores, take pride in the white blood I have, but I am also proud of the Indian blood and the black blood that mix in it." It appeared absurd, he said, to exclude nonwhites, for such a policy was completely at odds with reality in Venezuela, "where we are all as it has been well said '*café con leche*.'" Rather, he added, "I would say . . . 'Let him throw the first stone who feels free of black or Indian blood, or white blood as well.'" Like Marturet, Blanco also spoke of a Venezuelan race. "We are the cosmic race, still in formation," he stated, a race no more beautiful than any other. Moreover, he added, Venezuela also had a commitment to defend the principles of democracy, which they could not ignore because of some misguided notions on race held by deputies in the National Congress.[14]

Let there be no doubt: in 1943 the views expressed by Marturet and Blanco represented those of a minority of populist politicians, not the elites and their allies who dominated the congress and the executive office. The more conservative elites advocated whitening and stressed the need to contract European laborers. Above all, they wanted only workers from so-called superior cultures. Concomitantly, they refused to encourage immigration of blacks and Asians. As one contributor to the conservative newspaper *Ahora* put it in June 1943, black and Chinese immigrants would not improve Venezuela, for the nation hardly needed more people used to a low standard of living. In the author's words: "Chinese and blacks have over them the weight of centuries of suffering, hunger, and slavery. They are stoic races . . . accustomed to primitive ways of life. And Venezuela is tired of suffering. Venezuela wants to wake up, it wants exacting people who aspire to a better life than exists, far from the unhealthy hovel and the overseer's whip."[15]

In the same issue of *Ahora*, Dr. Héctor Maldonado, director of the Institute of Immigration and Colonization, made an equally blunt statement about race. "But why do we have to bring colored races, since we can attract already civilized classes of other races?" Maldonado preferred hardworking farmers from Lithuania, Poland, Yugoslavia, Romania, and Bulgaria to the Chinese and blacks. Other elites sought Italians and Spaniards. But whatever European group they touted, they all agreed with the essence of what Jorge Lusiani wrote in late 1944, when he argued that even though Venezuela had a hybrid race, it needed further crossing with

Europeans. Without European blood, he warned, Venezuela would degenerate and in so doing accent "the peculiar blackness of the majority until it regresses to black."[16]

Until the downfall of the Medina administration in October 1945, the Venezuelan government rigidly enforced the ban on nonwhite immigration to Venezuela. In fact, some officials took such a rigid position that before the outbreak of World War II, they sometimes refused to let black and Philippine seamen disembark United States ships at Venezuelan ports. Although Venezuelan government officials assured representatives of the United States State Department that this treatment of the sailors resulted from actions taken by mistake by local authorities, the situation nevertheless typified the general level of antipathy of Venezuelans toward nonwhite foreigners.[17]

For the most part, the Venezuelan public did not pay much attention to immigration questions. One exception occurred in June 1944 when overzealous Venezuelan immigration agents denied two black boxers permission to enter Venezuela. The incident stirred up some interest among fight fans, especially, but also gave political satirists an opportunity to point out the folly of refusing to let blacks enter a country with a substantial black population. Humorists, ever conscious that Venezuelans of all political stripes did not support the Germans' Aryan ideology, reminded their readers of the Venezuelans' vulnerability on racial matters. Both *Panorama* and the national humor magazine *Fantoches* ran cartoons showing a stork carrying a black baby to Venezuela, with captions to the effect that blacks could not enter the country. Another humor magazine, *Morrocoy Azul,* printed a cartoon pertaining to the same theme that depicted a black couple with a white baby. In response to her husband's obvious display of anger for having given birth to another man's child, the wife defended herself saying, "But, my love, it was the stork who brought me this because they do not allow blacks to enter Venezuela."

Immigration obviously became a dominant target of attack by humorists. The leftist newspaper *Ultimas Noticias* (Caracas) published a drawing of three dark-skinned immigration officers, all with definite negroid features, turning away a black who wanted to enter Venezuela. In desperation, the latter asked, "But what if I am a little sunburned, then can I pass?" A satirical piece in *Morrocoy Azul* suggested that a distinguished black jurist would have to become consul in Higuerote, a coastal town in the predominantly black region of Barlovento, because if he took a diplomatic post outside of Venezuela, he might not be permitted back into his homeland. In a less serious manner, *Fantoches* included a cartoon showing a Venezuelan boxer stretched out on the mat for the count, with his black adversary standing in a neutral corner watching the referee. The poor

Venezuelan, holding his aching head in his gloves, muttered to no one in particular: "Caray! Why didn't they prohibit the entry of blacks before this one came?"[18]

The good-naturedness of such humor suggests that most Venezuelans felt relaxed about race. Usually rare, such cartoons did not try to make strong racial statements. They show that Venezuelans readily laughed at themselves. Such jokes drew the public's attention to reality, as did cartoons that reminded the average Venezuelans of their tricolored origins. Not infrequently, a cartoonist might draw something like a three-colored youngster born on October 12, or the Day of the Race, to prod Venezuelans to accept racial mixing and to reject the threat to Venezuela inspired by German racism. And, even though they continued to treat blacks in basic stereotypical ways—that is, exaggerated negroid features, without individual identity—they nevertheless made no attempt to present any one race as either superior or inferior.

As a rule, until the time of the Todd Duncan affair, Acción Democrática's major political opponents concentrated on class instead of race as an issue. The Communists followed an orthodox Marxist path toward class struggle. Race never became a central part of their political campaigns. For their part, the Christian Democrats, or Copei, never attempted to attract blacks to their ranks. Led by Rafael Caldera, the party came into existence originally as a result of the efforts of a group of young Catholic nationalists. These politicians feared that Betancourt and his followers intended to establish a godless Marxist regime in Venezuela. To counter Acción Democrática's basically populist appeal, the *copeyanos* (members of Copei) first reached out for upper- and middle-class support. The resulting essentially white composition of the party's membership led to the following popular refrain attributed to *adecos:* "There are two things I shall probably never see: a woman pissing into a test tube, and a black member of Copei."

As for President Medina, his Partido Democrático Venezolano represented elements of the white elite who allowed the establishment of a moderate democratic political system. Beyond this outwardly democratic posture, both he and his followers showed no inclination to include the masses in their movement and generally overlooked their needs. Medina certainly did nothing to alleviate the problems of the nation's poor blacks. Nor did he try to include successful blacks in his administration. In 1944, a group of journalists actually sent him a letter in which they included draft resolutions and recommendations for a campaign to reduce the privileges of race and to remove all aspects of racial prejudice, but nothing in Medina's correspondence suggests that he seriously entertained the journalists' requests. Nor does evidence exist that demonstrates he took any interest in the announcement that hotels in Caracas refused to serve blacks such as Todd Duncan.[19]

Medina's silence on the Duncan incident seems puzzling in the light of the heat it generated. His opponents lost no time in turning the affair into a political issue. From the beginning, members of Acción Democrática led the attack on the hotels who excluded blacks. They made a nationalistic appeal to the multiracial majority by placing the blame for the incident upon foreigners and their allies among the oligarchy. On May 29, 1945, Rómulo Betancourt, the nominal leader of the party, delivered a scathing speech about the hotel managers when he introduced a proposal to the municipal council of Caracas to investigate the affair. He considered the incident uncharacteristic of Venezuelan behavior; furthermore, he accused the hotel managers and owners of having "the mentality of a Kentucky slaveholder." At his urging, the municipal council passed a resolution that prohibited any discrimination in public buildings.

A few days later, on June 2, the official AD party organ *El País* expanded these thoughts in an editorial stating the party's position in unequivocal terms. "Black does not exist in Venezuela either as a problem or as a caste. Because in Venezuela we are all *café con leche,* some with more coffee and others with more milk, according to the graphic statement of a sociologist whose lineage was white on all sides." Thus, like Betancourt, the editors of *El País* attributed the racist behavior of the hotel managers to their foreign origins, claiming, "It is possible to believe that the managers who committed this absurdity might not be Venezuelan."[20]

On June 4, another member of AD, Manuel Rodríguez Cárdenas, delivered an ardent speech to the national senate in which he also blamed foreigners for having imported racism of the North American variety to Venezuela. A *pardo* from the state of Yaracuy, he denied that Venezuelans practiced racial discrimination. But he admitted that the three hotels had refused to admit Todd Duncan and that shortly before that incident some Caracas hotels had turned away a group of Haitian newspaper correspondents who had come to Venezuela as delegates to the Third Inter-American Press Congress. As in the case of Duncan, he blamed the poor treatment of the Haitians on racism, for as he noted: "It mattered little that one was a university professor, a poet of quality, and a diplomat; it also did not amount to much that the other was a distinguished writer and Haitian biographer." Like Betancourt and others, Rodríguez Cárdenas imputed such racism to foreigners.

The idea that North Americans brought their brand of overt racial discrimination to Venezuela did not originate with either Betancourt or Rodríguez Cárdenas. This notion had existed for a long time. At the turn of the century, many Venezuelans feared that the spread of United States hegemony in the region would eventually bring segregation and North American racism to Venezuela. To many observers, foreign oil companies already practiced racial discrimination in the daily operation of their oil fields. In 1936, Ramón Díaz Sánchez used his novel *Mene* to accuse North American petroleum companies of having introduced segregated working conditions at their facilities in western Venezuela. In that novel, Díaz Sánchez dealt with the sufferings of a black laborer whom the oil companies blacklisted for having broken one of the rigid segregation codes in effect at the time.

In a similar way, Rodríguez Cárdenas explained to his fellow senators that the owners of the hotels that rejected Duncan had acted like North American racists. He warned that "through the caprice of a few, the racial problem is beginning to be planted in Venezuela." Of course, he admitted, a few Venezuelans believed that blacks looked ugly because of their flat noses and thick lips, but in the past such biases had not led to overt discrimination against blacks. Nor had those biases constituted a problem until the Duncan incident brought them to light. It now appeared to Rodríguez Cárdenas that an explosive situation existed in Venezuela. In no uncertain terms, he thought that racism such as he had seen during a trip through the southern United States might develop in Venezuela. At some future date more violations of the constitution might occur. This would divide the society between blacks and whites. To assure that racism did not grow, the senator from Yaracuy implored his colleagues to remember that "there does not exist in any part of the world a Venezuelan who is able to hide his black grandparent."[21]

By shifting the blame to foreigners, Acción Democrática partisans won considerable support for their position. For one thing, they did not offend other Venezuelans, who nominally accepted the creed of nondiscrimination. More important, they gave themselves ample room in which to maneuver. As leaders of a multiracial and multiclass popular movement, they knew full well that race constituted a potential problem for all Venezuelans. To a degree, they identified a white oligarchy as the common enemy of the Venezuelan masses. But they wanted to avoid open racial conflict, as such. Like nineteenth-century Venezuelans, they used a social definition of white, for the most part, and applied the term to the very rich and powerful individuals who controlled the bulk of the nation's economic, social, and political institutions.

In effect, they allowed their followers to accept the rhetoric about racial democracy, while also linking a portion of the white elite with foreign oil interests whom they accused of racism. AD members insinuated that those elites either willingly or unwittingly supported racial discrimination because of their role in bringing the foreign companies to Venezuela in the first place. Thus, the *adecos* avoided an open racial split, which they feared might have antagonized white middle-class supporters of their party, but at the same time, they raised the specter of racism as a tool of social control in the hands of a small minority with close ties to foreign business interests. In the long run, Acción Democrática strategists reasoned that they stood to gain more by forcing the elites to accept the consequences of their own statements about racial democracy. The removal of race as a barrier to social mobility would make it all the more possible for the *adecos* to succeed in their efforts to implement what constituted a bourgeois revolution.

Their strategy worked for the most part. Rodríguez Cárdenas' colleagues in the senate applauded his reaffirmation of the doctrine of nondiscrimination. J. Mauricio Berrizbeitia, a white senator from the eastern state of Sucre, referred to Venezuelan society as a single family. "We have not had distinctions between blacks, whites, and Indians," he said. Another eastern senator, Father C. Benítez Fonturvel of Nueva Esparta, who claimed to speak with the voice of a Christian "and a Catholic priest," proclaimed "the Christian equality of men before God and society." Typical of many whites, Fonturvel dealt with the question of equality in patronizing terms when he added, "I know many black people with white souls." These words, like those of Berrizbeitia, ultimately meant that many elites could not find fault with their fellow Venezuelans but, rather, pointed their accusing finger at foreigners, despite indications that they actually harbored basic antiblack prejudices of their own.[22]

Other members of the society followed suit. For instance, the June 2, 1945 issue of *Ultimas Noticias* ran a column by Pedro Boroes, who insisted, "The mark of our democracy is the absolute equality of all races." According to Boroes, the Venezuelan population constituted such a complex blend of black, Indian, and white that nobody could establish the exact proportion of any racial group in the mix. He fully accepted the myth that during the nineteenth century the social convulsions that accompanied the Federal War completed the process by which racial equality was achieved. Consequently, Boroes concluded that since Venezuelan democracy guaranteed equality, it seemed absurd not to repudiate all discrimination. The June 5 and 6 editions of the same leftist newspaper ran other articles which criticized the hotels. These, too, pointed out that the incident had provoked feelings of profound indignation among the public. While it acknowledged that racism existed elsewhere in the hemisphere, *Ultimas Noticias* unflinchingly stated: "Fortunately, we do not have a similar problem in our country, and we will not tolerate foreigners who might come in order to bring a similar calamity to our soil. . . . Whites and blacks, yellow, Indians, Semites or Aryans—all people in Venezuela are equals and ought to enjoy liberty and equal treatment."

Likewise, on the right, *El Nacional*, a generally conservative Caracas newspaper, noted that the resurgence of racial discrimination in Venezuela appeared unlikely, at best limited to only a few incidents. These they attributed to "Yankee imperialism and its national lackeys." According to *El Nacional*, the hotels served individuals from a country where racial discrimination still existed. North American oilmen came from a segregated society and did not want to mingle with blacks. Knowing this, the managers of the three hotels refused to risk the loss of business from this affluent clientele by serving black guests. As *El Nacional* pointed out, this behavior posed an inherent threat to Venezuelans. The United States had already transplanted its brand of racism in Cuba. If Venezuelans did not halt the penetration of North American influence in their country, it would soon be possible to imagine a similar situation in Venezuela: "Substitute sugar with petroleum, *habaneros* with *caraqueños*, and you will have created the exact image of what can happen in Venezuela." In fact, the editorial went on, several changes had already occurred. Some Venezuelans now chewed Wrigley's gum, read *Readers' Digest* selections, smoked mild cigarettes—and held racial prejudices. But the responsibility for all of this did not fall solely upon the Yankees. The article concluded thus: "We certainly know that our country does not lack the little creole—a typical product of imperialism—who makes one call him mister, who is servile with the gringo to the point of sharing the worst evil that the latter brings." [23]

Other conservatives took the same line. For instance, *Ahora* assured its readers: "We believe that this incident has nothing Venezuelan about it. Our true aristocracy is of an economic character and best responds to the heading plutocracy. The owners of wealth are those who least have blue eyes." [24] Writing for the same newspaper on June 10, 1945, Luis Barrios Cruz thought that Venezuelans had proven their anti-Aryan sympathies. Nevertheless, he found the fact that some hotels refused to let colored people use their facilities a truly disagreeable situation. As he argued, if Venezuelans practiced some form of democracy, it was precisely racial democracy. They simply did not make distinctions between races. A contribution to *Fantoches* echoed these sentiments, noting that if the hotels had been located in Berlin or New York, the Venezuelans would not have felt outraged, but since they were situated in Caracas, they had to judge the consequences of the hotels' actions because "whoever might have doubts about the purity of their blue blood takes a chance by entering these hotels, where the norms established by Adolf Hitler are alive and in force." [25]

Individuals of every color of the racial spectrum attacked the hotels, among them several prominent middle-class blacks. One black, Dr. Jorge Stronach, also singled out foreign attitudes as a root cause of racism in Venezuela. In an interview given to *Ultimas Noticias* he stated, "Racial discrimination, more than being a negation of national solidarity, constitutes a waste of talents and efforts that this country cannot well afford." Nevertheless, the incident bothered him because he did not want to let racism grow in Venezuela as it had in Cuba, Puerto Rico, and Panama. For that reason, he suggested that "the Aryans who neither want nor can endure the presence of our little 'toasted' Venezuelans can go elsewhere with their prejudices and their nonsense." In his estimation, only a handful of "little white criollos" accepted the notion of racial superiority in Venezuela. Therefore, he urged all Venezuelans who wanted to preserve a free republican system to reject racial hatred. Another black, the reporter Miguel Angel Sánchez, also refused to believe that racial discrimination existed in Venezuela. He thought that the hotel managers had blundered, largely because they lacked an understanding of the basic hospitality and kindness of Venezuelans. As he put it, they tried "to establish racial distinctions here where all of us legally enjoy equality."[26]

In retrospect, the public reaction, though short-lived, showed an overwhelming consensus among a wide sector against the hotels. Predictably, nationalistic statements by individuals from different political, social, and racial groups upheld the official doctrine of nondiscrimination fostered by twentieth-century elites. Foreign-owned hotels had impugned the Venezuelan national image as a racial democracy. In the eyes of most critics, foreigners introduced a dangerous racism of the sort found in the United States or Hitler's Germany. Thus, Venezuelans found it relatively easy to view the hotels' treatment of the Duncans as an aberration. Moreover, they easily convinced themselves that they had taken adequate steps to avoid further incidents of racial discrimination simply by enacting legislation against such behavior. They had, in effect, resisted the influence of imperialists who attempted to impose non-Venezuelan values upon the country.

Yet, given the historical context of the incident, it becomes increasingly clear that the nationalistic rhetoric did not necessarily mean that all Venezuelans held the same attitude on the subject. Despite the seeming consensus of opinion, many observers in 1945 missed the mark, as had José Gil Fortoul some fifty years before. To begin with, although the nation's elites accepted their own mixed racial origins and fostered a concept of racial democracy, they never adopted the idea of racial equality. Rather, they subscribed to the notion of social race first described in the 1890s by Gil

Fortoul, which placed a premium upon whitening in both cultural and racial terms. This, in turn, led them to set whitening of the entire population of Venezuela as their ultimate goal.

Their determination to whiten the population also led them to overlook the nature of discrimination in Venezuela, where most blacks continued to comprise a distinct poverty class. Instead of giving blacks equal status in a pluralistic society, they urged them to improve their lot through what they called whitening, an inexact process which involved miscegenation, education, and economic advancement. For the elites, racial democracy actually meant that all black and colored individuals could whiten themselves and their descendants socially through a number of steps, including specific economic, and cultural measures, as well as through actual racial mixing with whites. Their use of the platitudes of racial democracy did not obviate the elites' deep-seated mistrust of Venezuela's multiracial masses, whom they still considered incapable of self-government. Implicit in their thinking on the subject was the long-held belief of their forbearers either that through an extended process of assimilation and acculturation the nation's blacks would eventually disappear as a group or that those few blacks who remained would withdraw to remote enclaves, well out of sight.

Despite their support of whitening, the elites did not want any serious discussion of race to take place. They expected most blacks to live in poverty and saw no contradiction between this expectation and their advocacy of racial democracy. Following the Duncan affair they manifested this attitude either by defending the doctrine of nondiscrimination or by ignoring the incident altogether. Antonio Pardo Soublette, president of the Venezuelan Association of Concerts, professed surprise when Duncan's agents called him to protest the treatment their client received at the hotels. According to Pardo Soublette, he did not believe the agents at first and felt that they had made a mistake because, as he said, "I had never heard that there might be racial discrimination in Venezuela since it is unconstitutional and would expose its perpetrators to severe sanctions." He only reluctantly admitted that the government should remain alert to the threat posed by the hotels once he became convinced of the veracity of the charges.[27] Another member of the elite, Antonio Arraiz, director of the Caracas daily *El Nacional* and a member of the municipal council of Caracas, denied the charges of racism leveled against the hotels, defending them on the ground that they had been completely full at the time that Duncan arrived.[28] As noted, President Isaías Medina Angarita chose to ignore the incident. Ostensibly a moderate on political matters, Medina made no public statement on the issue, despite calls from the liberal press to take a strong stand against racism.

For a variety of reasons, Venezuelan middle-class blacks also did not discuss the question of racial discrimination in depth. Neither Jorge Stronach nor Miguel Angel Sánchez questioned the myth of racial democracy. Rather, they supported the nondiscrimination doctrine and repeated the same shopworn phrases uttered by white elites. For one thing, such individuals as Stronach and Sánchez had escaped the fate of most Venezuelan blacks, who lived in the shadow of their slave past as domestic servants, rural campesinos, and day laborers. In Venezuela, as in Brazil, these individuals did not jeopardize their social gains by identifying themselves with poor blacks. Furthermore, they sincerely thought of themselves as living examples of racial democracy at work. In their own eyes the basic social division in Venezuela resulted from class, not race.[29]

The fact that they did not speak out on matters related to race should not reflect a negative image of successful blacks. In Venezuela, as elsewhere in the Americas, the elites discouraged the organizing of black-consciousness movements. In contrast to the Brazilian experience, Venezuelans showed no inclination to idealize the African contributions to their culture. At midcentury, Venezuela had no black political organizations, as such, which articulated the aspirations of the nation's black minority.

Furthermore, as the gifted critic and writer Julián Padrón lamented shortly before his death in 1944, the nation had not produced a major black poet or novelist. To date, the mestizo novelist Rómulo Gallegos had written the best-known novel about the blacks of Barlovento, *Pobre negro,* and another mestizo, Guillermo Meneses, had published short stories in which he recorded the lives of poor black prostitutes, seamen, and coastal workers. But as Padrón pointed out, Meneses, like Gallegos, failed to penetrate the minds of his black characters and at best portrayed the mestizo poor of Venezuela.[30]

In 1943, the mulatto author Juan Pablo Sojo published his novel *Nochebueno negra,* which he based on his native Barlovento region. Called by one critic a "muted protest against an economic structure that forever relegates blacks to the bottom where there is little hope for change," the novel met with little literary success. According to most critics, it failed to win an audience because Sojo could not transform his knowledge of folklore into plausible fiction.[31] An earlier protest in 1936 by novelist Ramón Díaz Sánchez vividly depicted the plight of black workers and the ugly side of segregated lunchrooms, rest rooms, and living quarters in the oil camps; this novel, *Mene,* also went largely unnoticed.

Venezuela's lack of black cultural leaders contrasted with Cuba and Brazil, where black literary and political movements took place. In Venezuela only individuals of mixed racial origin made any significant contributions to the study of Venezuela's black heritage. Of those who wrote about blacks, the majority paid only scant attention to modern issues. For instance, during the 1940s, Eduardo Calcaño founded and directed a black theater group, which received praise for the level of its productions. But Calcaño made no effort to concentrate on Venezuelan black traditions, nor did he attempt to encourage a popular-culture movement among the nation's blacks. In fact, his theater's repertoire mostly included works written by North Americans, such as James Weldon Johnson, or Caribbean poets, including the Cuban Nicolás Guillen. Only on occasion did they present writings of Juan Pablo Sojo or perform dances and musical numbers drawn from Venezuelan sources.[32]

Just a few other individuals studied Afro-American culture in Venezuela besides Eduardo Calcaño. For one brief period during the 1940s and early 1950s, the most notable students of Venezuela's blacks—Juan Pablo Sojo, Carlos Siso, Juan Liscano, Alfredo Machado Hernández, and Miguel Acosta Saignes—wrote the bulk of the existing literature on African contributions to the formation of Venezuelan society. Of these writers, only Acosta Saignes received any formal training as a social scientist, in his case as an anthropologist at a Mexican university during a period of political exile. Though not a formal group, these individuals shared a number of common interests, especially the influence of Brazilian scholars Gilberto Freyre and Arthur Ramos, whose groundbreaking works they emulated. They also subscribed to Gil Fortoul's concepts of social race and racial democracy, which they incorporated into their own books. Although they dealt mostly with folklore and music, they attempted for the first time to undertake serious investigations of the historical role of blacks in the evolution of Venezuelan culture.

For the most part, their answers to complex questions about race and racial mixture proved simple. Basically, they saw blacks as important contributors to Venezuela's popular culture. But they also tended to emphasize the general disintegration of an independent black culture over a long period of years. In that way, they succeeded in reinforcing the myth of racial democracy. Their judgment that the assimilation of blacks progressed much further in Venezuela than in any other American nation led them to maintain that the blacks of modern Venezuela made up a different and more advanced racial group than blacks of Brazil, the Caribbean, or the United States.

In 1938, Sojo wrote *Tierras del Estado Miranda,* his first major book. In that work he selected economic conditions above those of race to account for lack of development. Essentially, he used the book to explain why the state of Miranda had not benefited from the oil boom that enriched many parts of Venezuela. Sojo did not blame the state's overall poverty on the blacks who lived there. As he noted, many of these poor people had already migrated to the cities and oil fields in search of work. They made up a group of industrious workers from all parts of the nation who took the initiative to seek better jobs than they found at home. Those who stayed also worked long, hard days to eke out their existence as *conuqueros* on their small plots of land. According to Sojo, nothing could change in Miranda until new roads integrated the region with the rest of Venezuela, new schools and libraries provided educational opportunities for the people, and new comprehensive hospitals and medical facilities helped the poor overcome diseases and malnutrition. Only then would the state emerge from ruin.

By 1943, Sojo shifted his attention from the economic conditions of his home state to an examination of the Afro-Venezuelans who resided in Miranda. In *Temas y apuntes afro-venezolanos,* a discussion of the folklore of Miranda, he presented a highly nationalistic interpretation of the assimilation of blacks into the prevailing Venezuelan society during the colonial era. He established as his central thesis that a process he called racial fusion took place so thoroughly during the colonial period that racism was eliminated from Venezuela. According to Sojo's theory, miscegenation and racial fusion produced Afro-Venezuelans who were far superior to blacks found anywhere else in the Western Hemisphere.

As he elaborated, racial mixing and the introduction to Christianity led Venezuelan blacks to forget their African cults and religious traditions. Catholicism replaced voodooism, witchcraft, and other African practices. For that reason, African religions never gained the strength among the descendants of Venezuelan slaves that they had among Haitians or Brazilians. In short, African superstitions, to use Sojo's language, gave way to Catholicism. To be sure, Venezuelans developed their own socioreligious structure, with tobacco smokers, evil eyes, demon possessors, amulets, and sorcerers; Sojo compared these to what North Americans called secret lodges or secret societies rather than to the African religions practiced in Haiti, Cuba, or Brazil. For that matter, Sojo added, superstitions and witchcraft really knew no racial bounds, for in Venezuela both whites and blacks performed these arts.[33]

Like most of his generation, Sojo also willingly embraced the myth of racial democracy. He never questioned the myth's basic premise, that blacks achieved great things in Venezuela only as they whitened themselves and their offspring. For him it seemed sufficient to note that blacks shared much in common with all Venezuelans. He thought that blacks did not create special social problems in Venezuela, as they did in most parts of the

Americas, because the great majority of them blended into the population at large, both spiritually and physically.[34] Moreover he argued, over the centuries, the descendants of African slaves lost their tribal consciousness, became "individualized," and no longer stood apart from the mass of the Venezuelan population. As Emiro Puchi Alborñoz noted, in Sojo's eyes the blacks "suffered the same misery and privation that the destitute classes suffered, whose resolution was joined with the economic and political problems of the country."[35] In that sense, Sojo did not see blacks as victims of racial discrimination, as such. Whites might not like black skin color, he argued, but they accepted most negroid features as part of a Venezuelan racial type. As he wrote in 1946, "In our country the pejorative term 'nigger' is unknown."[36]

Sojo's contemporaries reached essentially the same conclusions he had. In 1941, the journalist Carlos Siso independently put forth a similar explanation of race relations in a study he entitled *La formación del pueblo venezolano*. First published in Paris and New York in a one-volume edition, it appeared in 1953 in an expanded two-volume version printed in Caracas. Like Sojo, Siso dealt with the question of black Venezuelans from the perspective of their incorporation into a predominantly white European society. An advocate of white immigration (preferably from Italy), he felt that Venezuelan blacks ranked well above other black groups in the Americas. Their superiority he attributed to the positive influence that Spaniards had upon their African slaves during the colonial era.

Even in Barlovento, he argued, the Spanish influence proved so great that no African social or economic institutions survived, as elsewhere. "On the contrary," he wrote, "the social spirit of the black population of Barlovento is completely Venezuelan; and the black, considered individually, whatever might be his state of backwardness, has a notion of his individuality." Siso believed that black Venezuelans had abandoned their "grotesque" African religious practices and that most had adopted what he called "exaggerated manifestations of Catholicism." In a blatantly unflattering manner, he suggested that despite their seeming lack of reason, one could appreciate in the blacks of Venezuela an "intelligence which . . . is easily capable of development," so that a little education would lead to their "social and intellectual superiority over the Antillian black, the North American black, and even the Brazilian black."[37]

Siso's attitude toward blacks typified the latent racism of his generation. Like most Venezuelans, he held ambivalent feelings. He obviously placed blacks well below whites and mixed racial groups on his social scale. But he also maintained that racial discrimination did not exist in Venezuela. He explained the nature of his ambivalence in part by the way he traced the evolution of race relations. According to him, racial prejudices once caused problems for Venezuelans, but by the end of the nineteenth century, reasons for those prejudices no longer existed. Whitening offered Venezuelans of all colors and classes a way out of the racial dilemma.

As he pointed out, since colonial times individuals who lived in the multiracial society believed that they descended from the most civilized racial groups. This sentiment grew out of vanity, as much as anything. But because of the prevailing Spanish culture, Siso said, all of the colonists considered themselves Spaniards regardless of race. As he expressed it: "In effect, it is not the race but rather the origin of a people's culture, of their spiritual formation, of their mentality—their language, customs, religion—which determines their ethnic affiliation." Simón Bolívar recognized this fact in 1819, Siso reminded his readers. Since then, the Venezuelans' prejudices gave way to increasingly egalitarian feelings. Thus: "Nothing defines the Venezuelan character more than its profound love of equality." From the president through the most humble citizen, he added, "all Venezuelans are equal." In such a setting racial prejudices completely disappeared, according to his reasoning. A new orientation came into being in Venezuela, where there "are neither whites nor *pardos*." In Venezuela racial barriers existed only in an individual's imagination, not in fact.[38]

In 1944, Alfredo Machado Hernández offered a less patronizing interpretation of the contribution made to the Venezuelan national character by blacks. Influenced by Siso's *Formación del pueblo venezolano* (1941) and Laureano Vallenilla Lanz's *Desgregación e integración* (1930), Machado attacked the "false concepts" of European and North American racist theorists who attributed inferiority to racial mixing. He considered it a grave error to think of Africans as barbarous, savage, and primitive people.

His work demonstrated that the bulk of the African slaves who came to Venezuela left regions that had cultural levels well above those of the indigenous Americans, with the possible exceptions of the Aztecs and Incas. Furthermore, the Africans came from societies with high degrees of political, cultural, economic, and religious organization. They had lived in small monarchies, with well-established social structures. Most brought either agricultural or pastoral experience with them. As Machado explained: "In their industries and manual arts, the Africans knew how to work with iron, copper, and bronze for utilitarian ends; they had superior ceramics, baskets, and mud construction, from which derived . . . the *rancho* in the bulk of the present Venezuelan countryside." Because of their skills, the blacks played an important part in the economic development of the colony. Indeed, Machado felt that it was "only when the importation of

Africans increased that the haciendas and farms prospered. It was estimated by contemporaries that the work of one black was equal to that of
four indigenous people." [39]

As a cultural nationalist, Machado supported racial mixing. In contrast
to many, however, he did not see the process strictly as one of whitening,
for he thought that whites benefited as much from miscegenation as
blacks. In his estimation, the latter brought to the union a number of
beneficial attributes, namely resilience and an ability to work hard. As he
wrote: "Blacks, besides their adaptation to the tropics, had physical for-
titude, were used to sedentary labor and life in peasant groups, and possessed a mentality more near that of the white, however more advanced
than that of the indigenous." In brief, Machado felt that black blood had
improved the mixture of races in Venezuela because its addition led to
racial adaptations suitable to the "inhospitable" physical conditions of the
region. The process also helped blacks. By mixing with whites the Venezuelan blacks evolved toward a superior civilization, he claimed, unlike those
blacks in Surinam and Brazil who fled to the bush and remained as curious
"racial cysts" with all of their African characteristics intact. For Machado,
the mixture of white, black, and Indian produced "very interesting hybrids,
with superior characteristics." With considerable pride, he said that *mestizaje* and miscegenation allowed the Spaniards to succeed in their colonization efforts where Anglo-Saxons, Dutch, and French failed. [40]

As for the future, Machado turned to a more traditional view. For one
thing, he realized that racial mixing contributed to the disappearance of
pure blacks and Indians, a factor that he believed reduced racial prejudices
to a minimum. For another, he knew that Venezuela's *pardo* majority was
well suited to its environment. The addition of European immigrants
would improve that population even more, he thought. As he said: "We
should not infer, however, that our ethnic composition ought to remain
unaltered. There are advantages in improving and vitalizing it with new
blood which can blend with it, and we are sufficiently identified from a
national point of view so that we do not have to fear the loss of our own
physiognomy. We can assimilate great quantities of European blood without risk, and we ought to make every effort to accomplish this." [41]

Juan Liscano also contributed to the discussion of Venezuela's African
heritage. Best known as a musicologist, poet, and folklorist, Liscano wrote
two books on Afro-Venezuelan themes. The first, *Apuntes para la investigación del negro en Venezuela: Sus instrumentos de música*, appeared in 1947;
the second, *Folklore y cultura: Ensayos*, in 1950. Because he relied upon
Juan Pablo Sojo for many of his interpretations of the role of blacks in the
formation of Venezuelan society, he, too, treated the long process of assimilation as central to explaining the "de-Africanization" of Venezuelan

blacks. He maintained that the phenomenon called racial fusion "constituted one of the most important reasons for facilitating the integration of the ethno-African groups into the national life and Western culture." He also accepted the idea that the wars of the nineteenth century completed the process of mixing. In a contrast to the Brazilian and Cuban experience, Liscano wrote, Venezuelan whites, mestizos, mulattoes, blacks, and zambos fought shoulder to shoulder for common causes, which, in the long run, joined the groups into a Venezuelan type. With no strong African culture or group to bond the blacks together, he added, they never formed a cohesive African identity. As a result, blacks ceased thinking of themselves as Africans, even though their music, folklore, and religious practices preserved vestiges of a number of African traditions. In other words, blacks simply became part of a larger mix, for as he noted, "The colored population, composed of Indians, blacks, mulattoes, zambos, mestizos, and other mixtures, constitutes just about the majority of the nation."[42]

For Liscano, Machado, Siso, Sojo, and others, whitening of the race served a useful purpose. As had earlier historians and social scientists, they accepted the process as one of the basic tenets of the doctrine of racial democracy. For them, racial mixing accomplished two major objectives: it improved the "Venezuelan race," and it alleviated racial tensions. If they took a condescending attitude toward blacks, they nevertheless considered them a basic element of the new Venezuelan population. Unlike North American racists, who referred to miscegenation as mongrelization, they rejected the idea that racial mixing weakened the offspring. They also refused to believe that it blackened or otherwise darkened the progeny of mixed couples. On the whole, they viewed miscegenation as both a whitening and a strengthening process. Since they did not want a static racial situation to exist, they advocated the continued gradual assimilation of blacks into a whiter race, a process they readily traced back to the colonial period.

Of course, not every scholar shared these ideas. A most notable exception, Miguel Acosta Saignes departed dramatically from the orthodox path followed by those few individuals who studied Venezuelan blacks. His training as an anthropologist equipped him with a different methodology. Also, he approached his investigations from a Marxist perspective. These two factors led him to conclusions different from those of his contemporaries, who brought few technical skills to their research. He believed that contrary to the majority opinion among students of Afro-Venezuelans, a long process of racial and cultural mixing actually Africanized whites and *pardos* rather than Hispanicized the blacks. Whereas earlier studies of Venezuela's population, such as those by Pedro M. Arcaya, emphasized the mestizo aspects of the population, Acosta Saignes demonstrated the need to consider the nation's African roots. As he once stated, "The history of the process of the Venezuelan culture is, then, the history of the indigenization and Africanization of the Spaniard in our land."[43]

In essence, Acosta Saignes tried to use scientific study of Afro-Venezuelans to put them in the best light. To begin with, he opposed the loose terminology employed by his untrained predecessors. He used the term *Afro* rather than *black* to avoid what he considered the unnecessary racist connotations of the latter. He also felt the need to give a more complex explanation of Venezuela's racial heritage. Unable to condone the use of either pure race or pure culture as a means of discussing the supposed superiority of one group over another, he dismissed skin color, stature, texture of hair, and color of eyes as having any scientific meaning. To his way of thinking, racial characteristics could be described, but otherwise they meant nothing. Nutrition, class, and economic conditions counted more. The poor remained undernourished, and thus weaker and less mentally capable than their richer countrymen. Race did not cause their basic problems, he argued; they stemmed from poverty and alienation.

As Acosta Saignes pointed out in 1948, in an essay entitled "Un mito racista: El indio, el blanco, el negro," he could not distinguish any intrinsic differences between whites, blacks, and Indians. This, in turn, led him to accept the multiethnic origins of Venezuela's spirit as the result of what he called transculturation. By that he meant that culture, geography, and such internal developments as political and social struggles combined historically to form a pluralistic society in Venezuela. In his estimation, until the completion of a scientific examination of the origins of modes of production, class structure, and social strata, the empty arguments about whites, blacks, and Indians "only hide the ignorance, ineptitude, and lack of knowledge of the modern scientific disciplines."[44]

Acosta Saignes' caveat moved few individuals to change their minds about race. The majority adhered to the more popular view of race. The prevailing concept of racial democracy appealed to them because it placed blacks in a subordinate social position without distorting the Venezuelans' orthodox position that racial prejudice and discrimination did not exist in their nation. Such an attitude suited an age of rapid change. As Venezuela's economy expanded, driven both by petroleum revenues and by diversification spawned by the wartime, a burgeoning middle class demanded a larger role in society. In their push to move upward socially as well as economically, Venezuela's tricolored *pardo* majority readily approved the idea of racial democracy. They felt that their time had come, and they sincerely abhorred any restrictions on their socioeconomic mobility that might result from race.

Given this climate of opinion, the leaders of Acción Democrática wisely supported racial democracy as a means of creating a truly egalitarian socioracial order. If they acted out of political expediency, they did so because they wanted to break the control of the conservative oligarchs who systematically excluded the Venezuelan masses from political activities. Hindsight suggests that some AD members harbored strong feelings against Antillian blacks and that several actually preferred to whiten Venezuela's population.[45] But the party's public rhetoric during and after the mid-1940s demonstrated a remarkably open-minded bent. As nationalists they blamed racism on foreigners whom they depicted as imperialists who came to Venezuela to exploit the oil fields. But they also made racial democracy an essential part of their nationalist reform party platform. For them racial democracy meant social mobility for nonwhites. To their credit, they committed their party to a policy of turning rhetoric into reality through political action.

Shortly after the Duncan affair simmered down as a public issue, the Acción Democrática party came to power. In October 1945, a military-civilian coup toppled the Medina administration. The coup paved the way for AD to become the ruling faction of a provisional government. Between late 1945 and October 1948, the so-called *trienio,* AD politicians introduced a series of popular reform measures aimed at redistributing the nation's wealth, land, and political power, as well as at changing the national educational system, the highway transportation network, and the federal bureaucracy. When Rómulo Gallegos won the presidential election in October 1947, the party's middle-class revolution seemed on the move. The Gallegos administration implemented an extraordinary number of basic social and economic reforms aimed at reducing the traditional powers of the wealthy oligarchs. But the rush to bring about change ultimately met with bitter opposition from conservative groups, namely those who controlled the major industrial groups, the banks, and the commercial establishments, as well as from high-ranking army officers. A year after his election, another military coup removed Gallegos from office. During the following decade, a military dictatorship led by Marcos Pérez Jiménez dismantled the AD reform programs and forced the party's leaders underground or into exile.

Acción Democrática's short-lived rule upset the elites for a number of interrelated reasons. Its agrarian reform, petroleum strategy, antichurch posture, and attempts to restrict military privileges ranked high as causes for its overthrow. But evidence exists that suggests the party's racial policies also contributed to its undoing. During most of the twentieth century, conservative governments had excluded blacks from positions in the federal bureaucracy, as well as from elite social circles. Administrations prior to AD's systematically denied education to the masses and offered little or no help to facilitate their entry into either the public or private sectors of the economy. At best, most poor blacks could aspire to become shopkeepers or grocers.

Under Acción Democrática, life for many blacks changed for the better. Blacks and mulattoes began to hold more jobs in the federal bureaucracy, as well as in other public institutions. In general, nonwhites made significant strides during the brief interlude of *adeco* rule. Even the society pages of the most widely read Caracas newspapers showed pictures of nonwhites, instead of whites only. As a result, a number of elites became upset. According to one observer, the elites resented AD's encouragement of blacks and "rabble" to occupy high government offices and "to interact with the best families of Caracas." Another source, Laureano Vallenilla Lanz, Jr., a respected member of the *caraqueño* elite, also added the issue of race to a list of reasons why he opposed the populist *adecos* and why he supported their removal from power.[46]

When President Gallegos announced in a positive sense, in September 1948, that "now the blacks are ruling," he further angered many already nervous conservatives. Obviously, he used the term figuratively to describe the down-and-out working class of "Juan Bimbo" campesinos and laborers who made up the rank and file of Acción Democrática. But his opponents did not all see it that way. Even liberal oligarchs, such as Arturo Uslar Pietri, took umbrage at the president's choice of words. Uslar accused Gallegos and his party of using race to divide the country. "Venezuela is not a country of either whites or blacks," he asserted, for both represented minorities. To say that blacks should rule, he continued, struck him as patently absurd; in a democracy no group had the right to rule. Furthermore, most Venezuelans were mestizos, not black or white. Thus, Uslar Pietri rejected outright what he considered Gallegos' idea of black supremacy. Rather, he called for unity among all races. As he maintained: "Whoever speaks of blacks or whites, whoever involves racial hatred or privileges, is denying Venezuela. In Venezuela, in political and social matters, there are neither whites nor blacks, neither mestizos nor Indians. There are only Venezuelans."[47]

In many ways Uslar Pietri and Gallegos actually held common views on the basic issues of race in Venezuela. Both men believed in the principle of racial democracy. Neither wanted racial discrimination or prejudice to split Venezuelan society along solely racial lines. But they saw the questions related to race from opposing sides. Gallegos accepted the inclusion of *pardos* and blacks in the new governmental structure as a healthy sign because it marked the end of predominantly white elitist rule. He equated the presence of blacks in his administration with the rise of middle- and lower-class citizens to political power. This fit his blueprint for mass action. Understandably, Uslar Pietri, a beneficiary of the previous system which monopolized control in the hands of a small group of so-called white oligarchs, felt concerned that the darker-hued majority might overrun the white minority. Like his nineteenth-century predecessors, who feared that black rule might lead to pardocracy, Uslar thought that the rise of blacks might signal the end of civilization, or social control based on the privileges of wealth and social class.

Uslar Pietri's comments deserve special attention for another reason. They demonstrated how much his own attitudes about race had advanced in a decade. In 1937, he described the average colored Venezuelan as an inferior breed of person. He advocated whitening the population as the only means of saving Venezuela from destitution and backwardness. By 1948, he agreed with the prevailing sentiment that Venezuela constituted a mestizo nation, with clear white and black minorities. He eschewed racism of any sort. This metamorphosis owed in large part to the influence of cultural nationalists, such as Liscano and Sojo. These scholars had blended the ideas of social race put forward by an earlier generation of Venezuelan thinkers, such as Gil Fortoul and Vallenilla Lanz, with new ideas about racial mixing emanating from the Brazilian schools of anthropology and sociology led by Gilberto Freyre. Uslar Pietri's ambivalence, typical of most Venezuelans, resulted from his inability to reconcile his own misgivings about the aptitude of blacks with his hope that at some future date the question of race would become a moot point in a truly tricolored society. In other words, he did not think that blacks could serve as competent civil servants, but he accepted the idea that they could be incorporated into some sort of new racial amalgam without serious or damaging side effects.

Some two months after Gallegos claimed that the blacks were in power, a right-wing military *golpe* swept him from office. Though not overtly racist in intent or purpose, supporters of the coup moved quickly to undo Acción Democrática's social and economic experiments. The new government won the wholehearted support of the conservative oligarchs, who feared the rise of the colored Venezuelans. From the perspective of the underclasses, the whites had regained control. By the time that Marcos Pérez Jiménez consolidated his authority as dictator, the nation's blacks lost what they had gained under AD. Pérez Jiménez undertook projects that reassured the traditional elites that he would protect their property and status. He also moved to continue the official whitening project begun during the 1930s by Alberto Adriani. Among other things, he opened the nation's frontiers to Italians and Spaniards who at long last moved to Venezuela in significant numbers following the end of World War II. He also reimposed the ban on the immigration of blacks, which *adecos* failed to remove from the books during their short tenure in office.[48]

Nevertheless, by midcentury Venezuelans had achieved a remarkable degree of racial harmony, despite class conflicts. Even during the dictatorship of Pérez Jiménez, the idea persisted that Venezuelans lived free of the racial discrimination and prejudice found in other American societies, most notably the United States. As in Brazil, the myth of racial democracy became entrenched as the official explanation for the lack of overt discrimination like that found in North America. Though many individuals continued to think of blacks as inferior, if asked they quickly denied being racists. Rather, they explained that they based their feelings about blacks on the belief that the latter, as poor people, lived differently than the rest of their fellow Venezuelans.

EPILOGUE

IN 1978, Austrian-born anthropologist Angelina Pollak-Eltz unequivocally stated that since 1958 economic conditions in Venezuela had improved so markedly that blacks now had equal opportunities with other racial groups for work and social advancement. She based her observation on a survey of one hundred males who lived in low-income apartments in Caracas owned by the Banco Central de Venezuela. Blacks from Barlovento made up half of the participants. The other fifty comprised individuals of all races from other parts of the nation. According to her: "The conclusion of this summary is that segregation based on skin color does not exist and that, once having reached a certain middle-class level, even though low, the attitudes, norms, and values of the ascending urbanized groups are notably homogeneous and they do not contemplate either the person's region or racial origins and antecedents." She also thought that behavior patterns usually attributed exclusively to blacks actually characterized all social groups that lived under similar economic conditions, regardless of skin color. For her, class held more importance than color. In her estimation, among the working class "a well-defined color barrier does not exist." [1]

Not surprisingly, Pollak-Eltz's conclusions did not raise any eyebrows among Venezuelan scholars and politicians, most of whom accepted the basic tenets of Venezuela's creed of racial democracy. All said and done, despite some severe methodological and analytical shortcomings, Pollak-Eltz simply restated the basic Venezuelan creed in the guise of social science. Like Brazilians, Venezuelans would not admit that racial discrimination existed in their country. And, as a corollary, they considered any expression of racial discrimination foreign in origin or un-Venezuelan. Thinking Venezuelans of all races considered racial democracy a natural result of miscegenation and the long-term lack of racial discrimination. In this fashion, they joined their countryman Andrés Eloy Blanco in viewing themselves as a tricolored *café con leche* people, descended from European, Indian, and African ancestors.

As Pollak-Eltz correctly noted, race, as such, did not hold a central place in the thoughts of most Venezuelans. Whites and *pardos* especially overlooked race. For them class and culture were far more important in determining the social worth of individuals. Therefore, most Venezuelans joined scholars like Pollak-Eltz in rejecting the possibility that racism of any kind existed in Venezuela. They sincerely believed that they lived in a racial democracy, free of prejudice and racial discrimination.

In this regard, it should be kept in mind that throughout the present century Venezuelans defined racism in terms of the virulent, hate-filled type of discrimination and segregation found in the United States; they have not considered the subtle forms of discrimination they practice as racism. Rather, they think of racism as an open conflict between distinct racial groups, a type of behavior that they believe they have avoided over a long period of time. Indeed, they call such behavior un-Venezuelan, and since gaining their independence they have eschewed the violent and overt racism practiced by their white neighbors in the North.

Because they regarded the closed system of race relations found in the United States as true racism, they usually overlooked any signs of discrimination in Venezuela. This was possible because by their definition whites and blacks had relatively little direct contact over the last hundred years. In their minds these two minority groups lived apart from each other on a socioeconomic scale and constituted minorities at opposite ends of the socioracial spectrum. Most blacks lived in poor, rural, and isolated enclaves scattered along the northern coastal crescent. The majority of whites lived in urban centers and made up a wealthier group. Although occasional contact between whites and blacks occurred, it usually amounted to exchanges between individuals rather than groups.

In Venezuela, as elsewhere in the region, generations of elites have maintained a somatic image of themselves that has emphasized their whiteness. Concomitantly, although they do not deny the black heritage of the population at large, they have systematically discounted its influence upon the upper and middle sectors of their society. More to the point, they have insisted that the nation's multiracial majority comprised mestizos, not people of predominantly African descent.

Separation contributed to diminished racial tensions. This obviously does not mean an absence of tension, for no modern Latin American society has escaped some form of racial division, due to the very nature of their multiracial populations. Given the relative lack of racial tension, Venezuelan whites never implemented an exclusionist policy based solely on race. For that reason, they deny that any form of racism exists in their homeland; whether this is so is irrelevant. Myths and legends can only be proved, never disproved. They depend in large part upon some elements of truth, both in their origin and in their continued support. The type of racial harmony found in Venezuela during the present century, when compared to the discord in the United States, gave impetus to the Venezuelans' acceptance of their creed of racial democracy. That blacks as well as whites have supported the creed only reinforces it. Such behavior also demonstrates the degree to which the official doctrine of nondiscrimination and the lack of prejudice have permeated all levels of Venezuelan thinking on the subject.

Of course, acceptance of the myth of racial democracy always has depended on the perspective of the observer. For their part, white elites do not consider themselves racists because they do not use race as a means of oppressing blacks. They have never intimidated the black minorities by the use of force and violence, nor have they resorted to institutionalized or legal forms of discrimination as a means of social control. Furthermore, they attribute their negative ideas about blacks to economic and cultural factors, not race. They believe that poverty, stemming from the common experience of the blacks' slave ancestors, and not race, explains the plight of most poor blacks. In a sense, they maintain that blacks have never escaped from the psychological traumas inflicted upon their race by the slave experience, which left them totally unprepared for living in modern societies. Uneducated, unskilled, and unprepared, the slaves and their descendants never adjusted to the rigors of a modern capitalistic society. According to this train of thought, at some future date a combination of education, economic gain, and cultural assimilation may change all of this, but for the time being the blacks are trapped in the heritage of their slave background.

Such thinking on the part of Venezuelan elites has led to some rather interesting, if contradictory, results. For instance, during the past few decades white Venezuelans have participated in the celebration of major Afro-Venezuelan holidays, such as St. John the Baptist's day on June 24. On that day, thousands of people flock to the Barlovento region, especially the beaches of Higuerote, where they take part in day-long festivities. Teams of black drummers frenetically beat out Afro-Venezuelan rhythms on huge drums known as *tambores* which they have made out of hollowed tree trunks. On this holiday, and several others, whites readily join blacks and *pardos* in acclaiming part of their nation's African heritage.

But, on the negative side, they more frequently think of Barlovento only as "a piece of Africa." The region's black residents have become exotic and peripheral people; the national press treats them as curiosities, victims of disasters, or subjects of quaint human-interest stories. Somehow, Barlovento lingers on as a land inhabited by happy-go-lucky descendants of slaves, who still speak African dialects, eat African food, and maintain African culture. As summed up by the lyrics of a popular folk song: "Barlovento, Barlovento, ardent land of drums, land of *fulías* and fine women."[2]

In this sense, little has changed over two centuries. In the late eighteenth century, Archbishop Mariano Martí noted the blackness of the Barlovento population. By the middle of the twentieth century, such writers as Juan Pablo Sojo, Luis Alberto Paúl, and José Arana perpetuated this image of Barlovento's people as overwhelmingly black. They described the residents of the region as poor but honest workers, most of whom, in Arana's words, were "direct descendants of slaves brought over by the Spanish."[3] The idea of Barlovento as an extension of Africa had become so ingrained in the thinking of Venezuelans that in 1967 the government accused Cuba of having landed Congolese guerrillas along the Barlovento coast in an effort to gain popular support for the Venezuelan insurgents operating in the district. Allegedly these Cuban-trained African soldiers spoke the same dialects as residents of Barlovento. Though wrong, this claim demonstrated the popular notion that blacks in Barlovento were as African as they were Venezuelan.

Such misconceptions about black Venezuelans does not constitute racism. Rather, it reflects the ambivalent and sometimes ignorant nature of elitist racial attitudes. Though they harbor no outward antipathy toward blacks, the elites nevertheless assume the backwardness and poverty of all blacks, even to the point of referring to them as Africans on occasion.

Yet, from time to time in the past decade, some individuals have raised the specter of racism in their observations of modern Venezuela's social problems. Journalists Luis García Goartaya, Rosa Haydee Sánchez, and Juana De Avila have discussed the presence of what they have termed latent racial discrimination. In 1974, anthropologist Miguel Acosta Saignes, once a proponent of racial democracy theory, raised the issue of racial discrimination in a eulogy for a black surgeon; he suggested that whites discriminated against blacks for racial as well as economic reasons. The article, which appeared in the Caracas newspaper *Ultimas Noticias*, concluded with a statement that white elites actually veiled their antiblack racial biases in the rhetoric of class consciousness. White Venezuelans, Acosta said, claimed that they had nothing in common with blacks, who because of their poverty lived differently from whites. Not until he thought about how the surgeon (a friend of his) had never fit into the social world of the whites did Acosta begin to change his mind about discrimination. As he

realized that whites had not invited the successful black to join their exclusive clubs, Acosta saw the larger pattern of discrimination in a new
light. Money had not whitened his friend. He remained an outsider among
the elites because of his race. In ruminating this fact, Acosta noted that
whites held strong prejudices against blacks of all classes, wealthy individuals as well as impoverished black workers.[4]

In April 1975, Kalinina Ortega wrote an article for a daily national
newspaper describing an example of another kind of discrimination that
frequently occurred against poor blacks. During the construction of luxury condominiums at Cata Beach near Ocumare de la Costa, contractors
acted with impunity against poor black residents of the properties adjacent
to the beach. These blacks, mostly fishermen and farmers, were forced to
leave their homes to relocate on marginal lands in the nearby mountains,
where they lacked adequate water and roads. Throughout the procedure
local and national government officials refused to protect the blacks from
the encroachment of the developers on their traditional lands. In Ortega's
view, the black fishermen, subsistence farmers, and rural workers experienced misery and suffering because nobody would come to their assistance. In her words, they still suffered the "stigma of slavery" and lived
imprisoned in "the narrow straights of their social poverty, cultural limita-
tions, and juridical penury."[5]

An even more strident protest against racial discrimination came from
the pen of a Haitian human rights activist. In 1975, Luc B. Innocent published a short pamphlet entitled *Si Haiti no fuera negra*, in which he accused Venezuelan government officials of racism because of their unwill-
ingness to join the protest against the human rights abuses committed by
the Duvalier regime. According to Innocent, Venezuelans would have
acted differently if Haiti were not a black nation. Apparently Venezuelans
did not think of Haitians as equals. From Innocent's perspective, as a resident exile in Venezuela, the Venezuelans' refusal to take action against
Duvalier led him, and other Haitians, to perceive them as racists, not unlike those they encountered in the United States.

Liberals within the Catholic church also have drawn attention to racist
undercurrents in recent years. In 1979, a leading Catholic newspaper, *La
Religión*, ran an editorial that questioned the validity of the myth of racial
democracy. According to its author:

> It is said that Venezuela is a liberal country, free of racial and religious
> prejudices. This thesis one raises high with pride and insistence.
>
> We do not believe it would be a very big sin to dissent a bit. In spite
> of our evident *mestizaje*, which ought to bring us intimate satisfaction,

we have made some observations in our beloved country which, for some time, have not ceased to bother us, as Christians and as Venezuelans.

The fact that a subtle prejudice exists in our beloved Venezuela seems undeniable to us, despite our history, our Christian traditions, and our manner of being. Occasionally there appears in the press some note about whether there was segregation in a hotel, or whether some bar threw some little black *cumbacumba* into the street. . . .

We do not believe that this racial prejudice might have been brought here by foreigners. It is very old. Older than the immigration. It is the product of the badly understood creole "*mantuanismo.*" [snobbery] We do not remember now that any beardless "*musiu*" [foreigner] with cat eyes might have happened to snub a black in the Plaza Bolívar or might have left a bus when a Barlovento mulatto got on and sat down beside him. No! We are frank. We, the creoles, who belong to the nobility of coffee, cacao, and petroleum—we are the ones who have racial prejudices in this country. In this new Venezuela of petroleum and "cinco y seis" [a weekly horse-racing lottery], there is no scarcity of he who believes he is a "baron" with the *b* of burro.[6]

In 1982, the liberal Catholic journal *SIC* dedicated an issue to a similar discussion of prejudice and discrimination in modern Venezuela. It, too, stated that Venezuelan blacks faced subtle but real forms of discrimination and prejudice and that despite the existence of a policy of nondiscrimination, Venezuelans had a racial problem of their own making. More recently, historians Manuel Pérez Vila and Luis Castro introduced the subject of racial discrimination in lectures they delivered at a symposium on Venezuelan history sponsored by the Universidad Metropolitana. Both men felt that questions related to discrimination merited further historical research.[7]

Most Venezuelans know that some subtle forms of racial discrimination still exist in their nation. Occasionally they acknowledge the fact that blacks meet with some not so subtle discrimination. Despite conscious efforts to change the behavior of the majority, vestiges of the hierarchical colonial society based on racial supremacy linger on. For most blacks still mired in poverty, this means that the concept of racial democracy holds little more than a hollow promise for improved social status at some future date, depending upon their ability to improve their lot economically. For the minority of blacks who have moved upward, it means that they must assimilate themselves into a white culture. Whitening has become a prerequisite for social mobility, both in cultural and racial terms. Blacks generally have to shun the most obvious aspects of their origins and conform to white norms.

Social mobility comprises only part of the larger picture. In politics blacks have made tremendous strides since the mid-1940s, and especially since the return of populist parties to power in 1958. Under Acción Democrática, and to a lesser extent Copei, blacks have gained access to political power at the national level as well as at local and regional levels. They have also constituted part of the leadership of a number of smaller splinter parties. Under a democratic form of government, they have succeeded as governors, party officials, and members of the national congress. They have served as cabinet officials and as heads of important ministries. Blacks have important leadership roles of trade unions, hold high positions in the police force of Caracas and other major cities, and increasingly make their presence felt at the nation's universities. In comparison to other Latin American nations, the progress of blacks in Venezuela since the 1960s has been extraordinary.

As Acosta Saignes and others point out, racial problems still exist in some areas of national life. But given the pragmatic approach Venezuelans have taken in the past, the subtle forms of discrimination may erode. Whether or not they do, Venezuelans will continue to insist that they base their discrimination upon class and economic factors—a claim they can not prove convincingly. The populist leaders, especially the leadership of Acción Democrática, have not tried to push for radical changes on the social and economic fronts. Since their return to power in 1958, they have cut back on programs aimed at reducing the power of the elites. The old social order still exists, as does the economic system which put petroleum at the disposal of the state but otherwise restricted economic development to a rich and powerful oligarchy of monopolistic capitalists. This compromise has added significantly to an environment in which racial democracy—whether real or perceived—can exist with few questions asked.

All things considered, Venezuelans deserve recognition for having overcome the seamiest aspects of race relations. Venezuela's *pardos* comprise a majority and operate openly in a society that accepts them as they appear. Their multiracial origins do not hold them back. Nor do they have to deal with questions of racial pluralism on a daily basis. As for whites, they have an option. They can retreat to exclusive clubs and cliques and ignore the gains of other racial groups, or they can acknowledge their belief that they live in a racial democracy, secure that in any case they set the norms for cultural advancement. Only blacks realize the full implications of the lingering prejudice that operates below the surface. They, probably more than any other racial group in Venezuela, realize that Venezuelans want only a little *café* with their *leche*.

NOTES

1. The Myth of Racial Democracy

1. *El País* (Caracas), April 25, 1944. Translation by author. All translations are by author unless otherwise noted.

2. For a survey of current research on race relations in Brazil see Pierre-Michel Fontaine, ed., *Race, Class, and Power in Brazil.* Andrews' findings appear in *The Afro-Argentines of Buenos Aires, 1800–1900.*

3. See Sidney Kronus and Mauricio Solaún, *Discrimination without Violence: Miscegenation and Racial Conflict in Latin America,* and H. Hoetink, *Slavery and Race Relations in the Americas: Comparative Notes on Their Nature and Nexus.*

4. Juan Pablo Sojo, *Temas y apuntes afro-venezolanos,* p. 33.

5. Mario Briceño-Iragorry, *Mensaje sin destino y otros ensayos,* p. 124.

6. Hoetink, *Slavery and Race,* p. 192. Pierre-Michel Fontaine makes a strong case for this argument in "Blacks and the Search for Power in Brazil," in *Race, Class, and Power,* ed. Fontaine, pp. 56–72.

7. Magnus Mörner, *Race Mixture in the History of Latin America,* pp. 89–90, 136–139; Magnus Mörner, ed., *Race and Class in Latin America,* pp. 214–215; and Leslie B. Rout, Jr., *The African Experience in Spanish America: 1502 to the Present Day,* pp. 254–255.

8. José Gil Fortoul, *El hombre y la historia: Ensayo de la sociología venezolana,* p. 24.

9. *El Cojo Ilustrado* 4, no. 73 (January 1, 1895): 16.

10. Olga Briceño, *Cocks and Bulls in Caracas,* pp. 110–111.

11. See Andrews, *Afro-Argentines,* for details of this process.

12. For a thorough discussion of the historiography of race relations in modern Brazil, see Thomas E. Skidmore, "Race and Class in Brazil: Historical Perspectives," in *Race, Class, and Power,* ed. Fontaine, pp. 11–24.

13. A great deal more attention has been paid to race relations in Brazil than to

those in any other Latin American nation. Among the studies are the following: Florestan Fernandes, *The Negro in Brazilian Society;* Carl N. Degler, *Neither Black nor White;* Thomas E. Skidmore, *Black into White: Race and Nationality in Brazilian Thought;* C. R. Boxer, *Race Relations in the Portuguese Colonial Empire, 1415–1825;* Gilberto Freyre, *The Mansions and the Shanties: The Making of Modern Brazil, New World in the Tropics: The Culture of Modern Brazil,* and *The Masters and the Slaves: A Study in the Development of Brazilian Civilization;* Donald Pierson, *Negroes in Brazil: A Study of Race Contact in Bahia;* Octavio Ianni, *Raças e clases sociais no Brasil,* 2d ed.; A. J. R. Russell-Wood, *The Black Man in Slavery and Freedom in Colonial Brazil;* and Arthur Ramos, *The Negro in Brazil.* Also refer to the essays in *Race, Class, and Power,* ed. Fontaine.

14. Because no Venezuelan census has listed people by race since the mid-nineteenth century, exact figures on the racial composition of the nation do not exist. I have based my estimates on the following: Elizabeth Yabour de Caldera, *La población de Venezuela: Un análisis demográfico;* Mörner, *Race Mixture in Latin America,* p. 2; Angel Rosenblat, *La población indígena de América desde 1492 hasta la actualidad,* pp. 20–21; and Chi-Yi Chen and Michel Picouet, *Dinámica de la población: Caso de Venezuela,* p. 21. Castro's poem first appeared in *Válvula* 1, no. 1 (January 1929), and was reprinted in Julian Padrón, *Obras completas,* pp. 20–21.

15. For examples of this debate, see Miguel Acosta Saignes, "Un mito racista: el indio, el blanco, el negro," *Revista Nacional de Cultura,* no. 67 (March–April, 1948), and *Elementos indígenas y africanos en la formación de la cultura venezolana;* Juan Liscano, *Apuntes para la investigación del negro en Venezuela: Sus instrumentos de música;* Carlos Siso, *La formación del pueblo venezolano: Estudios sociológicos,* 2 vols.; Juan Pablo Sojo, *Tierras del Estado Miranda: Sobre la ruta de los cacahuales,* and *Temas y apuntes;* and Luis Felipe Ramón y Rivera, *La música afrovenezolana.*

16. As quoted by Luis Beltrán Prieto Figueroa, *De una educación de castas a una educación de masas,* p. 181.

2. The Colonial Legacy: Racial Tensions in a Hierarchical Society

1. Guillermo Morón, *A History of Venezuela,* pp. 55–56.

2. Angel Rosenblat, *La población indígena y el mestizaje en América,* vol. 2, p. 15.

3. For the most complete compilation of colonial population figures, see John V. Lombardi, *People and Places in Colonial Venezuela.* General figures for Venezuela in 1800 appear in James Lockhart and Stuart B. Schwartz, *Early Latin America: A History of Colonial Spanish America and Brazil,* pp. 282–287. For Caracas in 1787 and 1809, see P. Michael McKinley, *Pre-revolutionary Caracas: Politics, Economy, and Society 1777–1811,* pp. 9–11.

4. McKinley, *Pre-revolutionary Caracas,* p. 14, and Federico Brito Figueroa, *El problema tierra y esclavos en la historia de Venezuela,* pp. 144, 149–150, and 162.

5. Morón, *History of Venezuela,* p. 55.

6. See Sojo, *Temas y apuntes,* pp. 9–11, 13–20, and 39–40; Liscano, *Apuntes,* pp. 6–11; Juan Liscano, *Folklore y cultura: Ensayos,* pp. 65, 70, and 77–91; Siso,

La formación del pueblo venezolano, vol. 1, p. 509, and vol. 2, pp. 430–435 and 451–452; and Alfredo Machado Hernández, "La función económica de las razas de color en la formación del estado venezolano," *Revista de Hacienda* 9, no. 16 (June 1944): 11–19. Anthropologist Angelina Pollak-Eltz deals with these themes in two short books, *La familia negra en Venezuela* and *María Lionza: Mito y culto venezolano*. For comments on music, see Ramón y Rivera, *La música afrovenezolana*.

7. John V. Lombardi, *Venezuela: The Search for Order, the Dream of Progress*, pp. 7–40 and 71–92.

8. For a description of the Caracas cacao elites, see Robert J. Ferry, "Encomienda, African Slavery, and Agriculture in Seventeenth-Century Caracas," *Hispanic American Historical Review* 61, no. 4 (November 1981): 609–635.

9. Lombardi, *People and Places*, pp. 68–69.

10. McKinley, *Pre-revolutionary Caracas*, pp. 46–62.

11. Ibid.

12. Ibid., pp. 19–20.

13. Jean Joseph Dauxion-Lavaysse, *Viaje a las islas de Trinidad, Tobago y Margarita y a diversas partes de Venezuela en la America-Meridional*, p. 273.

14. Pedro M. Arcaya, *Insurrección de los negros de la serranía de Coro*, p. 24.

15. For descriptions of life in the late colonial era, see Jean Joseph Dauxion-Lavaysse, *A Statistical, Commercial and Political Description of Venezuela;* Francisco J. Depons, *Travels in South America during the years 1801, 1802, 1803, and 1804. Containing a Description of the Captain-Generalship of Caracas and an account of the discovery, conquest, topography, legislature, commerce, finance, and natural production of the country; with a view of the manners and customs of the Spaniards and Native Indians;* Alexander von Humboldt and Aimé Bonpland, *Personal narrative of Travels to the equinoctial Regions of America during the Years 1799–1804;* and Mariano Martí, *Documentos relativos a su visita pastoral de la diócesis de Caracas: 1771–1784*, 7 vols.

16. The following authors adhere to this orthodox position: Morón, *History of Venezuela;* Sojo, *Temas y apuntes;* Liscano, *Apuntes;* Siso, *La formación del pueblo venezolano;* Pollak-Eltz, *La familia negra;* Gil Fortoul, *El hombre y la historia;* Laureano Vallenilla Lanz, *Cesarismo democrático: Estudios sobre las bases sociológicas de la constitución efectiva de Venezuela;* and Pedro M. Arcaya, *Estudios de sociología venezolana*.

17. Sojo, *Temas y apuntes*, p. 11.

18. See Miguel Acosta Saignes, *Vida de negros e indios en las minas de Cocorote, durante el siglo XVII*.

19. I am indebted to Herbert Eder for his thorough discussion of the *conuco* as an important part of Venezuela's food production.

20. Pollak-Eltz, *María Lionza*.

21. Miguel Izard, *Orejanos, cimarrones y arrochelados*, pp. 45–51.

22. Ibid., pp. 31–43.

23. Martí, *Documentos*, 2:655.

24. Depons, *Travels in South America*, p. 127.

25. For a thorough description of elites in Caracas between 1710 and 1810, see McKinley, *Pre-revolutionary Caracas*, pp. 13–18, 25–31, and 77–97. For an ex-

cellent study of the social development of Caracas at the end of the colonial era, see Kathleen Waldron, "A Social History of a Primate City: The Case of Caracas, 1750–1810" (Ph.D. diss., Indiana University, 1977).

26. The codes are found in Ermila Troconis de Veracoechea, *Documentos para el estudio de los esclavos negros en Venezuela*, pp. xxi and 133; Rafael Angel Rondón Márquez, *La esclavitud en Venezuela: El proceso de su abolición y las personalidades de sus decisivos propulsores José Gregorio Monagas y Simón Planos*, p. 29; and Lombardi, *Venezuela*, p. 48.

27. Veracoechea, *Documentos*, p. 286.

28. Dauxion-Lavaysse, *A Statistical, Commercial and Political Description*, pp. 72–73.

29. For more on the *gracias al sacar*, see Rout, *The African Experience*, pp. 156–161; McKinley, *Pre-revolutionary Caracas*, pp. 116–119; and Santos Rodulfo Cortes, *El régimen de 'las gracias al sacar' en Venezuela durante el período hispánico*, 2 vols.

30. Depons, *Travels in South America*, pp. 176–177.

31. Ibid., p. 178.

32. This and the subsequent discussion of resistance and rebellion is based on Miguel Acosta Saignes, *Vida de los esclavos negros en Venezuela*; Federico Brito Figueroa, *Las insurrecciones de esclavos negros en la sociedad colonial venezolana*; Carlos Felice Cardot, *La rebelión de Andresote*; and *Juan Fco. de León: Diario de una insurgencia, 1749*, ed. José Antonio de Armas Chitty.

33. See Acosta Saignes, *Vida de esclavos*, pp. 249–274. He and Brito Figueroa fix the figure of runaways at some thirty thousand. For further treatment of the theme, see Rout, *The African Experience*, p. 112, and McKinley, *Pre-revolutionary Caracas*, pp. 120 and 122–124.

34. For details see Armas Chitty, ed., *Juan Fco. de León*. Also see Brito Figueroa, *Las insurrecciones*, pp. 49–53; and Carlos Felice Cardot, "Rebeliones, motines y movimientos de masas en el siglo XVIII venezolano," in *El movimiento emancipador de Hispanoamerica*, vol. 2, pp. 72–74. For Nirgua, see Rout, *The African Experience*, p. 112, and Dauxion-Lavaysse, *Travels in South America*, pp. 70–72.

35. For accounts of the Coro uprisings, see Arcaya, *Insurrección de los negros*; Brito Figueroa, *Las insurrecciones*, pp. 59–77; Rout, *The African Experience*, pp. 114–116; McKinley, *Pre-revolutionary Caracas*, pp. 124–125; and Pompeyo Márquez, *El gesto emancipador de José Leonardo Chirinos*. Reports of the Coro revolts of 1796 and 1799 can be found in Archivo General de la Nación (AGN), Real Audiencia, Provisiones 1796, VIII, folios 210–212, and Provisiones 1799, XIV, folios 295–299.

36. John V. Lombardi, "The Abolition of Slavery in Venezuela: A Nonevent," in *Slavery and Race Relations in Latin America*, ed. Robert B. Toplin, pp. 232–233. For a longer discussion of the participation of slaves in the struggle for independence, see John V. Lombardi, *The Decline and Abolition of Negro Slavery in Venezuela, 1820–1854*, pp. 35–53. In his many books on the subject of Venezuelan slavery, Federico Brito Figueroa also subscribes to the theory that slaves destroyed much of the plantation culture during the wars of independence.

37. Vicente Lecuna, *Selected Writings of Bolívar*, vol. 1, p. 181.

38. See Lecuna, *Selected Writings*, vol. 1, p. 223, and vol. 2, p. 490; and Rout, *The African Experience*, pp. 175–179.

39. Bolívar to Santender, Magdalena, July 8, 1826, in Lecuna, *Selected Writings*, vol. 2, p. 624.

40. John Hawkshaw, *Reminiscences of South America from Two and One Half Years' Residence in Venezuela*, pp. 206–208.

41. Ibid., p. 208.

42. Ibid.

43. Randall Hudson, "The Negro in Northern South America, 1820–1860," *Journal of Negro History* 49, no. 4 (October 1964): 226–229.

44. The best account of emancipation remains Lombardi, *Decline and Abolition of Negro Slavery*. See especially pp. 135–142 for Monagas' reasons for liberating the slaves.

45. Salvador de Madariaga, *Bolívar*, p. 524.

46. Ibid., pp. 524 and 556; Rout, *The African Experience*, pp. 176–177; and Hudson, "The Negro in Northern South America," p. 229.

47. For their respective views, see Walter Dupouy, ed., *Sir Robert Ker Porter's Caracas Diary, 1825–1842: A British Diplomat in a Newborn Nation;* and John G. A. Williamson, *Caracas Diary, 1835–1840: The Journal of John G. A. Williamson, first diplomatic representative of the United States to Venezuela,* ed. Jane Lucas de Grummond.

48. Dupouy, ed., *Sir Robert Ker Porter's Caracas Diary,* p. 574. Italics in original.

49. Ibid., p. 559. Italics in original.

50. Ibid., p. 517. Italics in original.

51. For instance, see Williamson, *Caracas Diary,* p. 57.

52. Ibid., p. 219. Porter's comments appear in Dupouy, ed., *Sir Robert Ker Porter's Caracas Diary,* p. 959; for Porter's report on a rebellion that occurred in 1836, see p. 935.

53. Dupouy, ed., *Sir Robert Ker Porter's Caracas Diary,* p. 959. Italics in original.

54. Ibid., p. 972. Italics in original.

55. *Gaceta de Venezuela* (Caracas), December 22, 23, and 25, 1838.

56. The best treatment of the llanero revolts is Robert P. Matthews, "Rural Violence and Social Unrest in Venezuela, 1840–1858: Origins of the Federalist War" (Ph.D. diss., New York University, 1974), published in a Spanish version as *Violencia rural en Venezuela, 1840–1858: Antecedentes socio-económicos de la Guerra Federal.* Also see Federico Brito Figueroa, *Tiempo de Ezequiel Zamora.*

57. As quoted by Porter, in Dupouy, ed., *Sir Robert Ker Porter's Caracas Diary,* p. 1068. Italics in original.

58. AGN, Interior y Justicia, 1853, tomo CDLXXXI, folios 335–336.

59. Besides Lombardi's *Decline and Abolition of Negro Slavery,* see José Manuel Núñez Ponte, *Estudio histórico acerca de la esclavitud y de su abolición en Venezuela,* and Rondón Márquez, *La esclavitud en Venezuela.* According to Matthews, "Rarely did slaves form a contingent themselves, but willingly mixed with escaped criminals and other outlaws" ("Rural Violence," pp. 182–184). For typical examples of advertisements for runaway slaves, see *El Liberal* (Caracas), September 26, 1835;

Gaceta de Venezuela (Caracas), December 22 and 23, 1838; and *Diario de Avisos* (Caracas), January 15, 1851; February 19, 1851; May 31, 1851; December 20, 1851; February 6, 1854; and February 9, 1854.

60. See *Diario de Avisos,* March 29, 1854, for reported disturbances and minor violence that followed announcement of emancipation in Caracas and Valencia. For a historian's description of the slaves' celebrations of liberty see Rondón Márquez, *La esclavitud en Venezuela,* p. 64, and Francisco González Guinán, *Historia contemporánea de Venezuela,* vol. 5, p. 370. A particularly gloomy view of emancipation appeared in a letter to the editor signed by "Un Abolicionista" in *Diario de Avisos,* March 25, 1854.

61. For the Federalists' objectives, see Guillermo Alvear to Elías E. Landaeta, Coro, October 2, 1858, Archivo de la Academia Nacional de la Historia (ANH), Colección M. F. Tovar (Tovar), carpeta 7, folio 4, and a pamphlet found in ANH, Tovar, carpeta 7, folio 55. For a general statement see Lombardi, *Venezuela,* pp. 186–190.

62. "Opúsculo histórico de la revolución desde el ano 1858 a 1859: Facción de los Indios Guanauto, Hacienda Palmo," pp. 110–111, microfilm, Fundación Boulton, Caracas.

63. Ibid., pp. 36–40. Also see Matthews, "Rural Violence," pp. 182–184.

64. "Opúsculo histórico," p. 38; Matthews, "Rural Violence," p. 280; and Juan Alderson to Manuel F. Tovar, Curiepe, March 26, 1858, ANH, Tovar, carpeta 5, folio 32.

65. Anonymous to Tovar, no date, ANH, Tovar, carpeta 20, folio 138.

66. Ibid. Also see "Medidas," ANH, Tovar, carpeta 20, folio 108.

67. "Opúsculo histórico," p. 215. For typical pejorative statements about the Federalists, see ANH, Tovar, carpeta 9, folio 17; carpeta 10, folio 127; carpeta 11, folio 1; carpeta 14, folio 42; carpeta 15, folio 130; and carpeta 20, folio 70, no. 11. Also see *El Constitucional* (Caracas), May 26, 1860.

68. Pbro. Antonio Asejo to Dr. Ovidio Linardo, San Antonio, August 18, 1860, ANH, Tovar, carpeta 15, no. 19. Also see Tovar, carpeta 11, folio 41, and carpeta 14, folio 130.

69. Ramón Páez, *Travels and Adventure in South and Central America: Life in the Llanos of Venezuela,* p. 51.

70. Germán Carrera Damas has disputed this thesis in *Boves: Aspectos socioeconómicos de su acción histórica.*

71. For a late example of this tradition, see Morón, *History of Venezuela,* pp. 27–28.

72. Páez, *Travels,* p. 3; and Carl Sachs, *De los llanos,* p. 152.

73. See Nelson Reed, *The Caste War of Yucatán.*

74. Charles Daniel Dance, *Recollections of Four Years in Venezuela,* p. 165; Edward B. Eastwick, *Venezuela: or Sketches on Life in a South American Republic; with the History of the Loan of 1864,* pp. 32 and 195; Friedrich Gerstacker, *Viaje por Venezuela en el año 1868,* p. 73; Thomas C. Dawson, *The South American Republics,* pt. 2, pp. 393–394.

75. *Gaceta Federal de Venezuela* 1, no. 26 (December 21, 1858): 101–103. For

more details on revolts and conscription, see Matthews, "Rural Violence." Also see Rondón Márquez, *La esclavitud en Venezuela*, p. 67; Walter E. Wood, *Venezuela: or Two Years on the Spanish Main*, pp. 44 and 84–85; and Venezuela, Ministerio de Fomento, *Memoria* (1867), p. 110.

76. The correspondence concerning Padrón is found in ANH, Tovar, carpeta 10, folio 109, and carpeta 15, no. 157.

3. Whitening the Population, 1850–1900

1. Paulo de Carvalho-Neto, "Folklore of the Black Struggle in Latin America," *Latin American Perspectives* 5, no. 2 (Spring 1978): 53–87.

2. See "Folklore venezolano," *Cultura Venezolana* 12, no. 96 (August 1929): 427–429.

3. Ibid. For an excellent collection of songs and poems, see Luis F. Ramón y Rivera, *Cantares: La poesía en la música folklorica venezolana*.

4. "Folklore venezolano," pp. 427–429.

5. Ibid.

6. See *El Cojo Ilustrado* 1, no. 5 (March 1, 1892): 77; 1, no. 12 (June 15, 1892): 179; 2, no. 43 (October 1, 1893): 365; 2, no. 44 (October 15, 1893): 386; 3, no. 62 (July 15, 1894): 273; 4, no. 87 (August 1, 1895): 465; 4, no. 88 (August 15, 1895): 505; 4, no. 90 (September 15, 1895): 574. For a later example of this genre, see the article "Un tipo popular," *El Nuevo Diario* (Caracas), February 6, 1924, which presented an interview with an old black peanut vendor named Malabar. Also see *Elite* 7 (February 6, 1932): 334, which ran a photo section entitled "The Rustic City" which showed black shoeshine boys, a black milkman, a black candy maker, and a black vendor.

7. Margaret Amanda Pattison, *The emigrants vade-mecum, or Guide to the "Price grant" in Venezuelan Guayana*, p. 21. Italics in original.

8. Edward B. Eastwick, *Venezuela: or Sketches of Life in a South American Republic; with the History of the Loan of 1864*, p. 179.

9. Carl Sachs, *De los llanos*, pp. 155–156. For later opinions see William E. Curtis, *Venezuela, a Land Where It's Always Summer*, pp. 151, 153, 169–170.

10. William Barry, *Venezuela: A Visit to the Gold Mines of Guyana, and Voyage up the River Orinoco during 1886*, p. 49.

11. Ira N. Morris, *With the Trade-Winds: A Jaunt in Venezuela and the West Indies*, p. 117.

12. Curtis, *Venezuela*, pp. 156–157.

13. Ibid., p. 159.

14. Ibid., p. 160.

15. *El Eco Popular* (Caracas), March 3, 1840. For a similar observation, see *El Republicano* (Caracas), June 11, 1845.

16. This theme runs throughout Eastwick's descriptions of Venezuela in the mid-1860s found in his *Venezuela*.

17. *El Comercio* (Puerto Cabello), July 16, 1864. In the first edition of this news-

paper, its editor, J. A. Segrestaa announced his intention to publish everything related to "the three great elements that form the base of our public wealth and which we have mentioned; industry, commerce, and agriculture" (ibid., July 2, 1864).

18. *El Comercio,* January 30, 1865.

19. *Correo de Zulia* (Maracaibo), September 19, 1863.

20. *Correo de Zulia,* August 22, 1863.

21. See *Diario de Avisos* (Caracas), January 12, 1875, for a translation of an article from the *Boston Daily Advertiser,* December 17, 1874; and Wood, *Venezuela,* p. 87, for descriptions of Venezuelan workers.

22. For a thorough discussion of this problem, see Matthews, "Rural Violence." An example of the vagrancy laws that upheld labor contracts and curtailed idleness can be seen in *Ordenanzas, expedidas por la Hon. Diputación Provincial de la Portuguesa en sus sesiones ordinarias de 1856,* pp. 55–61.

23. This account, and that in the following paragraphs, derived primarily from travel accounts and descriptions of nineteenth-century Venezuela noted in the bibliography. Also see Hudson, "The Negro in Northern South America," pp. 225–239, and Alfred Jackson Hanna and Kathryn Abbey Hanna, *Confederate Exiles in Venezuela.*

24. *El Comercio* (Puerto Cabello), February 13, 1865. For discussions of former slaves as rural poor, see Salvador de la Plaza, *La reforma agraria,* p. 14; Fernando Ignacio Parra Aranguren, *Antecedentes del derecho del trabajo en Venezuela, 1830–1928,* p. 54; Jonathon N. Leonard, *Men of Maracaibo,* pp. 138–142; and Federico Brito Figueroa, *El problema tierra y esclavos,* pp. 316 and 350–354.

25. *El Venezolano* (Caracas), May 2, 1843. Also see José Eustaquio Machado, *El gaucho y el llanero,* p. 14, and Izard, *Orejanos, cimarrones y arrochelados,* pp. 46–48.

26. H. M. and P. V. N. Myers, *Life and Nature under the Tropics; or Sketches of Travels Among the Andes, and on the Orinoco, Rio Negro, and Amazons,* p. 17. Italics in original.

27. Rafael Villavicencio, *La evolución,* p. xvi. For another example of his views, see "Discurso pronunciado ante la ilustre universidad en el acto de la repartición de premios, el dia 8 de Diciembre de 1866," *El Federalista* (Caracas), December 11 and 12, 1866.

28. A number of works deal with positivism. See Elías Pino Iturrieta, *Positivismo y gomecismo;* Arturo Sosa, *La filosofía política de gomecismo: Estudio del pensamiento de Laureano Vallenilla Lanz;* Carlos Salazar, "Metología de la historia," in *El concepto de la historia en Laureano Vallenilla Lanz,* ed. Germán Carrera Damas; and Juan Penzini Hernández, *Vida y obra de José Gil Fortoul, 1861–1943.*

29. Aristedes Rojas, *Objetos históricos de Venezuela en la exposición de Chicago: Estudios acerca de ellos,* p. 25.

30. Aristedes Rojas, "El cancionero popular de Venezuela," *El Cojo Ilustrado* 2, no. 30 (March 15, 1893): 100.

31. José Gil Fortoul, *El Cojo Ilustrado* 4, no. 73 (January 1, 1895): 15.

32. For this exchange see Jesús Muñoz Tébar, *El personalismo i el legalismo,* and José Gil Fortoul's review of that work in *La Opinión Nacional* (Caracas), May 9, 1891.

33. José Gil Fortoul, *El hombre y la historia*, pp. 24 and 27. Also see Penzini Hernández, *Vida y obra de José Gil Fortoul*, p. 101.

34. *El Cojo Ilustrado* 4, no. 73 (January 1, 1895): 16.

35. Muñoz Tébar, *El personalismo*, pp. 10–23, 29–42, and 198–201, and Gil Fortoul's comments in *La Opinión Nacional*, May 9, 1891.

36. See *El Cojo Ilustrado* 4, no. 73 (January 1, 1895): 14–15.

37. Ibid., p. 15.

38. Ibid., and Gil Fortoul, *El hombre y la historia*, pp. 24–27.

39. *El Cojo Ilustrado* 4, no. 73 (January 1, 1895): 14–15.

40. Found in Arturo Uslar Pietri, "Venezuela necesita inmigración," *Boletín de Cámara de Comercio de Caracas* 26, no. 284 (July 1937): 6941.

41. *El Monitor Industrial* (Caracas), August 3, 1858.

42. For brief reviews of immigration policies, see Susan Berglund, "Las bases sociales y económicas de las leyes de inmigración venezolanas, 1831–1935," *Boletín Academia Nacional de la Historia* 65, no. 260 (October–December 1982): 951–962 and Ermila Troconis de Veracoechea, *El proceso de la inmigración en Venezuela*.

43. See Roberto Moll, "Lecciones de economía venezolana," *Revista de Fomento* 4, no. 55 (April–June 1944): 85, and Curtis, *Venezuela*, pp. 237–242. For basic information on immigration at midcentury, see *Diario de Avisos* (Caracas), January 4, 1851.

44. José Tomás Machado to Ministerio de Relaciones Interiores y Justicia, Ciudad Bolívar, July 6, 1850, as published in *Diario de Avisos*, August 13, 1850.

45. *Diaro de Avisos*, June 3, 1854.

46. Venezuela, Congreso de Valencia, *Debates* 3 (October 6, 1858): 273.

47. This description is based upon an extensive reading of Venezuelan newspapers, official ministry reports, travelers' accounts, and documents found in the Archivo General de la Nación (AGN). Also see Manuel Pérez Vila, "El gobierno deliberativo: Hacendados, comerciantes y artesanos frente a la crisis, 1830–1848," in Fundación John Boulton, *Política y economía en Venezuela, 1810–1976*, pp. 35–89; Robert P. Matthews, "La turbulenta decada de los Monagas, 1847–1858," ibid., pp. 93–127; and Benjamin A. Frankel, "La Guerra Federal y sus secuelas, 1859–1869," ibid., pp. 131–162. For a frank contemporary account, see Ministerio de Fomento, *Memoria* (1867), pp. 108–116. For comments about the effects of the war on education, see ibid. (1863), pp. 30–37. According to that organ, fighting not only interrupted the education of students who went off to war but also used up funds so that the government did not have money available to finance public education.

48. Ministerio de Fomento, *Memoria* (1865), p. 34. In 1864, Eastwick made a similar observation in a discussion he had with President Juan C. Falcón: "I then said I had visited the richest districts of Venezuela and was quite convinced of the enormous productiveness of the soil; but there were two things wanting, *brazos y dinero*—'labor and capital'" (Eastwick, *Venezuela*, p. 203).

49. Ministerio de Fomento, *Memoria* (1866), p. 13, and Jacinto R. Pachano, *Colección de documentos oficiales, artículos de periódicos, ensayos literarios y correspondencia privada del General Jacinto R. Pachano*, p. 36.

50. For example, see *Diario de Avisos* (Caracas), March 15 and 16, 1876.

51. Ibid., March 28, 1876.

52. *El Opinión Nacional*, March 20, 1891; *Boletín de la riqueza pública de los Estados Unidos de Venezuela*, November 28, 1891, p. 334; and José Manuel Hernández Ron, *Tratado elemental de derecho administrativo*, vol. 2, p. 168.

53. I am indebted to Ramón Velásquez for sharing his opinion about this information. I found evidence of extensive immigration from Trinidad to Venezuela in Trinidad, "Report of the Protector of Immigrants for 1889," *Council Papers*, no. 29 (1890), p. 5. For an example of a scientific racist argument in favor of white immigration and against other racial groups, see *El Derecho* (Caracas), December 21 and 26, 1892. Also see Domingo Alberto Rangel, *Capital y desarrollo*, vol. 1: p. 79; William M. Sullivan, "The Rise of Despotism in Venezuela: Cipriano Castro, 1899–1908" (unpublished Ph.D. diss., University of New Mexico, 1974), p. 27; and Hernández Ron, *Tratado elemental*, vol. 2: pp. 143–191.

54. Carnevali to Febres Cordero, El Callao, June 7, 1887, Archivo y Biblioteca de Dr. Tulio Febres Cordero, Mérida. I am grateful to Arturo Muñoz for this reference.

55. Wood, *Venezuela*, pp. 85–86.

56. Ibid. Also see Leonard, *Men of Maracaibo*, p. 106, and Lindon Bates, Jr., *The Path of the Conquistadores: Trinidad and Venezuelan Guiana*, p. 135.

57. Lemos to Hernández, Ciudad Bolívar, October 29, 1892, ANH, Hernández Collection, No. 8; Wood, *Venezuela*, p. 87; Haggard to Salisbury, Caracas, November 16, 1898, Public Record Office (PRO), Foreign Office (FO), 80/389/48–52, no. 18; Curtis, *Venezuela*, p. 242; Sullivan, "Rise of Despotism," p. 167; Loomis to Secretary of State, Caracas, July 16, 1900, National Archives (NA), Department of State (DS), Record Group (RG) 52, Roll 17; Haggard to Salisbury, Caracas, March 22, 1900, PRO FO 80/404; Loomis to Hay, Caracas, March 4, 1901, NA DS RG 52, 569; Lemos to Bax-Ironside, Ciudad Bolívar, August 25, 1903, PRO FO 199/170; Bax-Ironside to Lansdowne, Caracas, September 5, 1903, PRO FO 80/455; Lemos to Bax-Ironside, Ciudad Bolívar, January 16, 1904, PRO Colonial Office (CO), 295/429/5849; Bax-Ironside to Lansdowne, Caracas, March 13, 1904, with enclosures of Bax-Ironside to Lemos, Caracas, February 13, 1904, and Lemos to Bax-Ironside, March 5, 1904, PRO CO 295/429/13057; Bax-Ironside to Lansdowne, Caracas, August 23, 1904, PRO CO 295/429/180; and Bax-Ironside to Cartwright, Caracas, February 12, 1906, PRO FO 80/371/164.

58. Haggard to Salisbury, Caracas, November 16, 1898, PRO FO 80/389/48–52, no. 18.

59. Lemos to Haggard, Ciudad Bolívar, November 8, 1898, PRO FO 80/389/55–60.

60. Trinidad, "Report of the Protector of Immigrants for 1889," *Council Papers*, no. 29 (1890): 5.

61. Trinidad, "Immigration: Report of the Protector of Immigrants for 1894," *Council Papers*, no. 108 (1895): 4.

62. Ministerio de Fomento, *Memoria* (1893), p. 26; *El Derecho* (Caracas), December 26, 1892; and Hernández Ron, *Tratado elemental*, vol. 2: p. 169.

63. *El Derecho* (Caracas), December 26, 1892.

64. Loomis to Secretary of State, Caracas, September 10, 1898, enclosure, NA DS RG 52, 194. Loomis sent a copy of Haggard to Salisbury, Caracas, June 25, 1898, as it appeared in the *Gazette* (Port of Spain, Trinidad), September 3, 1898.

65. I am indebted to Thomas Orum for much of this information that he graciously shared with me.

66. See *El Derecho*, January 14, 1893.

67. *El Conciliador* (Caracas), December 21, 1900.

68. Scruggs to Secretary of State, Caracas, June 28, 1892, NA DS microfilm M79-T43, vol. 42.

69. Johnson to Washington, August 30, 1906, Con. 323 Booker T. Washington Papers, Library of Congress.

4. Positivism and National Image, 1890–1935

1. *El Pregonero* (Caracas), July 18, 1901.

2. Lima wrote a series of articles on immigration that appeared in *Eco Industrial* (Barquisimeto), February 7, 8, 17, 19, and 21, 1902.

3. Ibid.

4. For examples of Táchiran self-images, see Juvenal Anzola, *De Caracas a San Cristóbal*, pp. xiii and 210; Isidoro Laverde Amaya, *Un viaje a Venezuela*, pp. xii–xiii, 120, and 168; and Alejandro Trujillo, *El Táchira ante la historia contemporánea de Venezuela.*

5. "Rafael Bolívar y Benjamín Ruiz, un mismo personaje," *Boletín del Archivo Histórico de Miraflores* (*BAHM*) 11, no. 68 (January–June, 1971): 3–19; Rufino Blanco Fombona, *De cuerpo entero: El negro Benjamín Ruiz;* Vicente Dávila, *Problemas sociales,* vol. 1, pp. 160–162; "Monseñor Jaurequí, Revolucionario (Octubre–Noviembre de 1900)," *BAHM* 17, no. 87 (September–October, 1975): 239–310; "El ejército de Antonio Fernández Cordero," *BAHM* 3, no. 10 (January–February, 1961): 27; "La defensa de Antonio Fernández," *BAHM* 3, no. 11 (March–April, 1961): 21; Sullivan, "Rise of Despotism," p. 108; Plumacher to Secretary of State, Maracaibo, September 19, 1899, NA DS, RG 52, Roll 17; Plumacher to Secretary of State, Maracaibo, March 22, 1900, NA DS, RG 52, Roll 17.

6. James W. Johnson to Booker T. Washington, Puerto Cabello, June 6, 1906, in *The Booker T. Washington Papers,* ed. Louis R. Harlan and Raymond W. Smock, vol. 9: pp. 28–29.

7. Blanco Fombona, *De cuerpo entero,* pp. 10 and 13.

8. See *La Voz del Pueblo* (Caracas), October 14 and 15, 1907, and the prologue to Julian Pardo, *Todo un pueblo,* written by José María Vargas Vila.

9. For examples of such treatment of Castro, see *Cipriano Castro en la caricatura mundial.*

10. Pardo, *Todo un pueblo,* pp. 12–13.

11. Rufino Blanco Fombona, "La evolución de Hispano-América," *Obras selectas,* p. 312.

12. Blanco Fombona, *Obras selectas,* pp. 1192–1193.

13. *El Pregonero* (Caracas), October 16, 1901.

14. James W. Silver, *Mississippi: The Closed Society,* p. 6.

15. Johnson to Washington, Puerto Cabello, April 9, 1908, in *Washington Papers,* ed. Harlan and Smock, vol. 9: pp. 494–495.

16. *La Linterna Mágica* (Caracas), June 19, 1900.

17. Carlos Gómez, *Contribución al estudio de la inmigración en Venezuela,* pp. 76–77.

18. *El Cojo Ilustrado* (Caracas) 17, no. 386 (January 15, 1908): 55–57.

19. Ibid., p. 57, and Gómez, *Contribución al estudio de la inmigración,* p. 22.

20. P. L. Bell, *Venezuela: A Commercial and Industrial Handbook,* pp. 21–23; Luis Cordero Velásquez, *Gómez y las fuerzas vivas,* 2d ed., p. 118; Sullivan, "Rise of Despotism," p. 27; and Susan Burglund, "Las bases sociales y económicas de las leyes de inmigración venezolanas, 1831–1935," *Boletín Academia Nacional de la Historia,* no. 260 (October–December 1982), pp. 953–964. As Burgland points out, oil companies got around the restrictions against black immigration by bringing Antillian laborers to the oil fields on temporary work visas, which did not make them eligible for permanent residency.

21. Bates, *The Path of the Conquistadores,* pp. 135–136, 174, 198, and 283; Arthur O. Friel, *The River of Seven Stars,* pp. 43 and 54; Leonidas R. Dennison, *Caroni Gold,* pp. 16–18, 39–40, 124, and 135.

22. For a brief discussion of this law, and others pertaining to immigration during this period, see Berglund, "Las bases sociales y económicas," pp. 953–964.

23. "El peligro de la inmigración de color," *Boletín de la Cámara de Comercio de Caracas* 13, no. 131 (October 1, 1924): 2577–2578.

24. Ibid.

25. A. Legendre, "La obra de la civilización blanca en peligro," *Boletín de la Cámara de Comercio de Caracas* 25, no. 152 (July 6, 1926): 3333–3337.

26. César Zumeta, *La ley del Cabestro,* pp. 4–15.

27. Ramón Tello Mendoza, *Intimidades,* pp. 159–161.

28. Alfredo Machado Hernández, *Ensayo sobre política sociológica hispano americana y en especial de Venezuela,* pp. 20–24. Machado Hernández wrote his study under the guidance of Estaban Gil Borges and José Santiago Rodríguez.

29. Machado Hernández, *Ensayo sobre política,* pp. 33 and 44–55.

30. See Laureano Vallenilla Lanz, *Críticas de sinceridad y exactitud,* pp. 162–168, 182, and 207.

31. Ibid., pp. 171–179, and Vallenilla Lanz, *Disgregación e integración,* p. 151.

32. Laureano Vallenilla Lanz, "El crisol de la nacionalidad," *Cultura Venezolana* 12, no. 94 (May–June 1929): 5–9.

33. Julio C. Salas, *Civilización y barbarie,* pp. 15–18, 32–57, 77–79, and 123–124.

34. Jesus Semprúm, "Una novela criolla," *Cultura Venezolana* 2, no. 14 (June 1920): 178–184. Italics added by author.

35. Mariano Picón Salas, "De la raza y de las razas," *Cultura Venezolana* 5, no. 35 (November 1922): 141–146. For variations on the same theme, see Diego Carbonell, "Por la raza," *Cultura Venezolana* 1, no. 1 (October 1918): 51–54, and J. Trujillo Arraval, "Cuales son las mejores razas," *Cultura Venezolana* 8, no. 64

(June 1925): 350–359. The latter argued that no pure racial classifications existed and that if racial mixing had actually ruined humanity, then some catastrophe would have occurred thousands of years ago. Rather, he thought that "it seems clear that a certain degree of racial mixing actually stimulates intelligence and human progress" (ibid., p. 359).

36. *Ahora* (Caracas), February 4, 1936.

37. *Fantoches*, September 21, 1927, p. 8; and ibid., April 25, 1925, p. 7.

38. Ibid., January 11, 1928, p. 8.

39. *Elite*, November 6, 1926.

40. *Fantoches*, May 22, 1929, p. 8. For other examples of such cartoons, see the following: ibid., December 5, 1932, p. 9; ibid., April 1, 1924, cover; ibid., October 28, 1924, p. 8; ibid., October 27, 1927, p. 9; ibid., August 2, 1928, p. 5; ibid., September 9, 1928, p. 4; ibid., January 23, 1929, p. 11; ibid., August 8, 1929, p. 5; and *El nuevo diario* (Caracas), August 31, 1932. For one of the most devastating and humorous satires written on the subject of whitening, see Leo [Leoncio Martínez], "Salta atras," in *Los humoristas de Caracas*, ed. Aquiles Nazoa, pp. 254–277, a one-act farce about a black child born to white parents.

41. Alberto Adriani, "Venezuela y los problemas de la inmigración," *Cultura Venezolana* 9, no. 76 (October 1926): 83–92, later published in *Labor venezolanista* by the same author and in *Revista de Fomento* 2, no. 15 (August 1939): 273–283.

42. Adriani, "Venezuela," pp. 83–92.

43. Ibid.

44. Ibid., pp. 89–91.

45. Bell, in *Venezuela*, pp. 22–23, notes that European commercial ventures succeeded but that otherwise European immigrants who lacked capital or credit did not prosper. For attitudes toward Italians, see *El Nuevo Diario*, March 24, 1912; June 24, 1912; and October 21, 1912.

46. *Venezuelan Herald* (Caracas), January 15, 1900, reprinted a letter from a Mrs. Fearn to the *New York Tribune*.

47. Johnson to Washington, Puerto Cabello, August 30, 1906, Con. 324, Booker T. Washington Papers, Library of Congress.

48. Bates, *The Path of the Conquistadores*, p. 283.

49. Leonard Caro, *Venezuelan Gilt: Some South American Reminiscences*, p. 38.

50. Hendrick De Leeuw, *Crossroads of the Caribbean Sea*, pp. 159–160.

51. Dorothy Mills, *The Country of the Orinoco*, pp. 14, 45, and 107.

52. Aurelio de Vivanco y Villegas and Galvarino de Vivanco y Villegas, *Venezuela al día: Venezuela Up to Date*, vol. 1, p. 36.

53. See *El Heraldo* (Caracas), February 6, 1934.

5. Race and National Image in the Era of Popular Politics, 1935–1958

1. I am indebted to Mr. and Mrs. Duncan for information they gave me during an interview at their Washington, D.C., home on November 27, 1973. Besides their account of the incident, see the following: *El Nacional* (Caracas), May 24 and 29, and June 3, 1945; *Ultimas Noticias* (Caracas), June 6 and 7, 1945; *Fantoches*

(Caracas), June 8, 1945; *El Vigilante* (Merida), June 9, 1945; *El País* (Caracas), June 2, 1945; and *Ahora* (Caracas), June 11, 1945.

2. Duncan interview, November 27, 1973.

3. *Ahora*, October 13, 1943.

4. Steve Ellner, *Los partidos políticos y su disputa por el control del movimiento sindical en Venezuela, 1935–1948;* Steve Ellner, "Populism in Venezuela, 1935–1948; Betancourt and Acción Democrática," in *Latin American Populism in Comparative Perspective,* ed. Michael C. Conniff, pp. 135–149; Robert J. Alexander, *Rómulo Betancourt and the Transformation of Venezuela;* and Rómulo Betancourt, *Venezuela: Oil and Politics,* trans. Everett Bauman.

5. Betancourt, *Venezuela,* p. 213.

6. Vicente Dávila, *Labores culturales,* p. 42, and *Campañas de "La Esfera": Editoriales sobre el problema agropecuaria de Venezuela,* pp. 43–46.

7. *El Luchador* (Ciudad Bolívar), January 18, 1936.

8. *Panorama* (Maracaibo), August 27, 1936. Julio Godio, "Venezuela: La gran huelga petrolera de 1936 y la lucha por la democracia," *Desarrollo Indoamericano* 20, no. 77 (April–June, 1980): 39–50, gives a thorough analysis of the strike. He claims that *Panorama*'s propaganda had no impact and did not divide the Venezuelan and Antillian workers.

9. *El Universal* (Caracas), July 28, 1937. Uslar Pietri's essays appeared between July 17 and July 30, 1937. He republished them as "Venezuela necesita inmigración," *Boletín de la Cámara de Comercio de Caracas* 26, no. 284 (July 1937): 6940–6947, and as a pamphlet entitled *Venezuela necesita inmigración.*

10. Alberto Adriani, *Labor venezolanista,* pp. 51–59. See his "Venezuela y los problemas de la inmigración," *Cultura Venezolana* 9, no. 76 (October 1926): 83–92, reprinted in Ministerio de Fomento, *Revista de Fomento* 2, no. 15 (August 1939): 273–283. For more of Adriani's antiblack views, see his "La primera etapa de una política económica," *Revista de Fomento* 2, no. 15 (August 1939): 268–272, and "La colonización en Venezuela," ibid., pp. 286–296.

11. Betancourt, *Venezuela,* pp. 222–224.

12. Venezuela, Cámara de Diputados, *Diario de debates* 3, no. 23 (June 21, 1943): 4–9.

13. Ibid., pp. 4–5.

14. Ibid., pp. 8–9.

15. *Ahora,* June 22, 1943.

16. *Ahora,* November 14, 1944.

17. See NCAAP to Marshall, December 11, 1939; National Maritime Union of America to Murray, December 13, 1939; and National Maritime Union of America to Smith, December 26, 1939, National Archives, DSRG 59, 831.111/1451.

18. *Panorama* (Maracaibo), August 2, 1944; *Fantoches,* August 4 and 11, 1944; *Ultimas Noticias* (Caracas), August 1, 1944; and *Morrocoy Azul,* August 4, 1944.

19. See Venezuelan Congress of Journalists to President Medina, March 1, 1944, Miraflores, Presidential Archives, carpeta March 1944, 1–9. My thanks to George Schuyler, who first drew my attention to this document. Also see his "Political Change in Venezuela: The Origins of Acción Democrática, 1936–1945" (Ph.D. diss., Stanford University, 1975), p. 229.

20. See Consejo Municipal (Caracas), *Actas* (January–June, 1945), "Acta de la sesión ordinaria celebrada el dia Martes 29 de Mayo de 1945," pp. 11–12.

21. Venezuela, Congreso Nacional, Senado, *Diario de debates* 2, no. 19 (June 9, 1945): 8–11.

22. Ibid., p. 10.

23. *El Nacional* (Caracas), June 3, 1945.

24. *Ahora* (Caracas), June 11, 1945.

25. *Fantoches,* June 8, 1945.

26. *Ultimas Noticias,* June 5 and 6, 1945.

27. See *El Nacional,* June 3, 1945.

28. *La Esfera* (Caracas), June 2, 1945.

29. For a discussion of a similar color dilemma in Brazil, see J. Michael Turner, "Brown into Black: Changing Racial Attitudes of Afro-Brazilian University Students," in *Race, Class, and Power,* ed. Fontaine, pp. 73–94.

30. Julian Padrón, *Obras completas,* pp. 139–140. Also see *Venezuela 1945,* pp. 542–544, and Guillermo Meneses, *La balandera "Isabel" llegó esta tarde.*

31. Richard L. Jackson, *Black Writers in Latin America,* pp. 112–121; *Venezuela 1945,* p. 544; Juan Liscano, book review in *El Nacional,* August 8, 1943; and Guillermo Meneses, *El Nacional,* October 20, 1948. Also see Miguel Angel Mudarra, *El Estado Miranda,* p. 78.

32. For information about Calcaño's group see *Ultimas Noticias,* July 14, 1944; September 8, 1944; December 2, 1945; and February 8, 1946. Also see *El País* (Caracas), November 29, 1945. For Betancourt's attitudes on the issue of culture, see his *Venezuela,* p. 213.

33. Sojo, *Temas y apuntes,* pp. 9–11, 13–20, 31–33, and 39–40.

34. Ibid., pp. 31–33.

35. Comments that appeared in *El Nacional,* January 9, 1944.

36. *El Nacional,* August 14, 1946.

37. Carlos Siso, *La formación del pueblo venezolano,* vol. 1, p. 509.

38. Ibid., vol. 2, pp. 430–435 and 451–452.

39. Machado Hernández, "La función económica," p. 11.

40. Ibid., p. 14.

41. Ibid., p. 19.

42. Liscano, *Apuntes,* pp. 6–11, and *Folklore y cultura,* pp. 65, 70, 77–78, and 81–91.

43. Acosta Saignes, *Elementos indígenas y africanas,* p. 4.

44. Miguel Acosta Saignes, *Un mito racista: El indio, el blanco, el negro,* pp. 4–6, 10, and 12–15. Acosta developed his ideas in two other works, *Vida de negros e indios en las minas Cocorote, durante el siglo XVII,* and *Los descendientes de africanos y la formación de la nacionalidad en Venezuela.*

45. For a brief discussion of Acción Democrática's immigration policies, see pertinent parts of Susan Burglund Thompson, "The 'Musiues' in Venezuela: Immigration Goals and Reality, 1936–1961," (Ph.D. diss., University of Massachusetts, 1980).

46. See José A. Silva Michalena, "Conflict and Consensus in Venezuela," (Ph.D. diss., Massachusetts Institute of Technology, 1968), pp. 138–139; Laureano Va-

llenilla Lanz, Jr., *Escrito de memoria,* p. 109; and Schuyler, "Political Change in Venezuela," pp. 230–234. A review of the society pages of conservative newspapers, such as *El Nacional* and *El Universal* of Caracas, during the period 1945 to 1948 reveals that mulattoes and blacks began to enjoy a more active role in Caracas high life than in any previous period. Events covered by the dailies included weddings, graduation ceremonies, birthday parties, confirmations, baptisms, funerals, family and professional gatherings, and public functions.

47. *El Nacional,* October 20, 1948.

48. For details of Pérez Jiménez's immigration policy, see *Caracas Journal,* September 25, 1950.

Epilogue

1. Angelina Pollak-Eltz, *La familia negra,* pp. 11 and 146.

2. For extreme examples of such reporting, see an article by Ramón del Valle entitled "Barlovento, Barlovento . . . Tierra ardiente: Un pedazo de tierra africana sembrado en Venezuela," *Ultimas Noticias* (Caracas), December 18, 1942, and a photo titled "Black Grief" in ibid., May 16, 1945. The words to the song "Barlovento" appear on the album *Venezuela: Folklore y Esperanza* recorded by Los Guaraguao, Suramericana del Disco, LPV 0208.

3. José de Arana, *Barlovento,* pp. 77–78. Elsewhere Arana states: "In towns such as Curiepe and the majority of settlements of Barlovento, the predominant race among campesinos is the black race which descended from the old slaves. Upon crossing with the other races, the black race has improved itself notably" (p. 38). Luis Alberto Paúl, *Barlovento, riqueza dormida,* p. 75, makes similar observations, as did Mudarra, *El Estado Miranda,* p. 115, and Luis Fernando Chaves [Vargas], *Geografía agraria de Venezuela,* pp. 166–168.

4. *Ultimas Noticias,* December 15, 1974. I am also indebted to Professor Acosta Saignes for discussing this and other racial matters with me during my stay in Caracas in 1975.

5. Kalinina Ortega, "Bahia de Cata, un submundo de miseria," *El Nacional,* April 6, 1975.

6. *La Religión* (Caracas), May 31, 1979.

7. Manuel Pérez Vila, "Economía y sociedad del siglo XIX en Venezuela," *Apreciación del proceso histórico venezolano,* vol. 1, pp. 41–54, and Luis Castro Leiva, "El debate sobre el desarrollo del país en el siglo XIX," ibid., vol. 1, pp. 113–128.

BIBLIOGRAPHY

Archives

Archivo de la Academia Nacional de la Historia (ANH), Caracas.
Archivo General de la Nación (AGN), Caracas.
Biblioteca Nacional, Caracas.
Biblioteca Pedro Manuel Arcaya, Caracas.
Fundación Boulton, Caracas.
Hermotecaria de la Academia Nacional de la Historia (HANH), Caracas.
Public Records Office (PRO), London.
Library of Congress, Washington, D.C.
National Archives (NA), Washington, D.C.

Books, Pamphlets, and Articles

Acosta Saignes, Miguel. "Los descendientes de africanos y la formación de la nacionalidad en Venezuela." In *Anuario, Instituto de Antropología e Historia*, vol. 3,
pp. 35–42. Caracas: Universidad Central de Venezuela, 1966.
———. *Elementos indígenas y africanos en la formación de la cultura venezolana*. Ca-
racas: Universidad Central de Venezuela, [1956].
———. *Gentílicos africanos en Venezuela*. Caracas: Universidad Central de Vene-
zuela, Facultad de Humanidades y Educación, n.d.
———. "La población del Estado Miranda." In *El Estado Miranda: Sus tierras y sus
hombres*, pp. 91–109. Caracas: Editorial Sucre, 1959.
———. *Teoría de la estructura económico-social venezolana*. Caracas: Ministerio de
Educación Nacional, 1948.
———. *Un mito racista: El indio, el blanco, el negro*. Caracas: Ministerio de Educa-
ción Nacional, 1948.
———. *Vida de los esclavos negros en Venezuela*. Caracas: Hesperides, 1967.

————. *Vida de negros e indios en las minas de Cocorote, durante el siglo XVII*. Mexico City: Estudios Antropológicos, 1956.

————. *Zona circuncaribe: Período indígena*. Mexico City: Instituto Panamericano de Geografía e Historia, Comisión de Historia, 1953.

Adriani, Alberto. *Labor venezolanista*. Mérida: Talleres Gráficos Universitarios, 1962.

————. "Venezuela y los problemas de la inmigración." *Cultura Venezolana* 9, no. 76 (October 1926): 83–92.

Alexander, Robert J. *Rómulo Betancourt and the Transformation of Venezuela*. New Brunswick, N.J.: Transaction Books, 1982.

————. *The Venezuelan Democratic Revolution*. New Brunswick, N.J.: Rutgers University Press, 1964.

Alvarado, Lisandro. *Historia de la Revolución Federal en Venezuela. Obras completas*. Vol. 5. Caracas: Ministerio de Educación, Dirección de Cultura y Bellas Artes, Editorial Ragon, C.A., 1956.

Andrews, George Reid. *The Afro-Argentines of Buenos Aires, 1800–1900*. Madison: University of Wisconsin Press, 1980.

Anzola, Juvenal. *De Caracas a San Cristóbal*. Caracas: Tip. Emp. El Cojo, 1913.

Arana, José de. *Barlovento*. Caracas: Tipografía La Nación, 1945.

Arcaya, Pedro Manuel. *Estudios de sociología venezolana*. Madrid: Editorial-America, 1917.

————. *Insurrección de los negros de la serranía de Coro*. Caracas: [Instituto Panamericano de Geografía e Historia], 1949.

Arcila Farías, Eduardo. *Economía colonial de Venezuela*. Mexico City: Fondo de Cultura Económica, 1946.

————, Federico Brito Figueroa, D. F. Maza Zavala, and Ramón A. Tovar. *La obra pia de Chuao, 1568–1825*. Caracas: Universidad Central de Venezuela, 1968.

Arevalo Cedeño, Emilio. *El libro de mis luchas*. Caracas: Tipografía Americana, 1936.

Armas Chitty, José Antonio de, ed. *Juan Fco. de León: Diario de una insurgencia, 1749*. Caracas: Tipografía Vargas, S.A., 1971.

————. *Zaraza, biografía de un pueblo*. Caracas: Editorial Avila Gráfica, 1949.

Barry, William. *Venezuela: A Visit to the Gold Mines of Guyana, and Voyage up the River Orinoco during 1886*. London: Marshall Brothers, 1886.

Bates, Lindon, Jr. *The Path of the Conquistadores: Trinidad and Venezuelan Guiana*. London: Methuen and Co., Ltd., 1912.

Beebe, Mary Blair, and C. William Beebe. *Our Search for a Wilderness: An Account of Two Ornithological Expeditions to Venezuela and to British Guiana*. New York: Henry Holt and Company, 1910.

Bell, P. L. *Venezuela: A Commercial and Industrial Handbook*. Washington, D.C.: Government Printing Office, 1922.

Betancourt, Rómulo. "Las posibilidades históricas de Venezuela." In *America Latina de hoy*, edited by Eugenio Chiang-Rodríguez and Harry Kantor. New York: Ronald Press, 1961.

————. *Venezuela: Oil and Politics.* Translated by Everett Bauman. Boston: Houghton Mifflin, 1979.

————. *Venezuela, política y petróleo.* 3d ed. Caracas: Editorial Senderos, 1969.

Bingham, Hiram. *The Journal of an Expedition Across Venezuela and Colombia 1906 – 1907: An Exploration of the Route of Bolívar's Celebrated March of 1819 and the Battlefields of Boyacá and Carabobo.* New Haven, Conn.: Yale University Association, 1909.

Blanco Fombona, Rufino. *De cuerpo entero: El negro Benjamín Ruiz.* Amsterdam: Imprimerie Electrique, 1900.

————. *Dos años y medio de inquietud.* Caracas: Impresores Unidos, 1942.

————. *Obras selectas.* Prologue by Edgar Gabaldon Márquez. Caracas: Ediciones EDIME, 1958.

Boxer, C[harles] R[alph]. *Race Relations in the Portuguese Colonial Empire, 1415 – 1825.* Oxford: Clarendon Press, 1963.

Briceño, Olga. *Cocks and Bulls in Caracas: How We Live in Venezuela.* Boston: Houghton Mifflin Company, 1945.

Briceño-Iragorry, Mario. *Mensaje sin destino y otros ensayos.* Caracas: Biblioteca Ayacucho, 1987.

Brito Figueroa, Federico. *Historia económica y social de Venezuela.* 2 vols. Caracas: Universidad Central de Venezuela, 1966.

————. *Las insurrecciones de esclavos negros en la sociedad colonial venezolana.* Caracas: Editorial Cantaclaro, 1961.

————. *El problema tierra y esclavos en la historia de Venezuela.* Caracas: Mersifrica, 1973.

————. *Tiempo de Ezequiel Zamora.* Caracas: Talleres Avila/Arte, S.A., 1974.

Bruni Celli, Blas. *Estudios históricos.* Caracas: Imprenta Nacional, 1964.

Burglund, Susan. "Las bases sociales y económicas de las leyes de inmigración venezolanas: 1831–1935." *Boletín Academia Nacional de la Historia* 65, no. 260 (Caracas, October–December 1982): pp. 951–962.

Caldera, Elizabeth Yabour de. *La población de Venezuela: Un análisis demográfico.* Cumaná: Universidad de Oriente, 1967.

Cameron, Charlotte. *A Woman's Winter in South America.* London: Stanley Paul & Co., [1911?].

Campañas de "La Esfera": Editoriales sobre el problema agro-pecuaria de Venezuela. Caracas: n.p., 1939.

Cane, Miguel. *Notas de viaje sobre Venezuela y Colombia.* Bogotá: Imprenta de "la Luz," 1907.

Cardona, Miguel. *Temas de folklore venezolano.* Caracas: Ediciones del Ministerio de Educación, 1964.

Caro, Leonard. *Venezuelan Gilt: Some South American Reminiscences.* London: Hurst & Blackett Ltd., [1943?].

Carrera Damas, Germán. *Boves: Aspectos socio-económicos de su acción histórica.* Caracas: Universidad Central de Venezuela, 1968.

————, ed. *El concepto de la historia en Laureano Vallenilla Lanz.* Caracas: Imprenta Universitaria, 1966.

————. *Historia de la historiografía venezolana.* Caracas: Universidad Central de Venezuela, 1961.

Carvalho-Neto, Paulo de. "Folklore of the Black Struggle in Latin America." *Latin American Perspectives* 5, no. 2 (Spring 1978): 53–87.

Castro Leiva, Luis. "El debate sobre el desarrollo del país en el siglo XIX." In *Apreciación del proceso histórico venezolano,* vol. 1, pp. 113–128. Caracas: Universidad Metropolitana, 1985.

Chaves [Vargas], Luis Fernando. *Geografía agraria de Venezuela.* Caracas: Imprenta Universitaria (Universidad Central de Venezuela, Ediciones de la Biblioteca), 1963.

Chen, Chi-Yi. *Movimientos migratorios en Venezuela.* Caracas: Instituto de Investigaciones Económicas de la Universidad Católica Andrés Bello, 1968.

————, and Michel Picouet. *Dinámica de la población: Caso de Venezuela.* Caracas: Edición UCAB-ORSTOM, 1979.

Chiossone, Tulio. *Temas sociales venezolanos.* Caracas: Tipografía Americana, 1949.

Cipriano Castro en la caricatura mundial. Caracas: Instituto Autónomo Biblioteca Nacional: Fundación para el Rescate del Acervo Documental Venezolano, [1981].

Cordero Velásquez, Luis. *Gómez y las fuerzas vivas.* 2d ed. Caracas: Editorial LUMEGO, 1974.

Corlett, William Thomas. *The American Tropics: Notes from the Log of a Midwinter Cruise.* Cleveland: The Burrows Brothers Co., 1908.

Curiepe [Cantón], Venezuela. Consejo Municipal. *Memoria que presenta el Consejo Municipal del Cantón Curiepe a la H. Camara Provincial, 1859.* Caracas: Imprenta de V. Espinal, 1859.

Curtis, William E. *Venezuela, a Land Where It's Always Summer.* New York: Harper and Brothers Publishers, 1896.

Dalton, Leonard V. *Venezuela.* London: T. Fisher Unwin, 1912.

Dance, Charles Daniel. *Recollections of Four Years in Venezuela.* London: Henry S. King & Co., 1876.

Dauxion-Lavaysse, Jean Joseph. *A Statistical, Commercial and Political Description of Venezuela, Trinidad, Margarita and Tobago.* London: G. & W. B. Whitaker, 1820.

————. *Viaje a las islas de Trinidad, Tobago y Margarita y a diversas partes de Venezuela en la America-Meridional.* Translated by Angelina Lemo. Caracas: Universidad Central de Venezuela, 1967.

Dávila, Vicente. *Compañas de "La Esfera": Editoriales sobre el problema agropecuaria de Venezuela.* Caracas: Tip. Americana, 1939.

————. *Labores culturales.* Caracas: Tipografía Americana, 1936.

————. *Problemas sociales.* Vol. 1. Santiago, Chile: Imprenta Universitaria, 1939.

Davis, Richard Harding. *Three Gringos in Venezuela and Central America.* New York: Harper & Brothers, 1903.

Dawson, Thomas C. *The South American Republics,* Pt 2. New York: G. P. Putnam's Sons, 1904.

Degler, Carl N. *Neither Black nor White.* New York: Macmillan, 1971.

De Leeuw, Hendrick. *Crossroads of the Caribbean Sea.* New York: Julian Messner, Inc., 1935.

Dennison, Leonidas R. *Caroni Gold*. New York: Hastings House, 1943.

Department of State, Office of Public Affairs. *Venezuela: Oil Transforms a Nation*. Washington, D.C.: Government Printing Office, 1953.

Depons, Francisco J. [Pons, Francois Raymond Joseph de]. *Travels in South America during the years 1801, 1802, 1803, and 1804. Containing a Description of the Captain-Generalship of Caracas and an account of the discovery, conquest, topography, legislature, commerce, finance, and natural production of the country; with a view of the manners and customs of the Spaniards and Native Indians*. London: Longman, Hurst, Rees, and Orme, 1807.

Díaz Sánchez, Ramón. *Mene*. Buenos Aires: Editorial Universitaria de Buenos Aires, 1966.

Díaz Seijas, Pedro. *Ideas para una interpretación de la realidad venezolana*. Caracas: Jaime Villegas, 1962.

Dupouy, Walter, ed. *Sir Robert Ker Porter's Caracas Diary, 1825–1842: A British Diplomat in a Newborn Nation*. Caracas: Editorial Arte, 1966.

Dzidzienyo, Anani. *The Position of Blacks in Brazilian Society*. London: Minority Rights Group, 1971.

Eastwick, Edward B. *Venezuela: or Sketches on Life in a South American Republic; with the History of the Loan of 1864*. London: Chapman and Hall, 1868.

Ellner, Steve. *Los partidos políticos y su disputa por el control del movimiento sindical en Venezuela, 1935–1948*. Caracas: Universidad Católica Andrés Bello, 1980.

———. "Populism in Venezuela, 1935–1948: Betancourt and the Acción Democrática." In *Latin American Populism in Comparative Perspectives*, edited by Michael C. Conniff, pp. 135–149. Albuquerque: University of New Mexico Press, 1982.

Espinosa, Gabriel. "José Gil Fortoul: Filósofo, sociólogo, político, historiador," *Cultura Venezolana* 2, no. 13 (May 1920): 28–41.

El Estado Miranda: Sus tierras y sus hombres. Caracas: Editorial Sucre, 1959.

Estado Portuguesa, Venezuela, Leyes, estatuos, etc. *Ordenanzas, expedidas por la Hon. Diputación Provincial de la Portuguesa en sus sesiones ordinarias de 1856*. San Carlos: Impreso por Luis Pérez, 1857.

Ewell, Judith. *Venezuela, a Century of Change*. Stanford: Stanford University Press, 1984.

Felice Cardot, Carlos. *La rebelión de Andresote: Valles del Yaracuy, 1730–1733*. 2d ed. Bogotá: Editorial ABC, 1957.

———. "Rebeliones, motines y movimientos de masas en el siglo XVIII venezolano." In *El movimiento emancipador de Hispanoamerica*. Vol. 2. Caracas: Academia Nacional de la Historia, 1961.

Fernandes, Florestan. *The Negro in Brazilian Society*. Translated by Jaqueline D. Skiles, A. Brunel, and Arthur Rothwell. Edited by Phyllis B. Eveleth. New York: Columbia University Press, 1969.

Ferry, Robert J. "Encomienda, African Slavery, and Agriculture in Seventeenth-Century Caracas." *Hispanic American Historical Review* 61, No. 4 (November 1981): 609–635.

"Folklore venezolano." *Cultura Venezolana* 12, no. 96 (August 1929): pp. 427–429.

Fontaine, Pierre-Michel, ed. *Race, Class, and Power in Brazil*. Los Angeles: Center for Afro-American Studies, University of California, Los Angeles, 1985.

Freyre, Gilberto. *The Mansions and the Shanties: The Making of Modern Brazil*. Translated by Harriet de Onís. New York: Knopf, 1963.

————. *The Masters and the Slaves: A Study in the Development of Brazilian Civilization*. 2d ed. Translated by Samuel Putnam. New York: Knopf, 1956.

————. *New World in the Tropics: The Culture of Modern Brazil*. New York: Knopf, 1959.

Friel, Arthur O. *The River of Seven Stars*. New York: Harper & Brothers Publishers, 1924.

Fundación John Boulton. *Política y economía en Venezuela, 1810–1976*. Caracas: Italgráfica, 1976.

Gerstacker, Friedrich. *Viaje por Venezuela en el año 1868*. Translated by Ana Maria Gathmann. Caracas: La Imprenta Universitaria de Caracas, 1968.

Gerulewicz, Marisa Vannini de. *Italia y los italianos en la historia y en la cultura de Venezuela*. Caracas: Imprenta Nacional, Oficina Central de Información, 1966.

Gil Fortoul, José. *Historia constitucional de Venezuela*. 4th ed. Caracas: Ministerio de Educación, 1953.

————. *El hombre y la historia: Ensayo de la sociología venezolana*. Paris: Garnier, 1896.

Göering, Anton. *Venezuela, el mas bello país tropical*. Mérida: Universidad de los Andes, 1962.

Gómez, Carlos. *Contribución al estudio de la inmigración en Venezuela*. Caracas: Tipografía Americana, 1906.

Gómez Rodríguez, Carmen. *Materiales para el estudio de la cuestion agraria en Venezuela, 1829–1860: Enajenación y arrendamiento de tierras baldías*. Vol. 1. Caracas: Universidad Central de Venezuela, Talleres Gráficos de la Imprenta Universitaria, 1971.

Góngora Enchenique, Manuel. *Lo que he visto en Venezuela*. Caracas: Ediciones Góngora, 1952.

González Guinán, Francisco. *Historia contemporánea de Venezuela*. 15 vols. Caracas: Ediciones de la Presidencia de la República, 1954.

Gosselman, Carl August. *Informes sobre los estados sudamericanos en los años de 1837 y 1838*. Translated from Swedish by Ernesto Dethorey. Stockholm: Biblioteca e Instituto de Estudio Ibero-Americanos de la Escuela de Ciencias Económicas, 1962.

Grummond, Jane Lucas de. *Envoy to Caracas: The Story of John G. A. Williamson, Nineteenth-Century Diplomat*. Baton Rouge: Louisiana State University Press, 1951.

Hanna, Alfred Jackson, and Kathryn Abbey Hanna. *Confederate Exiles in Venezuela*. Tuscaloosa, Ala.: Confederate Publishing Co., 1960.

Harlan, Louis R., and Raymond W. Smock, eds. *The Booker T. Washington Papers*, vol. 9, *1906–1908*. Urbana: University of Illinois Press, 1980.

Harris, Marvin. *Patterns of Race in the Americas*. New York: Walker and Company, 1964.

Hawkshaw, John. *Reminiscences of South America from Two and One Half Years' Residence in Venezuela*. London: Jackson and Walford, 1838.

Hernández Ron, José Manuel. *Tratado elemental de derecho administrativo*. 3 vols. 2d ed. Caracas: Editorial Las Novedades, C.A., 1943, 1944, 1945.

Hill, Rolla B., and E. I. Benarroch. *Anquilostomiasis y paludismo en Venezuela*. Caracas: Editorial Elite, 1940.

Hoetink, H[arramus]. *Slavery and Race Relations in the Americas: Comparative Notes on Their Nature and Nexus*. New York: Harper and Row, 1973.

Hudson, Randall O. "The Status of the Negro in Northern South America, 1820–1860." *Journal of Negro History* 49, no. 4 (October 1964): 225–239.

Humboldt, Alexander von, and Aimé Bonpland. *Personal narrative of Travels to the equinoctal Regions of America, during the years 1799–1804*. 3 vols. Translated and edited by Thomasina Ross. London: H. G. Bohn, 1852–1853.

Humboldt, Alexander von, and Alexander Bonpland. *The Travels of the Baron von Humboldt and Alexander Bonpland in South America in the years 1799, 1800, 1801, 1802, 1803, and 1804*. Translated by Richard Hawkesworth. London: H. D. Symonds, 1806.

Hutchinson, William F. *A Trip to Venezuela and Curacao by the Red "D" Line: A Winter Excursion*. Providence: Providence Press Company, 1887.

Ianni, Octavio. *Raças e clases sociais no Brasil*. 2d ed. Rio de Janeiro: Civilizacao Brasileira, 1972.

Innocent, Luc B. *Si Haiti no fuera negra*. Caracas: n.p., 1975.

International Bureau of the American Republics. *Venezuela: Geographical Sketch, Natural Resources, Laws, Economic Conditions, Actual Development, Prospects of Future Growth*. Washington, D.C.: Government Printing Office, 1904.

Izard, Miguel. *Orejanos, cimarrones y arrochelados*. Barcelona: Sendai Ediciones, 1988.

Jackson, Richard L. *Black Writers in Latin America*. Albuquerque: University of New Mexico Press, 1979.

Jahn, Alfredo. *El desarrollo de las vias de comunicación en Venezuela*. Caracas: Lito-Tipografía Mercantil, 1926.

Johnson, James Weldon. *Along This Way: The Autobiography of James Weldon Johnson*. New York: The Viking Press, 1933.

Kottack, Conrad Phillip. "Race Relations in a Bahian Fishing Village." *Luso-Brazilian Review* 4 (1967): 35–52.

Kronus, Sidney, and Mauricio Solaún. *Discrimination without Violence: Miscegenation and Racial Conflict in Latin America*. New York: Wiley, 1973.

———. "Racial Adaptation in the Modernization of Cartagena, Colombia." In *Latin American Modernization Problems: Case Studies in the Crises of Change*, edited by Robert E. Scott, pp. 87–117. Urbana: University of Illinois Press, 1973.

Lacle, Antonio. *Las guerras internas de Venezuela i como han perjudicado su población: (Cuantos hijos le cuestan hasta hoy)*. Caracas: Taller Gráfico Lit. Tip., 1932.

Landaeta Rosales, Manuel. *La libertad de los esclavos*. Caracas: Imprenta Bolívar, 1895.

Lascano Tegui, Emilio. *Venezuela adentro: Turista en los llanos; pescador en Margarita; golondrina en el Táchira.* Caracas: Ediciones de "El Universal," 1940.

Laverde Amaya, Isidoro. *Un viaje a Venezuela.* Bogotá: Imprenta de "La Nación," 1889.

Lecuna, Vicente. *Selected Writings of Bolívar.* 2 vols. Edited by Harold A. Beirck. Translated by Lewis Bertrand. New York: Colonial Press, 1951.

Leonard, Jonathon Norton. *Men of Maracaibo.* New York: G. P. Putnam's Sons, 1933.

Lisboa, [Miguel Maria]. *Relación de un viaje a Venezuela, Nueva Granada y Ecuador.* Madrid-Caracas: Ediciones EDIME, 1954.

Liscano [Velutini], Juan. *Apuntes para la investigación del negro en Venezuela: Sus instrumentos de música.* Caracas: Tipografía Garrido, 1947.

———. *Folklore y cultura: Ensayos.* Caracas: Editorial Avila Gráfica, 1950.

Lockhart, James, and Stuart B. Schwartz. *Early Latin America: A History of Colonial Spanish America and Brazil.* New York: Cambridge University Press, 1983.

Lombardi, John V. "The Abolition of Slavery in Venezuela: A Nonevent." In *Slavery and Race Relations in Latin America,* edited by Robert B. Toplin, pp. 228–252. Westport, Conn.: Greenwood Press, 1974.

———. *The Decline and Abolition of Negro Slavery in Venezuela, 1820–1854.* Westport, Conn.: Greenwood Press, 1971.

———. "Manumission, *Manumisos,* and *Aprendizaje* in Republican Venezuela," *Hispanic American Historical Review* 59, no. 4 (November 1969): 656–678.

———. *People and Places in Colonial Venezuela.* Bloomington: Indiana University Press, 1976.

———. *Venezuela: The Search for Order, the Dream of Progress.* New York: Oxford University Press, 1982.

López, José Eliseo. *La expansión demográfica de Venezuela.* Mérida: Talleres Gráficos Universitarios, 1963.

López Mendez, Luis. *Obras completas.* Barquisimeto: Editorial Nueva Segovia, 1955.

Machado, José Eustaquio. *El gaucho y el llanero.* Caracas: Tip. Vargas, 1926.

Machado Hernández, Alfredo. *Ensayo sobre política sociológica hispano americana y en especial de Venezuela.* Caracas: Tipografía Americana, 1907.

———. "La función económica de las razas de color en la formación del estado venezolano." *Revista de Hacienda* 9, no. 16 (June 1944): 5–19.

Madariaga, Salvador de. *Bolívar.* New York: Schocken, 1969.

Magallanes, Manuel Vicente. *Historia política de Venezuela.* 3 vols. Madrid: Editorial Mediterráneo, 1972.

———. *Los partidos políticos en la evolución histórica venezolana.* Caracas: Editorial Mediterráneo, 1973.

Márquez, Pompeyo. *El gesto emancipador de José Leonardo Chirinos.* Caracas: Editorial Bolívar, 1949.

Martí, Mariano. *Documentos relativos a su visita pastoral de la diócesis de Caracas, 1771–1784.* 7 vols. Caracas: Academia Nacional de la Historia, 1969.

Massiani, Felipe. *El hombre y la naturaleza venezolana en Rómulo Gallegos.* Caracas: Ediciones de Ministerio de Educación, 1964.

Matthews, Robert Paul, Jr. *Violencia rural en Venezuela, 1840–1858: Antecedentes socio-económicos de la Guerra Federal.* Translated by Marie Françoise de Petzolde. Caracas: Monte Avila Editores, 1970.

McKinley, P. Michael. *Pre-revolutionary Caracas: Politics, Economy, and Society 1777–1811.* Cambridge/New York: Cambridge University Press, 1985.

Mendoza, Daniel [Rafael Bolívar Coronado]. *El llanero: Estudio de sociología venezolano.* Madrid: Editorial-America, [1918?]. First published in 1846.

Meneses, Guillermo. *La balandera "Isabel" llegó esta tarde.* Caracas: Editorial Elite, 1938.

Mills, [Lady] Dorothy [Rachael Melissa of Walpole]. *The Country of the Orinoco.* London: Hutchinson & Co., 1931.

Moll, Roberto. "Lecciones de economía venezolana." *Revista de Fomento* 4, no. 55 (April–June 1944): 81–163.

Moore, J. Hampton. *With Speaker Cannon Through the Tropics: A Descriptive Story of a Voyage to the West Indies, Venezuela and Panama.* Philadelphia: The Book Print, 1907.

Morillo González, Jesus. "El trabajo en Venezuela." *Ciencia y Cultura* 2, no. 6 (June 1957): 45–76.

Morisse, Lucien. *Excursion dans l'Eldorado (El Callao).* Paris: Association D'Imprimeurs, 1904.

Mörner, Magnus. *Race Mixture in the History of Latin America.* Boston: Little, Brown, 1967.

———, ed. *Race and Class in Latin America.* New York: Columbia University Press, 1970.

Morón, Guillermo. *A History of Venezuela.* Edited and translated by John Street. New York: Roy Publishers, Inc., 1963.

Morris, Ira Nelson. *With the Trade-Winds: A Jaunt in Venezuela and the West Indies.* New York: G. P. Putnam's Sons, 1897.

Mudarra, Miguel Angel. *El Estado Miranda.* Caracas: Editorial Relámpago, 1954.

Muñoz, Pedro José. *Breves apuntes acerca del negro en Iberamericana.* Madrid: CEBE, 1961.

Muñoz Tébar, Jesús. *El personalismo i el legalismo: Estudio político.* New York: A. E. Hernández, 1891.

Myers, H. M., and P. V. N. Myers. *Life and Nature under the Tropics; or Sketches of Travels Among the Andes, and on the Orinoco, Rio Negro, and Amazons.* New York: D. Appleton and Company, 1871.

Nazoa, Aquiles, ed. *Los humoristas de Caracas.* Caracas: Editorial Arte, 1966.

Nuñez Ponte, José Manuel. *Estudio histórico acerca de la esclavitud y de su abolición en Venezuela.* 2d ed. Caracas: Tip. Emp. El Cojo, 1911.

Pachano, Jacinto R. *Colección de documentos oficiales, artículos de periódicos, ensayos literarios y corespondencia privada del General Jacinto R. Pachano.* Caracas: Imprenta de G. Corser, 1868.

Padrón, Julian. *Este mundo desolado.* Caracas: Ediciones EDIME, 1954.

———. *Obras completas.* Mexico City: Union Gráfica, 1957.

———. *Parásitas negras (sainete de 3 actos y 7 cuadros).* Caracas: Elite, 1939.

Páez, Ramón. *Travels and Adventure in South and Central America: Life in the Llanos of Venezuela*. London: Sampson Low, Son, and Marston, 1868.

Palacio, Miguel Emilio. *Industria minera del Yuruary*. Caracas: n.p., 1937.

Pardo, Miguel Eduardo. *Todo un pueblo*. Caracas: Impresores Unidos, 1941.

Parra Aranguren, Fernando Ignacio. *Antecedentes del derecho del trabajo en Venezuela, 1830–1928*. Maracaibo: Talleres Gráficos de la Editorial Universitaria, 1965.

Pattison, Margret Amanda. *The emigrant's vade-mecum, or Guide to the "Price grant" in Venezuelan Guayana*. London: Trubner and Co., 1868.

Paúl, Luis Alberto. *Barlovento, riqueza dormida*. Caracas: Tipografía La Nación, 1944.

Peña, Vicente. *Cartilla antipaludica: Arreglada para el uso de los planteles de instrucción del Estado Guarico*. Caracas: El Cojo, 1912.

Penzini Hernández, Juan. *Vida y obra de José Gil Fortoul, 1861–1943*. Caracas: Ministerio de Relaciones Exteriores, 1972.

Pérez Vila, Manuel. "Economía y sociedad del siglo XIX en Venezuela." In *Apreciación del proceso histórico venezolano*, vol. 1, pp. 41–54. Caracas: Universidad Metropolitana, 1985.

Pierson, Donald. *Negroes in Brazil: A Study of Race Contact in Bahia*. Carbondale: Southern Illinois University Press, 1967.

Pineda, Rafael [Rafael Angel Díaz Sosa]. *Italo-venezolano: Notas de inmigración*. Caracas: Imprenta Nacional, 1967.

Pino Iturrieta, Elías. *Positivismo y gomecismo*. Caracas: Universidad Central de Venezuela, 1978.

Pittier, Henri Francisco. *El problema del cacao en Venezuela*. Caracas: Empresa El Cojo, [1934].

Plaza, Salvador de la. *La reforma agraria: Elemento básico de planificación de la economía nacional*. Caracas: Editorial Neveri, 1944.

Pollak-Eltz, Angelina. *Cultos afroamericanos (vudu y hechicería en las Américas)*. Caracas: Universidad Católica Andrés Bello, 1977.

———. *La familia negra de Venezuela*. Caracas: Universidad Católica Andrés Bello, 1974.

———. *María Lionza: Mito y culto venezolano*. Caracas: Universidad Católica Andrés Bello, 1972.

Ponte, Antonio José, ed. *Primeros actos del ejecutivo federal para la estadística de Venezuela, edición oficial*. Caracas: Imprenta Nacional, Jesus María Monasterios, 1871.

Prieto Figueroa, Luis Beltrán. *De una educación de castas a una educación de masas*. Havana: Editorial LEX, 1951.

Primer censo de la república: Decreto del Ilustre Americano General Guzmán Blanco, Presidente de la Republica. Caracas: Imprenta Nacional, 1874.

Pulido, Obdulio. *Ensayos de inmigración: Varios tópicos saneamiento*. Caracas: Cooperativa de Artes Gráficas, 1937.

Ramón y Rivera, Luis Felipe. *Cantares: La poesía en la música folklorica venezolana*. Caracas: Italgráfica, n.d.

———. *La música afrovenezolana*. Caracas: Imprenta Universitaria, 1971.

Ramos, Arthur. *The Negro in Brazil*. Translated by Richard Pattee. Washington, D.C.: Associated Publishers, 1951.

Rangel, Domingo Alberto. *Capital y desarrollo*. 2 vols. Caracas: Universidad Central de Venezuela, 1969–1970.

Reed, Nelson. *The Caste War of Yucatán*. Stanford: Stanford University Press, 1964.

Rodulfo Cortes, Santos. *El régimen de 'las gracias al sacar' en Venezuela durante el período hispánico*. 2 vols. Caracas: Academia Nacional de la Historia, 1978.

Rojas, Aristedes. *Estudios históricos: Orígenes venezolanos*. Caracas: Imprenta Nacional, Oficina Central de Información, 1972.

———. *Leyendas históricas de Venezuela*. 2 vols. Caracas: Imprenta Nacional, Oficina Central de Información, 1972.

———. *Objetos históricos de Venezuela en la exposición de Chicago: Estudios cerca de ellos*. Caracas: Imprenta y Litografía Nacional, 1893.

Rondón Márquez, Rafael Angel. *Crespo y la revolución legalista*. Caracas: Talleres Gráfica de la Controlaria General, 1973.

———. *La esclavitud en Venezuela: El proceso de su abolición y las personalidades de sus decisivos propulsores José Gregorio Monagas y Simón Planos*. Caracas: C. A. Tipografía Garrido, 1954.

Rosenblat, Angel. *La población indígena de América desde 1492 hasta la actualidad*. Buenos Aires: Institución Cultural Española, 1945.

———. *La población indígena y el mestizaje en América*. 2 vols. Buenos Aires: Nova, 1954.

Rout, Leslie B., Jr. *The African Experience in Spanish America: 1502 to the Present Day*. Cambridge: Cambridge University Press, 1976.

Russell-Wood, A. J. R. *The Black Man in Slavery and Freedom in Colonial Brazil*. New York: St. Martin's Press, 1982.

Sachs, Carl. *De los llanos*. Translated by José Izquierdo. Caracas: Ediciones EDIME, 1955.

Salas, Julio C. *Civilización y barbarie: Estudios sociológicos americanos*. 3d ed. Caracas: Talleres Gráficos Italgráfica, 1970.

Silver, James W. *Mississippi: The Closed Society*. New York: Harcourt, Brace and World, 1964.

Singh, Jenarine. *El cacao en la región de Barlovento*. Caracas: Editorial "Elite," 1934.

Siso, Carlos. *La formación del pueblo venezolano: Estudios sociológicos*. New York: Horizon House, 1941.

———. *La formación del pueblo venezolano: Estudios sociológicos*. 2 vols. Madrid: Editorial Garcia Enciso, 1953.

Skidmore, Thomas E. *Black into White: Race and Nationality in Brazilian Thought*. New York: Oxford University Press, 1974.

Sojo, Juan Pablo. *Temas y apuntes afro-venezolanos*. Caracas: Tipográfica La Nación, 1943.

———. *Tierras del Estado Miranda: Sobre la ruta de los cacahuales*. Caracas: Cooperativa de Artes Gráficas, 1938.

Solaún, Mauricio, and Eduardo Velez. "Racial Terminology and Discriminatory Integration in Latin America." In *Research in Race and Ethnic Relations*, vol. 4, pp. 139–159. Westport, Conn.: JAI Press Inc., 1985.

Sosa [Abascal], Arturo. *La filosofía política de gomecismo: Estudio del pensamiento de Laureano Vallenilla Lanz*. Barquisimeto: Centro Gumilla, 1974.

Sotillo Picornell, José C. *De como y por que conocé a Juan Santaella y de lo que hablé con el [Apuntes de una entrevista pintoresca con un cónsul de la dictadura]*. San José, Costa Rica: n.p., 1924.

Spence, James M. *The Land of Bolívar, or War, Peace, and Adventure in the Republic of Venezuela*. 2 vols. London: Sampson Low, Marston, Searle, & Rivington, 1878.

Sullivan, Edward. *Rambles and Scrambles in North and South America*. London: n.p., 1852.

Tejera, Miguel. *Venezuela pintoresca e ilustrada*. 2 vols. Paris: Librería Española de E. Denne Schmitz, 1875.

Tellería, Luis Oscar. *La experiencia migratoria venezolana*. Madrid: Ediciones Jornal, 1961.

Tello Mendoza, Ramón. *Intimidades*. Caracas: Tip. J. M. Herrera Yrigoyen & Ca., 1902.

Trujillo, Alejandro. *El Táchira ante la historia contemporánea de Venezuela*. San Cristóbal: Tipografía Cortes, [1939].

Uslar Pietri, Arturo. *Obras selectas*. Madrid: Ediciones EDIME, 1953.

Vallenilla Lanz, Laureano. *Cesarismo democrático: Estudios sobre las bases sociológicas de la constitución efectiva de Venezuela*. 3d ed. Caracas: Tipografía Garrido, 1952.

———. *Críticas de sinceridad y exactitud*. Caracas: Ediciones Garrido, 1956.

———. *Disgregación e integración*. Caracas: Tip. Universal, 1930.

———. *La rehabilitación de Venezuela: Campañas políticas de el Nuevo Diario (1915 a 1926)*. 2 vols. Caracas: Lit. y. Tip. Vargas, 1926–1928.

Vallenilla Lanz, Laureano, Jr. *Escrito de memoria*. Mexico City: Editorial Mazatlán, 1961.

Van den Berghe, Pierre L. *Race and Racism: A Comparative Perspective*. 2d ed. New York: John Wiley & Sons, 1978.

Velez Boza, Fermín. *El folklore en la alimentación venezolana*. Caracas: Editorial Sucre, 1966.

Veloz, Ramón. *Economía y finanzas de Venezuela desde 1830 hasta 1944*. Caracas: Impresores Unidos, 1945.

Venezuela, Consulado, New York. *Venezuela al dia/Venezuela Today, 1945*. New York: Consulate General of Venezuela in New York, 1945.

Venezuela, Ministerio de Fomento. *Memorias del Ministerio de Fomento*. Caracas: Ministerio de Fomento, 1865–1895.

Veracoechea, Ermila Troconis de. *Documentos para el estudio de los esclavos negros en Venezuela*. Caracas: Biblioteca de la Academia Nacional de la Historia, Italgráfica, 1969.

———. *El proceso de la inmigración en Venezuela*. Caracas: Biblioteca de la Academic Nacional de la Historia, 1986.

Villavicencio, Rafael. *Discursos leidos en la academia venezolano*. Caracas: Imprenta Bolívar, 1899.

———. *La evolución*. Caracas: Tip. Vargas, 1912.

Vivanco y Villegas, Aurelio de, and Galvarino de Vivanco y Villegas. *Venezuela al día: Venezuela Up to Date*. Vol. 1. Caracas: Imprenta Bolívar, 1928.

Waldron, Kathy. "Public Land Policy and Use in Colonial Caracas." *Hispanic American Historical Review* 61, no. 2 (May 1981): 258–272.

Ward, Edward. *The New El Dorado Venezuela.* London: Robert Hale Ltd., 1957.

Whitten, Norman E., Jr. "Ecología de las relaciones raciales al noroeste del Ecuador." *América indígena* 30, no. 2 (1970): 345–358.

Wickham, Henry Alexander. *Rough notes on a Journey Through the Wilderness, from Trinidad to Para, Brazil, By Way of the Great Cataracts of the Orinoco, Atabapo, and Rio Negro.* London: W. H. J. Carter, 1872.

Williamson, John Gustavus Adulphus. *Caracas Diary, 1835–1840: The Journal of John G. A. Williamson, First Diplomatic Representative of the United States to Venezuela.* Edited by Jane Lucas de Grummond. Baton Rouge, La.: Camellia Publishing Company, Inc., 1954.

Wood, Walter E. *Venezuela: or Two Years on the Spanish Main.* Middlesbrough, England: Jordison & Co., Ltd., 1896.

Wright, Winthrop R. "*Café con leche:* A Brief Look at Race Relations in Twentieth-Century Venezuela," *Maryland Historian* 1, no. 1 (Spring 1970): pp. 13–22.

Wright, Winthrop R. "Elitist Attitudes toward Race in 20th-Century Venezuela." In *Slavery and Race Relations in Latin America,* edited by Robert B. Toplin, pp. 325–347. Westport: Greenwood Press, 1974.

Zuloaga, Nicomedes. *Páez: Estudio histórico político.* Caracas: Imprenta Bolívar, 1897.

Zumeta, César. *El continente enfermo.* New York: n.p., 1899.

———. *La ley del cabestro.* New York: Unz & Co., 1902.

Dissertations

Ferry, Robert J. "Essays in the Society and Economy of Colonial Caracas, 1580–1810." University of Minnesota, 1980.

Floyd, Mary B. "Antonio Guzmán Blanco: The Evolution of Septenio Politics." Indiana University, 1981.

Lavenda, Robert H. "The First Modernizing Attempt: Modernization and Change in Caracas, 1870–1908." Indiana University, 1977.

Matthews, Robert P. "Rural Violence and Social Unrest in Venezuela, 1840–1858: Origins of the Federalist War." New York University, 1974.

Schuyler, George. "Political Change in Venezuela: The Origins of Acción Democrática, 1936–1945." Stanford University, 1975.

Silva Michalena, José A. "Conflict and Consensus in Venezuela." Massachusetts Institute of Technology, 1968.

Sullivan, William M. "The Rise of Despotism in Venezuela: Cipriano Castro, 1899–1908." University of New Mexico, 1974.

Thompson, Susan Burgland. "The 'Musiues' in Venezuela: Immigration Goals and Reality, 1936–1961." University of Massachusetts, 1980.

Waldron, Kathleen. "A Social History of a Primate City: The Case of Caracas, 1750–1810." Indiana University, 1977.

INDEX